TEST, MEASURE, PUNISH

CRITICAL PERSPECTIVES ON YOUTH SERIES
General Editors: Amy L. Best, Lorena Garcia, and Jessica K. Taft

Fast-Food Kids: French Fries, Lunch Lines, and Social Ties
Amy L. Best

The Kids Are in Charge: Activism and Power in Peru's Movement of Working Children
Jessica K. Taft

Growing Up Queer: Kids and the Remaking of LGBTQ Identity
Mary Robertson

White Kids: Growing Up with Privilege in a Racially Divided America
Margaret A. Hagerman

Coming of Age in Iran: Poverty and the Struggle for Dignity
Manata Hashemi

The World Is Our Classroom: Extreme Parenting and the Rise of Worldschooling
Jennie Germann Molz

The Homeschool Choice: Children, Parents, and the Privatization of Education
Kate Henley Averett

Growing Up Latinx: Coming of Age in a Time of Contested Citizenship
Jesica Siham Fernández

Unaccompanied: The Plight of Immigrant Youth at the Border
Emily Ruehs-Navarro

The Sociology of Bullying: Power, Status, and Aggression Among Adolescents
Edited by Christopher Donoghue

Gender Replay: On Kids, Schools, and Feminism
Edited by Freeden Blume Oeur and C. J. Pascoe

False Starts: The Segregated Lives of Preschoolers
Casey Stockstill

Fierce, Fabulous, and Fluid: How Trans High School Students Work at Gender Nonconformity
LJ Slovin

Policing Not Protecting Families: The Child Welfare System as Poverty Governance
Edited by Jennifer Randles and Kerry Woodward

Test, Measure, Punish: How the Threat of Closure Harms Students, Destroys Teachers, and Fails Schools
Erin Michaels

Test, Measure, Punish

How the Threat of Closure Harms Students, Destroys Teachers, and Fails Schools

Erin Michaels

NEW YORK UNIVERSITY PRESS
New York

NEW YORK UNIVERSITY PRESS
New York
www.nyupress.org

© 2025 by New York University
All rights reserved

Please contact the Library of Congress for Cataloging-in-Publication data.

ISBN: 9781479823383 (hardback)
ISBN: 9781479823390 (paperback)
ISBN: 9781479823437 (library ebook)
ISBN: 9781479823406 (consumer ebook)

This book is printed on acid-free paper, and its binding materials are chosen for strength and durability. We strive to use environmentally responsible suppliers and materials to the greatest extent possible in publishing our books.

The manufacturer's authorized representative in the EU for product safety is Mare Nostrum Group B.V., Mauritskade 21D, 1091 GC Amsterdam, The Netherlands. Email: gpsr@mare-nostrum.co.uk.

Manufactured in the United States of America

10 9 8 7 6 5 4 3 2 1

Also available as an ebook

CONTENTS

Preface: Finding Sandview High — vii

Introduction: A School under Threat of Closure — 1

1. The Creation of a "Bad" School: Divestment in an Inner-ring Suburb — 9

2. Schooling under Threat of Closure: State Surveillance and Punishment in Twenty-first Century Education — 25

3. "What Are We, Test Monkeys?" The Testing Regime Complex — 44

4. "Bad" Kids: The Stigma of a School under Threat — 59

5. On (Not) Fixing Racialized Policing through Neoliberal Accountability: Intensifying Pervasive Social Control beyond a Formal Suspension — 77

6. Go Get Them (and Not Me): Fostering Peer Antagonisms through School Policing Practices — 100

Conclusion: We Can't "Measure and Punish" Our Way Out of This — 119

Acknowledgments — 131

Appendix: Research Methods — 135

Notes — 145

Bibliography — 163

Index — 179

About the Author — 189

PREFACE

Finding Sandview High

Like many researchers, my path to writing this book was circuitous. It was 2007 and I had several part-time jobs while I was a student at Portland State University. By far the best paying of these jobs was as an after-school tutor in a local public high school for new immigrant students. To my surprise, when I arrived for my job training, the supervisor handed me a set of large glossy textbooks specifically designed to prepare new immigrant students to pass Oregon's standardized state exams. It felt like I had just been handed another version of the SAT prep textbooks that I recalled from my own high school experience and that I loathed because they were designed to teach how to take a specific standardized test rather than to teach for content. I learned that my supervisor for this new job was not from the school but rather part of a separate commercial entity that the school district had hired to help their individual schools improve the state test scores for new immigrant students. These students were in a "subpopulation" of the student body, labeled English Language Learners (ELL), and the school needed to improve ELL students' scores for state accountability purposes. Most of the students I met spoke very little English and had little idea what was even happening in their classes, let alone how to read and answer the sample test questions in our sleek textbooks. It was ridiculous. This experience was key in shaping my sociological interest in K-12 education and state policy and piqued my interest in studying how immigrant backgrounds served as a dimension of socially constructed inequalities like race, class, and gender.

Fast forward to the early 2010s. I had moved to New York City to attend the City University of New York (CUNY) Graduate Center. There, the struggle between private sector greed and the public good was rampant, both within and outside of education. Activists waged a fight for the city against state-led gentrification, through which public officials worked to sell the city to the highest bidder.[1] During that time, the national focus on neoliberal accountability in K-12 education reform was intensifying. The ostensive goal of these reforms was to reshape K-12 schools to act as and be treated more as part of the for-profit sector. The "right to the city" push that was taking place in New York refocused the critical conversations about neoliberal education reform onto the (very real) profit motivations apparent in the growing privatization spread over public schooling: the greedy investors, education consultant corporations, massive charter school conglomerates and the folks over at Teach for America, all aiming to benefit from the federal No Child Left Behind school improvement mandates. This kind of school accountability, with its roots in neoliberal ideology, offered a seat (or the whole school) to the private for-profit sector as punishment for low performance.[2] This conflict reached the halls of the CUNY Graduate Center as well: During the summers, our own public university housed training sessions for the city's largest and growing charter network.

The critical conversations in New York City about neoliberal education reform were taking place alongside similar fights in other large cities, including Chicago and Philadelphia. School closures were (and still are) a key state lever to drive reform. The federal government's (and consequently the states') justification for using the threat of school closures as a neoliberal accountability tool was that a struggling traditional public school could either learn from the private sector experts, or face market discipline, rising sanctions to reorganization, and on to the final blow of school closure. Either students would be sent to a different, ostensibly better school, or the former traditional public school could be converted into a charter school itself. The irony of course was that most kids did not go to a better school when theirs closed down.[3] And as scholars like Eve Ewing documented,[4] students and their advocates felt such deep pain when their public school was being closed that some of them even staged hunger strikes to try to prevent it.

However, the struggles to save public schools in large gentrifying urban centers were strikingly different than what I saw in "Sandview," my pseudonym for the small inner-ring suburban community that I came to study. Considering that case required that I reorient my analytic perspective, which previously had been wholly immersed in central cities like the one in which I was living at the time. Unlike New York, in Sandview there were no charter schools circling to take over, no city wealth to bargain for, and no mass of activists raring to fight back. What the small community of Sandview (fewer than 30,000 people) did share with these large urban centers was the ongoing burden of neoliberal accountability pressures that threatened to close their public schools. As the title of this book suggests, I became increasingly concerned about the *threat* of school closure itself, especially because it seemed to create more state surveillance and less time for the care of students attending the school, most of whom were Black and Latinx youth from very modest income families.

So, why did I study Sandview and its high school, and how did I end up there specifically? Initially, it was because I had planned to build on a prior study about K-12 public schools in suburban new immigrant destinations (the subject of my master's thesis and a subsequent journal article). My time in Portland as an after-school tutor took place at the end of that study and led me to think about the role of state pressure in encouraging unreasonable testing practices for new immigrant youth. And, learning about the struggles related to neoliberal education policy in big cities like New York helped me to think about why Sandview, a small public school in an inner-ring suburb, was different, and how these differing challenges were largely invisible from the discussions in and about big cities. From spending time at the school, listening to students and their adult advocates, I came to center neoliberal accountability and also broadened the study's scope to all of its students, those from immigrant and non-immigrant family backgrounds. I started to see what I came to call the school's "testing regime" as a punitive experience for students, and made connections between it and the school's growing obsession with social control of the students in order to improve their commitment to test prep. I saw both of these school structures (academic and disciplinary approaches) were linked together, both motivated by the state's neoliberal approach to school improvement: the threat of closure.

I began to think of day-to-day school life at Sandview High School as a pressure cooker. School assemblies put more and more pressure on students to pass the state exams, with constant appeals to students to step up their work. The school's leadership constantly berated students to work harder and more efficiently with their teachers as they drilled again and again for test practice. They reinforced the same message to the teachers: Work harder, more efficiently, and tailor their teaching materials to improve student test scores. Simultaneously, the school cracked down on student discipline, which was also part of its school improvement plans with the state. To help enforce attendance, the school added a student tracking system connected to their ID cards and followed up with students they identified for attendance issues. Students hid in the bathrooms, so the school started locking them. Cameras were installed everywhere in the school, but many students still found places to hide and avoid the testing drills. It all felt intensely punitive, controlling, and, importantly, motivated by the threat of closure. The situation didn't feel very "market-centered." Sure, there were education consultant companies that made money from Sandview High's improvement programs. There were also private security companies who were paid a great deal to implement the new student surveillance services. These were part of the school's improvement plan with the state, which included improving students' attendance and lowering disciplinary infractions in addition to improved state test scores. However, it actually wasn't market-centered because the state was the entity continuously monitoring and coercing all of this through the federal mandate that New York State intervene in "low-performing" schools.

As I argue throughout this book, neoliberal education reform for underperforming schools boils down, in practice, to ushering in more coercive and surveillant state programs for working-class students of color to confront inside their schools. Broadening the frame in this way helps clarify what is "neoliberal" about neoliberal education reform, when the main narrative had previously been about privatization. Most schools under threat of closure for low performance do not get shut down, and thus, in most of these cases, the education system is not privatized. But the *threat* of closure looming over these schools motivates their leaders to implement a series of reform efforts that inculcate a more punitive school context. This set of practices is one of the means by which traditional public schools serving students living with stark social disadvantages are being pulled apart. Essential work must be done to repair our public K-12 schools so that every child can have a positive, safe, and rewarding education, but neoliberal experimentation is not the right way to do it.

Introduction

A School under Threat of Closure

The first time I met with students at Sandview High School, one young man inquired with downcast eyes, "Are you here because we're so bad?"[1] We were sitting in a classroom after school with a group of students and another tutor. We had just been talking about TV shows filmed in Brooklyn and I mentioned that I lived in Brooklyn, a fact that made me instantly interesting to students, but also raised the question of my presence at the school. One student jumped in and said, "I can't wait to leave here, when I leave, I'm never coming back." Another student chimed in, "Man I can't wait to leave. Why would you come here if you live in Brooklyn?" I replied that I was a researcher and that I study schools. I was there because I was interested in what they had to say about their education. I explained that there were a lot of changes to schooling and I felt like I hadn't heard much from students themselves about their perspectives. The students repeatedly explained that the reason they were "bad" was because students' average state exams scores were "too low." They were also aware of the stakes. Their school was under huge state pressure to increase those test scores. So, as another student put it, "The state" was going to "come and get us" and "shut the school down" if students' exam scores did not go up.

School shutdowns are the focus of most books on distressed schools enduring state-led reform.[2] And, as the mass school shutdowns in cities like Chicago and New York illustrate, school closure is a credible threat. Yet on average, fewer than 3 percent of all schools targeted for dissolution due to low performance are closed.[3] This suggests that the emblematic position for these types of schools is mainly one of unending, intense stress and detriment. *Test, Measure, Punish* critically shifts the focus from school shutdowns to the more typical situation within these strained public schools—operating under persistent risk of closure.

Throughout this book, I argue that threatening schools with closure has distorted education to become more punitive, in ways that remain largely unexamined. Many K-12 schools today are like Sandview High: distressed and facing escalating sanctions if they do not improve by state metrics. These state sanctions incentivize repressive school regimes embodied by nonstop test drills and strict student conduct rules. But the scholarship tends to look only at harsh student discipline and security regimes when examining the growing prison-like conditions of many public schools. It also overlooks the role of state improvement policies in driving authoritarian discipline practices toward students.

I analyze how these new punitive schooling conditions for troubled schools reproduce racial inequalities, focusing on how students make sense of those changes. The state's stipulations for struggling schools target Black and Latinx student populations supposedly to combat ongoing racial inequities in education; I find that, in actuality, those same state conditions detract from these students' educational experience, in part by engendering harmful racializing messages to students about who they are and what they deserve. This inquiry also highlights the *structural* element of how racial inequality is reproduced in schools. As I find, none of the school professionals working directly with students at this school thought the states' school reform programs were good ideas.

Sociologists have long explored schools as a key site of youth socialization, shaping youth beyond formal academic lessons.[4] In particular, sociologists identify how schools tend to differently socialize youth for their future roles in ways that help reproduce race, class, and gender inequalities.[5] This book examines how and why a particular model of schooling, which aims to address racial inequalities, actually creates new harm for students it purports to be helping, while also uncovering new dimensions of youth socialization in school related to citizenship, identity, and race relations. I trace how the school's testing and security regimes made students feel dejected, criminalized, and suspicious of the system, their peers, and themselves.

Test, Measure, Punish reveals how threatening school closure expands the carceral state. School restructuring policies are justified as temporary actions but will only be removed when the school meets unreasonable goals, all but guaranteeing that most stressed schools persist "under threat." Other sociological studies have explored the merging of schools and the penal system, and how this merger is racially stratified.[6] My analysis connects increased carcerality with the neoliberalization of K-12 schools, including key state efforts to improve troubled public schools. Since the 2003 "No Child Left Behind Act" (NCLB), the main federal funding source for schools serving youth from class-disadvantaged families has transformed into a policing apparatus. The shift was explicitly led by neoliberal principles, which look to market-based solutions for improving public services. This book argues that these neoliberal solutions also include new punitive and surveillant features. After NCLB, this federal funding stream became highly conditional: If schools did not meet certain state academic targets, then they had to restructure.[7] These austere directives have crafted a more punitive learning environment than what existed before.

The book's case study choice of a stressed *suburban* school serving mainly Black and Latinx students is also important. Books on the racialization of youth in stressed schools largely do not examine suburban cases, even though many suburban schools increasingly show the same racialized injustices that Jonathan Kozol famously identified in urban sites as "savage inequalities."[8] This oversight is particularly troubling because stressed suburban schools are more vulnerable to state pressures than schools located in large central cities due to their relative invisibility, small-scale and geographic dispersion, as well as limited helping institutions and related infrastructure. This book exposes the full impact of school restructuring on suburban schools.

This book draws on a case study of a high school in upstate New York, which I call Sandview High School. The school's name and its location (Sandview) are both pseudonyms, as are the names of the people described in this book. The primary study data are two years of critical school ethnography (more than three hundred hours of fieldwork) and sixty-five in-depth formal interviews with students, school professionals, and community members. The student population is composed of nearly all working-class Black and Latinx youth, who increasingly live in a suburban environment.[9] In this school, nearly all the Latinx students are immigrants and most of them are undocumented. These student groups are the main targets of federal education reform policies. The book argues that the school's status as "under threat" was particularly harmful to these vulnerable student populations.

Test, Measure, Punish offers a new theory of schooling inequality that provides scholars, students, and the broader interested public with a deeper understanding of why state-led school reforms represent a new level of racialized citizenship in twenty-first century public education.

Road Map for the Book

Test, Measure, Punish advances the long tradition of critical ethnographic work studying students' experiences in school. These studies seek to reveal the role educational contexts play in reproducing racial inequalities. My book enriches the conversation about the role K-12 education plays in reproducing race, adding critical insight to the parameters of institutional racism in schools—rather than simply examining whether or not such racism exists.

Because the roots of this school's plight and others like it are related to a set of concentrated structural disadvantages, the kinds of state interventions I describe herein are misguided at best, and at worst constitute bureaucratic violence.

This text reveals how kids experience and interpret what is happening to them and how it matters for their futures. Most of the recent scholarship analyzing school routines and structures does not engage with students' perceptions of these routines and structures.[10] In cases where the literature does address students' subjectivities, it largely focuses on students' interpretations of their peer cultures.[11] That approach overlooks how students understand the new education practices, which is also an important part of how those practices affect students. This book remedies that gap, offering extensive student accounts to directly reveal how youth understand new educational practices at their school. Also, most books on racial inequality and K-12 school reforms focus on academic achievement outcomes.[12] In contrast, *Test, Measure, Punish* investigates how these schools shape youth political socialization, linking school regimes, youth subjectivities, and racialization. As a result, the book sheds light on overlooked social consequences of K-12 school reforms directed at minoritized student groups, revealing the striking ways that students learn devastating messages about their citizenship.

In chapter 1, "The Creation of a 'Bad' School," I explain why and how resource deprivation and opportunity hoarding unfolded in this community, leading to this school's predicament of being under threat of closure for low performance. Drawing on in-depth interviews with local older community members alongside analysis of statistical reports, public policy documents, and historical events, it illuminates how Sandview High became a "bad" school, in parallel with a shrinking resource base. This chapter also offers a major intervention in the literature by arguing that stressed suburban schools tend to have more challenges than their urban counterparts. The area local to Sandview High is part of a national trend in the growth of suburban poverty, and this chapter explores how this type of poverty concentration may be worse than that for similar populations in urban environments. It then foreshadows the next chapter, stressing how the state-led compulsory school reform policies set up stressed schools like Sandview to disappoint.

Chapter 2, "Schooling under Threat of Closure," resolves key misinterpretations of recent education reforms since NCLB, explaining why carcerality is central to understanding the neoliberalism of K-12 education. The literature describes how private for-profit companies drive the sanctioning of schools. In contrast to the existing scholarship, this chapter argues that education policy reforms for "low-performing" schools are at least as much about state carcerality as they are about private greed. Analyzing education reform policies, school documents, and interviews with Sandview High's teachers and students, it argues that threatening individual schools with sanctions is at least as important as privatization efforts to explain what has changed in twenty-first century schools. Describing this school's testing and security routines, the chapter argues that the scholarship largely overlooks how high-stakes testing is also a punishing experience (like punitive school security measures) and how rising school security measures are also part of state-led reform mandates for low-performing schools (like testing). Focusing on the school's vulnerable population of new immigrants from Central America, it stresses the absurdity and harm of the testing regime.[13]

Socialization in school, we might assume, includes learning that you have a right to respect, safety, and good public resources. Yet, in chapter 3, "What Are We, Test Monkeys?," I argue that schooling under the threat of closure imparts the lesson to youth that they are not entitled to a good education.[14] Drawing on students' narratives, it argues that the testing regime played a clear role in engendering students' cynicism about their education and thus eroding their confidence in state legitimacy. The chapter underscores how the messages that students learn in school are ultimately about their political membership. This is another layer of what sociologists call the "hidden curriculum," how school practices beyond formal lessons also include informal (i.e., largely unintentional) lessons, which prepare students' for their future adult roles. Analyzing students' perspectives through the lens of political incorporation explains how this type of school system reproduces social stratification beyond work and prison outcomes, clarifying how schools can prepare youth for unequal adult futures in political terms. As it is mainly African American and Latinx student populations from modest income families navigating this type of school structure, they are the ones learning to feel discredited from political engagement by the undermining of students' sense of entitlement to good public services, like education.

In chapter 4, "'Bad' Kids," I argue that being "under threat" engendered stigma for the students, which they then managed by distancing themselves from each other to save their dignity. The students wrestled with the contradictions of the school's meritocracy ethos and their own academic struggles. They got the message that the low average state exam scores at their school were typical for Black and Latinx students. Students felt ashamed to be in a situation where students' test scores were "too low"; the scores marked them as members of a racialized population. They resisted racialized devaluation by asserting themselves as markedly superior in comparison to their peers (what I call "super minorities") and blaming their peers as typical members of racialized populations with poor culture. As a result, they ended up supporting the "culture of poverty" myth, which places families and peer culture as the root obstructions for social mobility for disenfranchised populations. Thus, this chapter uncovers the role the school structure can play in the motivations behind student behavior. Navigating the testing regime left students feeling trapped and disrespected. This undercut students' potential for collective opposition to an ineffective education because it damaged students' ability to respect themselves on their own terms and to respect their peers.

Chapter 5, "On (Not) Fixing Racialized Policing through Neoliberal Accountability," argues that being a school "under threat" intensified the school's harsh disciplinary practices, which also had a range of negative social consequences for students. For one, the school was under state pressure to lower rates (and could be sanctioned for high rates) of formal student suspensions. Instead of punishing students less, the school penalized them more, but in ways not counted on the school's state evaluation. This chapter sheds new light on how school disciplinary practices beyond formal student suspensions treat Black and Latinx students' bodies as potential threats to be corrected. The analysis is intersectional, stressing the extreme ways Black youth were punished, Latinx students' distinct vulnerabilities as immigrants related to the school's security practices, and Black and Latina girls' struggles with the school's dress code. The neoliberal policy of school improvement, implemented through increasing pressure on the school, did not reduce Sandview High's punitive environment. If anything, it incentivized the school's harsh school-security regime to get worse.

The final substantive chapter, "Go Get Them (and Not Me)," drives home the overlooked harms of the increasingly harsh disciplinary practices that schooling under threat of closure produce. It explores how the school's security regime attached racialized criminal frames to students' behavior, and how this incentivized students to criminalize each other. Students' experiences with school punishment reflected prominent racialized criminal frames: Black youth were seen as "violent"; Latinx youth felt "illegal"; and Black and Latinx girls were made to feel "scandalous." Students then often viewed each other through these same criminal frames. Students were understandably anxious to avoid abuse in the school's security regime; and this chapter argues that perceived resource competition remains key to reproducing racial stratification, including the social and emotional resource of avoiding the pain of criminalization.

In the conclusion, "We Can't 'Measure and Punish' Our Way Out of This," I stress why the book's findings concern all who are interested in the freedom of disenfranchised youth. Arguing that the path to liberation for disenfranchised youth will require them to support each other, it explores the opportunities for eradicating educational policies that incentivize racialized relations and undermine crucial citizenship resources for youth.

1

The Creation of a "Bad" School

Divestment in an Inner-ring Suburb

"I could never live in a city," asserted Tara, a self-described "energetic" sixteen-year-old Sandview High School student. I had just been hanging out with her and her friend Chloe before I interviewed Tara after school. The girls texted once more before parting ways. Our prior conversation had focused on friendship; as best friends they dislike parting ways for the day. As we spoke, Tara explained with her usual big smile that cities were "too big" for her, then declared, "I have to live in the suburbs, I'm used to it." Tara was speaking about Sandview, New York, her hometown with a population of about 30,000 people. Sandview was also where she attended Sandview High, the sole public high school, along with about 1,000 other students. Many Sandview High students I met were like Tara, positive about the suburban quality of their setting. They named things they enjoyed, such as the slow pace of life, knowing where everything was, the many flowers and trees, the kind of place where people greet you when pass them on the street. Yet not all students agreed that this small-town feel was entirely good. Aisha, for example, stated, "They don't have that much stuff here for us to do," explaining, "The only thing teenagers do [here] is "go to their friends' house, or go to the mall, it's so simple and *boring*." Students also spoke about Sandview in pessimistic terms due to the high level of poverty. As a student named Jumaane told me, "It's a little depressing," elongating the last word as he spoke. Similarly, another student, Righteous, explained, "Sometimes I want a break from this place. I mean, all of my memories are here, but there is not a lot of motivation here." Overall students felt that things here were not as they would like them to be, most notably the excessive poverty surrounding them. Visible signs of this included the many boarded up buildings and stores catering to low-income patrons: paycheck cashing, money mailing, pawnshops, and dollar stores. The area local to

Sandview High is part of a national trend in the growth of racialized suburban poverty.[1] At Sandview High, roughly eight out every ten students live below the poverty line and most of these students are either African American or Latinx immigrants. Schools serving these student populations are also the ones struggling with low student performance outcomes and facing state discipline for it in our current system of school improvement programming.[2]

Rethinking Suburban Schools

The suburban character of Sandview High's surrounding community is largely outside of the popular imagination of schools under duress. In the public imagination, stressed schools serving mostly class-disadvantaged students of color are located in large urban centers.[3] Likewise, books about youth in strained public schools still largely do not examine suburban cases. Instead, most suburban case study analysis of racial inequalities in schooling focuses on affluent cases. These types of studies importantly examine racial inequalities in "best-case-scenario" schools that are racially integrated and well-resourced.[4] In contrast, my study of Sandview High analyzes the growing phenomenon of divested suburban schools, which neighbor both rich cities and rich suburbs. Examining stressed suburban schools is essential because these types of school are *more* vulnerable to state pressures than schools located in large central cities. This vulnerability is a result of their relative invisibility, small scale, and geographic dispersion, as well as a lack of helping institutions and related infrastructure.[5] As a result, analyzing a case study of a stressed suburban school exposes the full impact of school restructuring. Moreover, because suburban schools have often made the transition to being distressed only recently, investigating this type of situation can more clearly illustrate how our society makes "bad schools" happen.

Sandview High became a "bad" school for reasons related to changing conditions in the local political economy that divested the Sandview community and the financial base of Sandview High. This is important because it is those conditions that permitted the neoliberal state to intervene, coercing Sandview High into engaging in punitive school regimes with the threat of pending school closure. Part of the reason Sandview

High was considered "failing" was because the new standards labeled it so by the state. It did struggle, with only about half of its students graduating.[6] Yet, Sandview High also became a struggling school because of how local educational resources disappeared over time. Rising poverty rates adversely affected the funding of Sandview High. Like most districts in New York State, local school funding comes primarily from property taxes.[7] As a result of this resource deprivation, Sandview School District depends on state aid for more than two-thirds of its total budget, which still does not make up the difference in funding.

Sandview High was not always a struggling school; and the manner in which it lost its local financial resource base corresponds with Sandview High becoming a struggling school. That is, the political economic conditions in Sandview deteriorated *leading up to* new changes to education policy that epitomize the post–"No Child Left Behind" policy context the United States has been in nationally for over the last twenty years. Examining the history and role of private business decisions in the divestment of Sandview High School shows that where large employers laid down geographic roots—literally, by building up their infrastructure within or outside of a given county or city limit—played a huge role in the ensuing troubles Sandview High and its district experienced. Unpacking the deepening social inequalities in this specific case reveals how, as disadvantage grew, it led to devastating consequences for the school and the students it serves.

Malls, Jobs, the Factory, and the State

Pam is a joyful Black woman in her early fifties. I met Pam through her work in a community-based organization (CBO) aiming to support youth who are facing social disadvantages. There I also met and spoke with some of her coworkers. Like her, they are all older, Black, and have lived in the area since the 1970s. They are also parents of (now) adult children who attended Sandview High School during the school's better times. Like the other older community members I spoke with for this study, they all recall the Sandview District in the early 1980s being *high quality*. "The schools used to be very good," Pam tells me, motioning with her hands over the top of her office desk. She continued, "Now it's just a mess." How is it that Sandview High went from being "very good" to a "mess"?

The "mess" of Sandview High, as Pam put it, occurred in tandem with the city's conditions itself. Back in the 1970s to early 1980s, "The whole area was different," Pam stated. "It was wonderful, it was *beautiful*." One example of this beauty was a small "walking mall" where the "locals" easily accessed goods and visitors also came to do some of their shopping. "They had everything you could want," Pam recalled with pleasure. "There were record stores, all the big labels, Woolworth, Lucky, Blatts, everything was in this area." This local shopping center buttressed the community's economy and was also something people took pride in. But like many small towns, the growing arrival of corporate malls just outside Sandview fostered the local economy's downfall. Pam outlined Sandview's story, "Then you had a mall opened up outside of town, and that changed stuff . . . And then another one also outside of town opened too; and *that* was when the local businesses started to close." All of the long-term residents I spoke to told a story like Pam's: the onslaught of new corporate malls opening outside of the town's boundary—outside of where the town could collect any tax revenue—and how it fostered the closing of the local businesses. This process, in turn, undermined the local tax base and deepened local economic distress. These events were just one part of why Sandview's local economy declined, as the closing of a large factory in the area further halted economic prospects for a vast number of residents.

I met Michael and Joseph the same way I met Pam, through their jobs in a community-based nonprofit organization aiming to support class-disadvantaged youth in the Sandview area. In our conversations, both Michael and Joseph explained that the kids here struggled with school mainly because they experienced significant mental health problems due to family neglect, stemming from their parents' meager job prospects. As Joseph explained, "Now parents work 2–3 jobs and have no time to raise the kids; there used to be more time for families." Joseph said that previously there *were* better jobs available, so parents did not have to work two or three of them to get by. Like the other old-timers I spoke to, Michael and Joseph described the loss of factory jobs as the key factor in the town's transition to poverty. As Joseph put it, the loss of a particular "major employer" was "traumatic" to the working-class people of Sandview. The jobs lost were living-wage, working-class factory jobs. The loss of this employer also led to the "tributary organizations" going "down the drain too," Joseph explained. In other words, all of the local businesses suffered when a large employer disappeared. "It was a huge employer . . . I knew people who lost their jobs, took the buyout, retired . . . Before, it was, you work at [the plant], you going to have a job that would last a lifetime until you retire." Once the factory closed, "then, the tax base changed, which meant that basis to support the school district changed, schools could no longer depend on those taxes; so, it had a ripple effect of lost income but also lower tax income to the city and the lost capital, it changed the economy. Now, there is a deficit, that is *different*, more poverty." Thus, when the plant downsized, the entry-level jobs were cut. This, as well as the construction of malls outside the city limits, were major blows to the local industry, revenue base, and property values.

In her story, Pam also described how the plant's closing affected her family directly. "My sister was one of them that lost her job . . . She didn't have a college degree, all she had was those twelve years of experience with them . . . She [like the others]; they do a buyout, that money wasn't going to last them maybe two years." A lot of them, Pam explained, had worked there for more than a decade, "That's all they did, what happens to them? They're still young." She emphasized that there were "a range of manufacturing businesses closed down and people lost their jobs, but when one in particular closed, large numbers of people displaced when they shut down in the early '80s. They had a number of sites, they had a big building, and they shut most of that down, and they closed plants, and a *lot* of people got laid off. Now the poverty here gets worse every year." She described how she sees "despair and hopelessness" among the families, a feeling that is also prevalent in the schools.

Joseph and Pam's coworker Michael shared similar reflections but also extended his thoughts to the existing local retail economy, stating: "The jobs here now, the Gap, the laundry, McDonalds, are *go-nowhere jobs*, that is what they are designed to be." Michael's comments brought me back to a community forum I had attended a few years prior. I first met their colleague Ellen at this forum, and she then introduced me to all of them.

"Challenges for youth in Sandview" was the title of the community forum. Held in a small community center, it was an older building with interior walls heavily lined with wood paneling. The audience was mostly full, largely made up of service providers of some sort (as I was told by a forum participant). There was also at least one member of the city council, the school board, and (briefly) the school superintendent in attendance. At one point, Ellen stepped up to the podium in front to speak. With a poise that seemed to suppress strong emotions, she explained to the crowd that she and her colleagues could "train" youth, but there are "no living-wage jobs" for them, "just Target and Walmart." An older Black woman, Ellen urged the crowd of mainly White middle-aged individuals to understand that the most significant way that they could support the youth she served was to *hire* them. Later during the meeting, another older Black woman in the audience stood and echoed Ellen's point. She looked around the room and declared, "You say the kids are supposed to go to school and have hope, well why should they have hope when all they see is their parents fighting because they are stressed because they can't get enough work or a job at all." She continued, "Thinking about poverty, it's not just about skills, it is about lack of *jobs*." These comments were a direct contrast to the core of the discussion, which had lamented "broken families" and advertised the transient services various community and municipal entities offered to youth facing "challenges."

Attending this "Challenges" forum reminded me of how the high school students described their work experiences. On the one hand, some Sandview High students reported that any job was hard to come by, even those Michael would call go-nowhere jobs. As a student named Martín told me, "I don't know why no one here wants to hire me." Robert, another student, echoed this point. Robert gazed out the window of the passenger side of my car as I drove him home after his interview. We passed a series of popular fast-food restaurants. Robert shared, "I applied and none of those places would hire me."

Often, students with jobs worked *outside* of Sandview. These were also go-nowhere jobs, often the same types of jobs that their parents held. Some of the better jobs involved working at a mall just outside of town. Most often, the better jobs among the students' parents were also outside of Sandview, elder care jobs notable among them. Many immigrant students and their parents also worked in private small businesses just outside of Sandview, in construction, farming, domestic labor, or restaurants. Just beyond Sandview's tax boundaries, where these jobs are located, is a range of affluent communities; these affluent communities received cheap labor from Sandview residents without having to support any of the local services, including the schools, for the increasingly very modest-income population that resides in Sandview.

Double Free Riding

This relationship between Sandview and its affluent neighbors correlates with what scholars have called "suburban free riding," where rich suburbs get labor from working-class people in a city without paying the human costs, like support for city schools.[8] As such, affluent families can use the city infrastructure, which includes services provided by low-income communities, but not contribute their property tax dollars, which they put back into their suburban towns. This leaves low-wealth populations isolated. They strive to manage with an impoverished tax base, dealing with already-thin budgets stretched among high-needs populations. But in low-income suburbs like Sandview that exist outside rich cities, there is actually a *double free riding* problem.[9] In this case, wealthy suburbs border low-income ones, *and* the low-income suburbs have increasingly taken in the city's poorest population, who then labor in both the wealthy nearby suburbs and the unaffordable revitalized city center. Here, both the rich city and the rich suburbs benefit from the low-cost labor of class-disadvantaged populations—populations who live next door in low-wealth suburbs where there is zero tax base and that also must bear all the costs of the poor.

Importantly, the big factory in which so many people in Sandview worked until it closed was also built just outside of the town's boundary. As Roger, another old-timer I spoke with explained, because the plant's executives chose to locate just outside of Sandview's border, Sandview did not benefit from the business's tax revenue. The factory recruited a new affluent middle-class workforce, which also settled, along with their families, just outside of Sandview's boundary. These affluent newcomers then contributed to establishing and growing a resource base away from Sandview's schools and its local tax base. This was a deliberate move for the affluent to hoard resources, depriving Sandview.

Like many older residents, Roger largely blamed the breakdown of Sandview High on the fact that these new affluent White parents lobbied for a new public high school, to be built near the plant, just miles away from Sandview. Roger's four children (now adults) all attended the Sandview schools. He explained, "At the time [1970s], Sandview High School was high quality, it had this reputation region-wide. Then, they took all of the best teachers." He was visibly outraged, after all this time. The new public high school near the plant was the result of fierce grassroots lobbying on the part of White and affluent parents. This happened even as the New York State Department, at that time, was aiming to fully consolidate these two small districts, as well as those of other nearby small districts. Even now, that neighboring high school serves just over four hundred students, while Sandview serves more than a thousand. In other words, a new district was deliberately created to redistrict White and affluent students.

This redistricting, along with the choice of a major employer to build up industry just outside Sandview's city limits, fostered the isolation of the affluent and modest income families from each other in the Sandview region. This history set the stage for more recent White flight, which also undermined Sandview High School and its district's resource base. As education scholar Nikole Hannah Jones put it, "when White people leave, they take all of their resources with them."[10]

Navigating Place-Based Inequalities: White Flight, Gentrification, and New Immigration

Because many suburban schools increasingly show the same racialized injustices that Jonathan Kozol famously identified in urban sites as "savage inequalities," the rising suburban-to-suburban school inequalities can be considered a type of state-involved "violence."[11] Since Sandview's tax base is very low, Sandview High has inadequate funding to meet the students' needs. Sandview High has a crumbling school infrastructure, a vermin problem, overcrowded classrooms, outdated and incomplete textbooks, and few teachers with more than a couple of years of experience. But just down the road from Sandview High you will find (entirely public) "suburban" school districts with the best school features local tax money (and parent volunteers and private donations) can buy. And, for reasons related to racialized generational social inequities, students in the well-resourced schools tend to be White, while those in the nearby divested schools tend to be Black and Latinx.[12] The

Milliken v. Bradley US Supreme Court case (1974) affirmed that all of this is perfectly legal; plaintiffs of cases related to their local schools' racial segregation must prove clear intent to discriminate. It also made racial segregation between nearby districts that much easier to create.[13] In response, White families jumped the district boundary to develop their own "public" schools.

Today, almost all the students at Sandview High are Black or Latinx from modest income families. But this is recent. Historically, Sandview High was an integrated (Black and White) school with modest poverty rates among its students. From the 1990s to the present, White families left Sandview High as new Black and Latinx families moved in. Even in 2000, roughly one in four of Sandview High students were still White; by 2015, that number dropped to around one in ten. At the same time, the proportion of low-income Sandview High students increased, until by 2012, about four out of five Sandview High students were low-income.

Thus, consistent with persistent national patterns of how social inequality is racialized, as White students left Sandview High and Black and Latinx students came in, the average number of students living below the poverty line went up. And, at the same time, as public schools continue to be funded largely by local taxes, the resource base of the school went down. Furthermore, even beyond local taxes, more affluent families often also help their local schools with donations or volunteer hours because they have the resources to do so. When more affluent families leave, those shared resources do too. The rising poverty rates among Sandview High students meant that the school district increasingly had limited funding because of the low tax base.

Local education resources, like those used to fund individual schools, are tied to geography. The big picture in Sandview is that White students left Sandview High as more Black and Latinx students enrolled. Sandview High is surrounded by other suburban schools with relatively low poverty.[14] In its county, there are also other high-poverty suburbs next to still other low-poverty suburbs.[15] Most of the students in the neighboring school districts are also White. In the closest school district, whose high school is less than five miles from Sandview High, the number of students living below the poverty line is just about 10 percent. The race and class differences in the student population between Sandview High and its neighboring districts also parallel stark resource differences between these schools. This further corresponds to stark differences in student performance outcomes that are tightly monitored by the state—with huge and growing penalties for low performance.

Gentrification and New Immigration

Sandview's story in part is one of people moving in and out of political economic borders. As I learned from Sandview High students, many of them were not from Sandview, but rather came there from New York City. Either they had moved with their parents when they were younger, or their parents had moved to Sandview before they were born. The reason they moved was that NYC was just too expensive. "Lack of money" was the most succinct way that I heard this representative experience expressed. Most of these students were African American. The gentrification of New York City had pushed more working-class Black and Latinx families into suburbs like this one. As a result, Sandview was receiving many new African American students and Latinx students, most of them being class-disadvantaged.

The school itself was in a residential neighborhood and to me it looked similar geographically to the many other little towns I had driven through, either en route to Sandview, or while visiting friends in other nearby towns. These small towns were all "upstate" New York, which in this region meant just a short (often one- or two-hours') drive from NYC. Many of the people I met in this area, including Sandview, commuted to NYC for work. Nearly everyone I met traveled to NYC for entertainment. The last few decades had changed the character of these towns: Some are a bit larger, others smaller; many *used to* have thriving area businesses. These are what scholars call "inner-ring" suburbs of major central cities like NYC: nearby suburbs that offer aging, affordable, uncompetitive old housing stock where low-income residents go when they are pushed out of city centers with rising housing costs.[16]

Inner-ring suburbs contrast with the popular conception of suburban living as an upward step in social mobility. In fact, poverty has been growing in suburban contexts for the last two decades. This increase in poverty is highly racialized. Since the 1990s, suburbia broadly has become increasingly racially diverse. Now most of the Black and Latinx population in metro (non-rural) areas are living in suburban regions, with the greatest growth taking place in inner-ring suburbs.[17] And, like many low-income suburban contexts, an increasing number of Sandview High's students are immigrants.

Unlike the new African American students, most Latinx students immigrated to Sandview from Latin America. All of the Latinx students I met were from immigrant families, and nearly all of them were immigrants themselves. Almost all of the immigrant students were undocumented and came straight to the Sandview area after their initial arrival in various parts of the United States. In short, Sandview was their primary destination, even if they took a circuitous route to arrive there. There were also a small number of students whose families had immigrated from Jamaica. All of the immigrant students either identified as Black or Latinx, but not both. The Latinx immigrant student population was mainly from Mexico, Honduras, or Guatemala, but I also met students from the Dominican Republic, Nicaragua, and Costa Rica.

New migration from Latin America was also quite recent at Sandview. As one African American student named Tara put it, "Now there people here from all over," explaining, "I don't know why they're here; how did people find this place? A lot of people is just here out of nowhere." Alma is one of those new people. She arrived two years ago from the Dominican Republic. She described Sandview as "bien chiquita aca y muy afuera de la ciudad." (*It's very small here and far from the city.*) Alma and many of the students go to "la ciudad" (NYC) for a day trip or for shopping and entertainment with their families. Some also work in the larger nearby towns where there is more commerce and more people with money to hire them. Strikingly, two of the towns nearest to Sandview have greater than 350 percent of the student population of Tara and Alma's school. Those schools have a nearly all-White student population. The relative huge size of the student populations in those adjacent districts happened in ways that are related to the choice of individual White parents to leave, but also state policies that allowed for these districts to be created and sustained.

White Flight

The move of White families out of Sandview High was possible partly because of how New York State allowed school districts to be designed in this region, which consists of an above average number of small, often *very* small, districts. This outcome is largely the result of public policy advocated by White parents.[18] Probably the most contested local redistricting was the relatively recent creation of Trails High School, near Sandview High School. Affluent White parents lobbied the state to build Trails. Archival news coverage reveals that journalists and activists (and likely many more) recognized this as a forthright effort by these parents to hoard their wealth. They also saw that the change would predictably concentrate racialized wealth and poverty in the region. It did.[19] This was a dramatic example of the redrawing of public resources, but there were other, more discreet efforts in the region, as shown by the numerous small districts compared to other regions. Such a phenomenon is also quite common for highly stratified geographic regions outside of the New York region.[20]

White affluent families in the Sandview area acted on vested interests to shape school policies and practices. Importantly, those private family efforts are also linked to the acquiescence of public governance to these private social actor groups. They also parallel practices among private companies. Well-known mass national historic trends in segregation occur through realtors, banks, and private White homeowners—and often their "association" organizations. These corporate entities set up highly unequal political geographic contexts where people live, work, and go to school.[21] Some urban sociologists and critical geographers describe this as a process of sinking capital into land.[22] They stress that preexisting political structures like municipal boundaries and taxes make this process possible. It is the *accumulation* of land use laws over time that largely shapes what is and is not allowed, and, critically, the structure of school funding. This is an example of "opportunity hoarding," in which those with many advantages choose not to share with the disadvantaged people in their regional population. Such decisions are strategic, like choosing where a new company is built, just outside of a particular geopolitical boundary. The reason that White families could make the choice to leave Sandview High was the buildup all around them, including the many nearby districts to which they could relocate.

Thus, the divestment of Sandview High is related not only to private White families' decisions but also to ongoing public policies that allow private individuals and companies to hoard resources in ways that systematically divested disadvantaged communities from opportunities to access social goods, like education. The state sustains new and old policies related to districts and funding schools that make individuals' decisions to exit possible. This reminds me of a whip-smart comment from one of my students at the end of a lecture on this subject: "Why don't we have just one big district for different large regions in a state?" The answer, of course, is because of actual and anticipated resistance from White affluent families.[23]

Suburban Poverty: The Worst-Case Scenario

Suburban schools like Sandview High have extra challenges when compared to large urban centers. Their small scale and scattered locations result in fewer comparative resources as well as invisibility. There are many underfunded schools in affluent cities like New York. Yet the city itself has funds that potentially can be tapped and city council members with some degree of localized power. In Sandview, all local political positions are part-time with nominal compensation, and the city itself is broke. City Council members receive less than $8,000 annually and the mayor receives less than $25,000. Furthermore, Sandview has no formidable teachers' union to push back on state reforms, in contrast to struggling large urban schools in cities like Chicago or Philadelphia.

Thus, growing concentrated poverty in the suburbs may actually be the worst possible situation for disenfranchised populations and the schools their children attend.[24] These types of places do not have formidable teachers' unions. Their small scale makes it harder to expand the existing limited community-based advocacy or organizing bodies. And, crucially, there is no city wealth to lobby for and few smaller local institutions with any political influence. In contrast, even the most devastated large inner-city centers can exert some pressure on a larger political unit that has some resources. For instance, New York City and Chicago have some of the most distressed public schools in the country. But these cities have huge budgets that can be directly lobbied for to help those schools. Their enduring struggle makes it clear that this is no easy task. However, in settings like much of upstate New

York, municipalities are legally divided into scores of small cities and towns.[25] And for those with low wealth like Sandview, there is no regional money to lobby for.

Looking Back, Looking Forward

At the same time that the resources were extracted, the Sandview District, and its singular high school, was increasingly targeted by the neoliberal state for "too-low" student academic performance. Sandview School District's (SSD) sole high school (Sandview High) is one of its schools on probation for academic performance nearly every year since 2005. New York State had labeled it "failing" because its students scored too low on the state's exams. But Sandview High had not always been low-performing by state standards. Even into the early 2000s, New York State's evaluations of Sandview High indicated that it was still in "good standing" with the state's expectations for school quality. But from the mid-2000s onward, it became a "failing" school: Students' graduation rates dropped and it failed on new state student performance standards. In part, Sandview High became a "failing" school due to the altered state standards themselves: The new exams were harder for students to pass. From the state's point of view, it was just "raising the bar." However, most critical analysts saw the new exams as problematic. The state narrowed curricula, reduced local control, offered insufficient implementation resources, and fixated on rebuking schools for noncompliance. Analysts also claimed that state exams were badly designed.[26]

The state's plan was that schools like Sandview High undergo one of their standardized improvement programs. The state's promise (or justification) had been that this top-down temporary new management with a plan would get Sandview High on the right track. Once it complied, Sandview High's leadership would regain control of its school. But restructuring did not help Sandview High. As of this writing, still just *half* of its students graduate. The short-term extra resources, the execution of state-led standardized and market-oriented reform plans tied to those funds did not improve those outcomes, and neither did the state's pressure to improve. Consequently, Sandview High continues to have more state-led interventions. As one local Sandview High community member and GED educator recently put it, "The state is running that school now."

How Sandview High Got to Where It Is Today

Sandview High's history illustrates how the school got to where it is today. This helps to explain why "schooling under threat of closure" did not work. The state's approach to school reform misconstrues a set of concentrated structural disadvantages. The state disparages the school and the population it serves for "failing" and then prescribes mandatory improvements with inadequate resources. The labeling process through new federal test score mandates has been a stigmatizing force, further framing the schools as "bad," while "good" becomes largely synonymous with "good state test scores." And, as we will soon learn, no one at the school (administrators, teachers, or students) thought these changes were good ideas. The reforms created new harms, and over time there were no tangible improvements in the outcomes based on state metrics.

Resource deprivation and opportunity hoarding expressed through a combination of public and private decisions related to school funding and assignments played a key role in why Sandview High became a "bad" school. Like national trends, Black and Latinx students at Sandview High have lower rates of academic achievement than White students, especially in standardized tests. But what those statistics actually mean is that there are deep differences in the average resources between those student groups that help them do well in school. As scholars continue to report, affluence and segregation *sharply* impact academic achievement.[27] As such, the isolation of wealth and disadvantage remain the key element to renewing the enduring "opportunity gap" for children's educational outcomes.[28] In this context (Sandview High), as in many others around the country, very poor suburbs exist next to very wealthy suburbs.[29] Schools are funded, and students are assigned, based on political geographic boundaries that we call districts. Nationally, carving out "districts" has been a strategy that those with many resources have exploited to block those with fewer resources from access. Scholars call this "opportunity hoarding," which is also related to the "resource deprivation" experienced by families with modest incomes.[30]

The uneven buildup of resources in this particular geography is exclusionary. It happened in a way that was related to a combination of private business decisions, public regulators, and choices by private individual White families. My analysis puts that specific history into a broader context to understand why some schools are "bad"; to understand the role of a suburban context; and to determine how this relates to neoliberal state reforms of said schools. While the rest of this book explores Sandview High School's plight to improve or be closed by the state, this chapter has explained why the neoliberal state was able to get involved in the first place: accumulations of divestment made possible through various means and moments of planned opportunity hoarding.

2

Schooling under Threat of Closure

State Surveillance and Punishment in Twenty-first Century Education

One day in school, when the state exam dates were getting close, a wide-eyed and scurrying school professional flashed me a nervous smile, then blurted with panic, "It's testing season," before rushing on. After this encounter, I continued walking to class through the school's main hallway. A large red poster broadcasting the diminishing days until state exams adorned the central passageway, immediately drawing the eye of anyone walking down the hall. Additional signs posted above students' lockers reminded them to follow school rules and prepare for the state exams. Beyond student lockers, a sign urged students to "work hard" and be on time to class. A few feet ahead, another sign prompted students to walk "respectfully." Yet, one sign dwarfed the rest: an eight-by-ten-foot poster entitled "Sandview High Data Wall." The Data Wall was part of Sandview High's official school improvement plan to better meet state testing benchmarks. It showed more than a dozen different bar charts, five additional sets of tables, and a series of explanations. These charts summarized the state test scores for different student cohorts, with a breakdown by subgroups of students as signified by acronyms, such as "ELLs" (English Language Learners). The Data Wall resembled slides from a PowerPoint presentation for school administrators. However, the actual reasoning behind the Data Wall was that exhibiting these valued data points to students and teachers would motivate them to better meet Sandview High's goals of boosting state test scores and reducing suspensions.

Despite the Data Wall's prominence, it was the large red sign counting down to the state exams that seemed to best echo the omnipresent pressure to improve on state test scores. "Stressful," "crazy," and feeling like their "entire professional career" was at stake was how teachers at

Sandview High described this pressure from the state. As one teacher put it, "If our students don't do well, we're up for a state takeover and that means new teachers." Their fears were justified: State sanctions for Sandview High as a "low-performing" school included the option to replace all teachers. There were also regular warnings during my time there that New York State might shut down Sandview High and replace it with a charter school.

Closing Sandview High had been an option as a traditional public school in New York State since the No Child Left Behind Act (NCLB) of the early 2000s. Sandview High had been on probation for academic performance nearly every year since 2005. It seemed to me that the state was never going to close Sandview High, that the threat of closure was their preferred tool, and it would disappear if the school was actually closed. I learned that Sandview High's case was common: on average, just 3 percent of schools threatened with closure for low performance are actually shut down, a statistic that has remained consistent throughout the post-NCLB era.[1] Importantly, there is real observed harm in school closings, yet, as analysts have noted, there is more to understand before schools are slated for closure than just the stark pain of the actual school closure process.[2] The fact that school closures do occur also strengthens the credible threat that it could happen to a specific school facing that risk.[3]

The fact that most of the time, "low-performing" schools persist under lasting state-led reform efforts is central to better understanding the problems surrounding neoliberal education reforms for low-performing schools since NCLB. Closure is the final pending sanction for schools like Sandview High, but in the lead-up to that possibility, these types of schools undergo endless evolving state-led restructuring programs that create stress and detriment for students, teachers, and other school professionals.

Neoliberalism and Twenty-first Century Education Reform

The state threatening Sandview High with school closure is a *neoliberal* approach to improving children's education. Neoliberal reforms reorganize public institutions and their underlying organizations to be more like businesses, a process also called "market orientation."[4] The professed aim of neoliberal governance is to shrink the work of the state, shifting public goods like education into the private sector (privatization) because this is believed to be a better way to get people the services they need.[5] Since the NCLB Act of the early 2000s, the federal government has used market-based solutions to improve low-performing public schools. These types of reforms include: bringing corporate consultants into individual public schools; having private companies sell schools extra test preparation services; and allowing charter schools to replace or compete with existing public school options.[6] From the view of the market-approach advocates, the public sector can either improve by acting more like the private sector or be replaced by it entirely.[7]

Since 2015, the key neoliberal education reforms of NCLB live on as the "Every Student Succeeds Act" (ESSA). The federal government has taken great pains to present this policy shift in 2015 as a departure from NCLB, but critics dispute that the rules have actually changed in substance.[8] Instead, critical scholars like sociologist of education Pedro Noguera maintain that the core "test and punish" approach of the prior system continues.[9] In particular, the ESSA continues the federal mandate that states engage in escalating interventions for low-performing schools, largely based on students' state test score averages.[10] These escalating state interventions typically include school closure.[11] Notably, "state takeovers" of public schools deemed low-performing is a growing trend around the country in the ESSA era, using the common tool of "test-based accountability and charter schools as an intervention strategy."[12] In short, states are opening new paths to public school shutdown. And, while the specific policies for intervening in low-performing schools change, their general "test and punish" treatment plan remains the same.

The risk of school closure for poor performance is a quintessential neoliberal school reform policy, according to advocates and critics alike.[13] For both groups, market-centered principals guide the strategy of closing low-performing schools to improve children's education.[14] The advocates of school closures believe that poor management is at the heart of a school's disappointing performance, and that thus it is best to either replace them with privately run charter schools or move children to a different school.[15] The advocates' professed plan is that "the educational market should select out those schools that fail to improve."[16]

On the other hand, critics of plans to close schools stress that private sector greed for prospective profit persuades promoters to stimulate options for school privatization as a strategy to manage low-performing schools.[17] Critics document how these sponsors have exploited the problem of neglected urban public schools, seizing an opportunity to privatize formerly public resources with the help of the federal government.[18] These critical scholars focus on large central cities and stress the contestation over public resources in those settings, including charter school networks "circling" to take over, as well as their location in "fought-over" gentrifying epicenters.[19]

Rising State Carcerality: The Punitive Nature of Neoliberal Accountability for Struggling Schools

I frame the situation for stressed schools under threat of closure as an increase in state carcerality, a type of punitive governance ushered in under the banner of market-oriented reform. The "carceral state" means coercive state intervention in people's lives, typically focusing on the criminal justice system.[20] My framing deepens the critical analysis of the neoliberal state because it is in contrast with the leading view that neoliberalism mainly uses privatization schemes to offer opportunities for capitalists' financial gains. Instead, I contend that, in the case of schools under threat of closure, the state maintains these schools in an endless situation of punitive restructuring under the auspice that it will discipline schools, and everyone in them, into a level of state compliance that is ultimately unattainable. It is a type of state-sanctioned purgatory that is undertheorized in a literature that emphasizes school closures.[21]

Much of the critical education scholarship has stressed how capitalist profit incentives drive overtly "neoliberal" K-12 education reform policies, suggesting that NCLB-style policies embody a shift to privatization of formerly public assets, including authority over K-12 public schools.[22] This scholarship has drawn from geographer David Harvey, suggesting that the neoliberal state takes a smaller role for the private sector to lead.[23] In contrast, political economists like Ben Fine and Alfredo Saad-Filho have explained that neoliberalism does not typically reflect state retreat.[24] But this type of insight still excessively stresses financial incentives, masking the role of political motivations. As education policy scholar Michael Apple has pointed out, NCLB de-democratized K-12 education through "massive recentralization" of power.[25] The ESSA is slightly less dramatic in this recentralization, but still requires states to test and punish low-performing schools. Since the ESSA's passage, many states have doubled down on the prior tools, expanding state laws to allow them to take over individual low-performing schools, which include even more paths to restructuring and closing these schools, replacing them with charter schools.[26] Thus, states are using the ESSA to further the credibility of closure as a threat.

When critical education scholars generally talk about the growing carceral state and its connection to schools, they are typically discussing harsh school discipline and the fortification of schools in ways that copy the criminal justice system.[27] Carceral state scholars like geographer Ruth Wilson Gilmore highlight how the explicit neoliberal turn in governance has relegated the state's legitimate work to the penal sphere.[28] These types of scholars build on Michel Foucault's claim that this shift to a larger carceral state is what maintains the state's validity in a context where its leaders contend that the state's role in supporting social welfare should be limited.[29] Sociologist of education Carla Shedd helpfully uses the term "carceral continuum" to reflect how schools have become more prisonlike, as well as the education system's parallels to the carceral state in neighborhoods, such as the ever-present threat of being hassled by police officers.[30] Additional aspects of the carceral state in this study include policies threatening schools with closure, coercion into top-down punitive school regimens focused on standardized testing, and the control of students' bodies through authoritative disciplinary practices to compel them to participate in onerous testing drills. Thus, the *ongoing* process of subjecting low-performing schools (like Sandview High) to increasing sanctions that include the threat of school closure is a means by which the carceral state is growing. Accordingly, neoliberal reforms are not just a way to separate people from public resources, such as when their public schools are shuttered (for private profit and austerity measures), but also a way to usher in the carceral state.[31]

Rather than withering away, the state's role grows as carceral schooling does, from designing and introducing new punitive forms of schooling to creating conditions for school professionals to work under threat of sanctions. These policies are largely driven in through elite state policy mandates that link funding to compliance. These policies undermine the ability of even the most caring professionals to help their students. Critically important, the changes target working-class students of color.[32]

Conditionality

Conditionality is a central element of what makes neoliberal education reforms for low-performing schools punitive.[33] The ostensive logic is that the state is merely holding schools accountable, which is the best way to improve education for disadvantaged student populations. States have threatened low-performing schools with potential closure since NCLB and have continued through the ESSA era. This is how policies work to usher in "market" logic, but with it come new punitive school conditions. These conditions also include how states like New York have embarked on new legislation such as New York's 2015 State Receivership Law.[34] This law, and others like it in other states, also explicitly expand punitive school conditions by threatening the potential for school closures as a tool to reform "bad" schools.[35]

Since NCLB, the ESEA (Elementary and Secondary Education Act of 1965, including its current ESSA version) requires states to identify and restructure their "lowest performing" public schools (those in the bottom 5 percent). The main difference with the ESSA is that the state is the one charged with doing the interventions; previously, the US Department of Education told states exactly what they had to do prescriptively. At stake is a state's access to ESEA money for their public K-12 schools with a high percentage of students living below the federal poverty line (Title I schools). As a result, states aim to comply largely to get this money. Since the ESSA, states have greater flexibility in exactly how they intervene in their low-performing schools, but they still must intervene. The ESSA requires states to undertake "more rigorous interventions" with schools remaining low-performing.[36] And, potential school closures have only expanded as an intervention tool in this more "flexible" ESSA policy context.[37] This is somewhat unsurprising given that many states' plans with the federal government for the updated ESEA under ESSA "look like NCLB 2.0."[38] As sociologist of education Pedro Noguera put it, the focus is still "accountability as measured by test scores."[39] The targeted schools' access to essential funding as well as the promise of greater local autonomy is linked to their agreement to try to improve by state standards. Thus, state compliance with ESEA comes at a particular cost for low-performing schools: restructuring.

At the school level, conditionality means tying indispensable school funding to implementing and prioritizing state-led market-oriented restructuring programs. The approach is to offer schools funding conditional on applying its reform instructions. The logic remains that with added temporary resources, pressure, and a state-led improvement plan, the "bad" school will improve. Schools the state labels low-performing must focus on increasing students' state exam scores and are pressed to do so by implementing market-oriented solutions, such as contracting private companies to train teachers and offer new practice tests for state exams. This is the case even though education experts are unconvinced that these indicators are useful measures of school quality.[40] Low-performing schools are forced to restructure to produce state-mandated metrics of achievement. If they do not meet these goals, the state will further discipline them. The state tells these schools that they can remain as traditional public schools if they meet certain external criteria developed by the state and private partners. Thus, it is the credible *threat* of dissolution that coerces individual schools into participating in state-led school restructuring.[41]

Federal and state entities have been able to compel individual school districts and their specific schools to implement their preferred policies. Neoliberal education reforms have ushered in endless compliance monitoring from more centralized and powerful governance entities, federal or state governments, to individual schools and their districts. Yet, while reform mandates shift government control upward, leaving little power to local school administrators, these local managers are then assigned blame for failing to meet state standards, even when they restructure their schools according to the state-led reform program. Thus, the state shifts the blame for failure to the local school administration.

Schooling under Threat of Closure at Sandview High

The first round of test-and-punish policies at Sandview High took place in the early 2000s. These policies shifted to become more powerful in 2012, and again in 2015 due to a new New York State law that ramped up the pressure on its public schools like Sandview High that had been on probation for the last three years or more. The school administration for Sandview High knew if they did not produce the results the state stipulated that they would be fired and replaced with new administrators. The local newspaper still (as of this writing) reports on the "constant turnover" among the top school administrator positions. Nearly all of the school's assistant principals and other top administrative positions change hands every year. There is also a new principal and a new superintendent every few years. Some of this turnover has been driven by episodic dismissals of top school administrators because they were found to be helping students cheat on the state tests. Others simply left. This constant turnover illustrates how much state pressure the school's administrators are under.

The school's leadership team called the state's 2012 intensification of Sandview High's sanctions "a time of urgency in getting those test scores up," in one exemplary quote from an interview with the local news media. This escalating pressure occurred because New York State identified Sandview High as one of the low-performing schools for deeper state-led interventions. New York put Sandview High (and the rest of its 5 percent lowest-performing schools) in probationary status so that the state could receive an ESEA "waiver" to prevent its losing federal funding because its public schools were not all meeting the updated federal benchmarks.[42] This was a new ESEA element introduced in 2012, designed to deepen governmental intimidation. The US Department of Education required states to dramatically improve their struggling schools, using added resources, pressure, and improvement plans. So, New York State increasingly intervened in Sandview High with the main goal of raising students' performance on the state's standardized tests. Under the newer system, New York State schools where students' average state test scores were below the state's targets had to undergo a state-directed school improvement process.[43]

Deepening the Threat: Expanding the Possibility of a State Takeover

While the NCLB era of the ESEA is over (currently replaced with the ESSA), the threat of school closure has actually seemed to deepen in part through new state takeover legislation. Evolving laws in states like

New York to take over individual schools, or whole districts, expand the possibility of a state takeover of these schools. Under these types of laws, schools are initially put into state "receivership." The essence of this type of state policy for low-performing schools is the use of a bigger stick. As one school receivership superintendent pointedly remarked in a media interview, "The state is expecting these schools to make things dramatically different in a short period of time when all the state is threatening them with is a bigger stick."[44]

Sandview High was one of 144 schools in New York State under "receivership," through a new state law ("New York Education Transformation Law") aimed at restructuring low-performing schools according to ESEA accountability standards in 2015.[45] This law placed schools in the lowest 5 percent of the state that had been so since the 2012–13 school year in "receivership," a ranking that was largely based on the students' low state test scores.[46] The new law broadened state powers to reform these types of schools, intensifying the state's earlier programs. These schools were under state pressure even before the new law, but the receivership made school closure an imminent threat if students' test scores did not improve, putting new fear and pressure on all the schools' stakeholders.[47] It also allowed New York State to assign an external manager to run the school for three years who could supersede any local school policies, dismiss all school employees, or request a new modified collective bargaining agreement.[48]

Being under receivership forced Sandview High to accept the terms of an even stricter improvement program: forgo local control, allow extensive restructuring. As Ms. Dobbs, Sandview High's (2015) superintendent, asserted in a public statement, the receivership would "intensify" their existing reform program. It required Sandview High to make "demonstrable improvement" in student attendance, state test scores, and various discipline indicators.[49] New York State specifies which indicators are available for selection and then chooses most of the metrics for the individual school.[50] Thus, the improvement mandates shifted government control toward one that was more top-down and standardized, leaving little power to local school administrators. This outcome is predictable: Neoliberal "NCLB-style" reforms were built on the notion that managerial issues were at the heart of schools' problems, which merited ignoring local leadership and hiring consultants.[51]

Sandview High was compelled to participate in New York State's receivership program under enormous state pressure. Importantly, no one in the school's leadership seemed to think the receivership, or the state's related efforts to reform Sandview High, were good ideas. In the last quarter of receivership, the Sandview High School administration completed a mandatory state survey document evaluating their experience with the program. As this document reveals, there was stark contrast between the reform program they were given and their own concerns for the school, as well as the approach they would have liked the state to take to support them. The school leaders at Sandview High used the section on the school's "unmet needs" to be critical of the state's restructuring programs. They cited their utmost unmet need was adequate, sustained, flexible funding.[52] They contrasted their school's unmet needs with the *temporary*, *restrictive*, and *insufficient* state funding offered for them as a low-performing school. They framed this desired funding as an issue of unaddressed "equity," describing how this funding could help their top needs of addressing "supports for high-needs populations" and "staff turnover." The school leadership also insisted that the state should provide opportunities to witness "high-performing districts/schools demonstrating effective practices" to model.[53]

Importantly, Sandview High's student outcomes did not improve as a result of the state's receivership program. In 2016, the graduation rate at Sandview High increased enough for New York State to remove it from the receivership program, but by 2018, Sandview High's graduation rate was back to its former lower levels. This drop occurred after a 2017 state inquiry into Sandview High's graduation data found widespread "improper and questionable" graduations, leading to the removal of nearly all top school administrators. Thus, in response to the incredible pressure they were under—and largely seeming to be buying time to stave off state inspectors—the school's leadership broke the rules to increase students' test scores and graduations. This outcome is the case in numerous struggling schools.[54] Strikingly, even when the graduation rate "increased," the improvement was still so slight that Sandview High remained in noncompliant status as a low-performing school, in the bottom 5 percent of New York State, keeping it under increased state scrutiny.[55] Thus, attaching badly needed (temporary) resources, because of historical and contemporary structural inequalities, to participation in punitive restructuring programs decided externally did not help raise the students' test scores. And while Sandview High's local leaders had little power, they were blamed for the failure, not the state improvement programs.[56]

Twin Regimes: Security and Testing

"Academic achievement" was "goal number one" and "safety and security" was "goal number two" according to Sandview High's website, reasonable goals for any school. But underneath these broadly worthy goals were state-led improvement plans that led the school to implement very particular twin school regimes that I refer to as *testing* and *security*. These regimes are linked in part through school improvement programs designed to restructure the school "for the better." Instead, they create a punishing environment for both students and school professionals.

Sandview High's Security Regime

"Security" was "goal number two" in Sandview High's District Comprehensive Improvement Plan (DCIP).[57] This is striking because Sandview High did not have a violence problem according to its own records.[58] The decision-making process to implement school safety practices at Sandview High is complex, but school policy documents show that the primary aim was to lower student misconduct. As a result, there were key changes in daily life at Sandview High via its state improvement plan related to "safety and security." The DCIP required Sandview High to raise student attendance and lower their suspension rates by enhancing "school culture and climate." So, following federal and state guidance and using the federal grant money attached to its reform plan, Sandview High purchased new student monitoring technology and metal detectors. It also installed new surveillance technology and added non-teaching security staff and a police patrol in 2013.[59]

Neoliberal federal and state education reform policies also broadly set the stage for Sandview High's efforts to meet its "Security" DCIP. First, one section of the ESEA, called the "Unsafe School Choice Option," required states receiving ESEA funds to provide more data gauging their safety levels (violent incidents) based on federal benchmarks. To comply, states had to create new school safety laws.[60] Consequently, New York State passed the SAVE Act (Schools Against Violence in Education), which created a uniform violent incident reporting system for New York State schools using Penal Law's definitions of crimes.[61] The SAVE Act also increased schools' ability to remove "disruptive" students and not count these sanctions as suspensions.[62] As a result, schools could use exclusionary punishment for many low-level school violations without those incidents counting on the school's student suspension rate, something it needed to keep low especially if it was a "low-performing" school. This change to the ESEA broadly was done as part of the shift toward the state holding schools "accountable" for how their students behave, including socially. It also changed the circumstances under which the state targeted low-performing schools for improvement, incentivizing these individual schools to ramp up securitization as a way to prove to the state that they are improving the school's climate.

States then devised standardized improvement plans that low-performing schools and districts with one or more low-performing school must implement, guided by federal rules. New York State uses a federal template called the "Diagnostic Tool for School and District Effectiveness," to review its lowest performing schools, and then selects one of the federally approved waiver programs.[63] For example, one option Sandview High had was the "Turnaround Model," through which the school received three-year federal grant funding attached to specific reforms. Most of the evaluation indicators involve students' test scores, but they also include student behavior metrics, measured largely by the number of incidents of student misbehavior.[64] In chapters 5 and 6, I show how the focus on improving students' obedience expanded punitive approaches to managing student discipline. In this way, "schooling under threat of closure" builds on analyses of how certain types of charter schools usher in socially controlling school regimes, also driven by neoliberal market-oriented school reforms epitomized by NCLB.[65]

The Testing Regime

Pressure in low-performing schools to improve students' state test scores is infamous, but a close look at school improvement plans illustrates how such a practice is unavoidable in low-performing schools like Sandview

High.[66] The incentive for the school's leadership and its teachers seemed simply too strong to engage in a different practice.

Everyone was "teaching to the test" and had an overly strict approach to teaching, the state's auditors critically reported following its inspection of Sandview High in 2014. Yet, because the state's standards were test-based, "raising academic achievement" became code for "teaching to the test." The teachers felt that the state had put them in an impossible situation. As one teacher explained, "The state is asking teachers to sprinkle our special dust on these kids . . . [and] if we haven't sprinkled that dust on them, then we are 'bad teachers'; and *that is stressful*. Especially if the state is saying, and the district is saying, and the administrators are saying, that this is something that can be used to get rid of teachers, or what they call 'bad teachers.'" This view was shared by the vast majority of Sandview High educators. As an independent survey of Sandview High teachers reported in 2015, about four out of five Sandview High teachers were either *worried* or *very worried* about their job security due to the students' performance on state or local tests.[67] This is also likely why a great many Sandview High teachers leave every year: The percentage of teachers teaching their first or second year at Sandview High is double the state average.[68] The total number of teachers also keeps dropping annually, which seems to suggest the problem of retention is even worse. Finally, about *half* of the teachers are "chronically absent" (10 days or more) every year. This is also two times the state's average for this issue. As one teacher told me, these absences were *precisely* about "burnout" due to increased work demands related to "testing." In addition, one of the substitute teachers told me that so many teachers were absent each day at Sandview that she could sub every day of the school year if she wanted to.

Auxiliary Tests

The state's contradiction went further: It required better student performance on its standardized tests, the addition of new "non-state" standardized tests into their classes, but did not want "teaching to the test." Sandview High added new auxiliary tests through contracts with state-approved corporations. On the surface, this was a straightforward market-centered approach to school improvement: Bring in the consultants, let them add new educational products. But these auxiliary tests were added through a state template for school improvement, meaning the state was still managing the school, just at a remote level. New York State's template is called District Comprehensive Improvement Plans (DCIPs), and my online search of Sandview High's recent history revealed nonstop DCIPs.[69] One "state-approved" product Sandview High purchased was the MAP (Measure of Academic Progress), an online test intended to gauge students' preparation for the actual state exams and evaluate the teachers.[70]

In practice, implementing the MAP test was a punitive policy. As one teacher described, MAP testing was a big deal even prior to the receivership, because of NCLB sanctioning: If they did not do well, this district was up for a state takeover, which they understood would mean new teachers. For one, its application was part of a school improvement plan that included a new process for firing teachers. This plan compelled Sandview High's local teachers' union to agree to a modified union contract, allowing them to be more easily fired based on students' MAP exam scores. The contract changes enabled these scores to have greater weight on the teachers' evaluations than before and any teacher with two low ratings had to be removed from the classroom.[71] This neoliberal approach to compelling what the state conceived of as greater teacher performance engendered fear and stress among teachers and threatened deeper sanctions on the school. As such, the expressly neoliberal reforms for Sandview High seemed to be at least just as much about carceral state expansion as they were about ushering in market-centered reforms.

In an interview I conducted with two Sandview High teachers, the fear and stress created by MAP testing was palpable. One of the teachers shook her head and stated, "The testing and teacher evaluations . . . it's so stressful and it gets worse every year," adding that if one did not know a teacher personally, "you have no idea what teachers are dealing with." The other teacher vented, "[Students] just get pulled out of their regular classes which are disrupted, the time for actual teaching . . . All this testing . . . And I'm not allowed to see the tests or what they are about, and there are supervisors in the room to supervise me and the kids." The MAP test was supposed to help improve students' education at Sandview High, but these teachers reported that it actually undermined students' learning: It reduced instructional time and it put extreme stress on teachers. One teacher said, "[Students] don't understand that it's our jobs that are being evaluated, it matters for my professional career." Both of these teachers had been punished for students having low MAP scores. One was being disciplined at the time of the conversation and the other had been the prior year. The one being disciplined was visibly astonished that the result of her poor evaluation meant that she needed to tailor the course more precisely to the MAP test. Thus, the key state recommended solution to poor test scores was to add more test preparation. Neither of these teachers thought this was effective pedagogy, but the conditions of the school reform program compelled them to implement it.

Teachers are still especially vulnerable in schools under state scrutiny. As sociologist of education Dara Shifrer demonstrated, when teachers move between "low-performing" and "high-performing" schools, their evaluations (still largely based on students' standardized test scores) change in ways that correspond with the low or high values associated with the schools' average student test score data.[72] In other words, teacher evaluations are based on bad data.[73]

"We Can't Do This Anymore"

In the two years I spent at Sandview High, I volunteered one to two times per week in a beginning ESOL (English for Speakers of Other Languages) classroom.[74] About 80 percent of the time that I was there, students were preparing for state tests. A typical day in class consisted of using a textbook or worksheet to prepare for a state exam. For one test-practice assignment, students were supposed to answer questions in English using complete sentences about a picture of a woman in a lab holding a test tube. "What is the setting, what is she doing, what might she be thinking?" When I sat with students, most of them couldn't read the instructions, let alone craft written answers to the questions. To begin, one student asked what the word "what" meant. The beginning ELL (English Language Learner) students, many of whom had recently arrived, were supposed to read whole sentences and answer questions in complete sentences in English. Many of the students tried to avoid the assignment by falling asleep. The teacher explained that she wanted to prepare them because they had six weeks of testing, for which they would be pulled out of class at different times. For another test preparation, the students had to listen to a tape and match words to pictures on their worksheets. The words included were often complex, such as "marsupial." At one point during the exercise, the teacher said to me quietly, "*I hate this.*"

On more than one occasion, students told me that they simply could not do these same exercises anymore. One day, several students exclaimed to me in Spanish, "Oh no, we've been doing this all week, no more." They had worked on a worksheet practicing the same sentences for an entire week. One sentence was, "I like to use my cell phone for texting." There were six pages of these statements. Several students in the class put their heads in their hands and told the teacher, "We can't do this anymore." In response, the teacher firmly shook her head and told them that they must. The students continued in chorus, "This is terrible, we can't do this anymore." Another day during class, I came across Carlos—a student in this class—hiding in an unlocked vacant computer lab. His eyes widened when he saw me, and he pleaded in Spanish that he could not go back to class because he could not do those endless test drills anymore.[75]

These days in the life of students under the testing regime show the harmfulness of the state's test-and-punish approach to "helping" Sandview High serve its new immigrant students, a very vulnerable student population at the school. The coursework was carried out through the explicitly neoliberal market-based reform mandate to improve their test scores. Yet, this does not provide meaningful opportunity for learning, which is likely why the teacher "hates this." These students are a captive population undergoing mechanistic tasks, forced into work for state funding. Yet, the state also criticized Sandview High for overtesting its students.

"Tried to keep a tight rein" on students' classroom participation and "suppressed the free exchange of ideas," the state's report concluded about Sandview High's teachers. This conclusion was based on observations of more nearly *half* of the teachers' classrooms at Sandview High.[76] Instead, the report's author recommended that Sandview High's teachers "promote open dialogue" in the classroom to improve their students' "deep applications of learning." The report was part of an external review Sandview High was required to undertake due to its low performance status, largely based on students' standardized test scores on the state's exams. I found this report during my regular online review of public documents related to Sandview High's enduring state evaluations.

I was struck by these state reviewers' comments about Sandview High teachers, because during my time observing and talking to students and professional staff there, it became shockingly clear to me that there was hardly any time for anything in class except test drills. Knowing this pressure and time constraint, it was no surprise to me that the state's reviewer observed that many of Sandview High's teachers tended to "keep a tight rein" on students' classroom participation.

My observation of one day in Ms. Turner's class highlights the stifling fallout of testing-oriented education. On this day in class, Ms. Turner introduced a new standardized test called the Writing Project. It was part of Sandview High's improvement plan to prepare students for a reading comprehension section of the state exam. Sandview High had recently purchased the test and paid associated consultants to train the teachers to implement it. The Writing Project was a major element of what the school's administration repeatedly cited as a new tool to better meet state performance expectations, measured by students' test scores on the state's standardized exams.

The subject matter of the reading for the Writing Project was child labor on tobacco farms in the United States. After the teacher explained the test to the students, a student named Jesus became visibly passionate about the topic because *he was* one of those children working on tobacco farms, not in the United States but rather in his home country of Guatemala. Incredulous, Jesus asked his teacher, "This happens in the United States?" All of the students inquisitively turned to look at him. He was flustered and seemed heartbroken to learn that exploitative child labor like he experienced in Guatemala was also happening in the United States. A pained look crossed the teacher's face, but she then abruptly stopped Jesus's talking, her eyes stopping to linger on the classroom clock. Ms. Turner said that they needed to double down and work faster to complete the school's required external assessment.

The state's external reviewers would likely label the moment described above as a teacher suppressing student discussion—and I agree. But from Ms. Turner's position, there was no time for Jesus to share his experiences and make what likely would have been a very relevant teaching point about the social problem that they were reading about in a way that would have engaged the students. Instead, the teacher had to get students to complete the assessment using standardized instructions.

Teachers like Ms. Turner are under extreme pressure to produce higher student test results on standardized exams. On one day in class, a man from the school district stormed into Ms. Turner's classroom twice on a single day to assert the importance of figuring out how to implement these new tests that the district had just paid for. Although I found him rude—he had literally interrupted her while she was teaching in front of her whole class—Ms. Turner did not seem startled at all and took his information politely in stride. I simply assumed that as a teacher in this type of school she was accustomed to this type of intrusion for new and evolving auxiliary testing requirements from the state.

Both students and teachers that I spoke to indicated to me that the teachers routinely ran out of time to cover the basic curriculum due to all of the extra state testing requirements. They meant not only additional drills for the state's exams, but also the auxiliary tests like the Writing Project that were part of the school's improvement program.

It should be no surprise to the state that this pressure tends to incentivize a repressive classroom management style. I had many conversations with Ms. Turner during my fieldwork and in none of those exchanges did it seem to me that she envisioned a teaching style focused on quelling student dialogue. Instead, she lamented how much time the auxiliary tests took from "actual teaching," and how all of the stress resulted in her inadvertently "snapping" at students because she was under so much pressure to get the students' performance metrics up to the levels the state desired. Certainly, there is pressure on all teachers to improve students' performance on state exams, but, as I explain in this book, this pressure is much more extreme in a school under threat of closure: At stake is the future of the school itself.

Deepening the Understanding of Neoliberalism

Schooling under threat of closure deepens the understanding of how neoliberalism's key feature is the creation of a larger coercive, carceral state. Post-NCLB ESEA programs are key policy tools that the federal government claims are its way of addressing the racialized social injustice of the poor quality of education many class-disadvantaged Black and Latinx students receive. These policies centrally include programs for struggling US K-12 public schools that offer *conditional* support to financially strapped schools with many working-class Black and Latinx students. The only way to get essential funding is to aggressively pursue market-centric strategies. These strategies for low-performing schools include restructuring that brings new corporate personnel, standardized tests, and security products into schools. And crucially, these policies to raise education standards often produce more disadvantage for already disenfranchised student populations by making their education worse than it was before.[77] This strategy assumes that the obstacles to success (academic or fiscal) are managerial problems, and not resource-based. But when the school does not improve, a new round of directives mandate more restructuring with the same basic priorities and strategies. Importantly, the replacement of NCLB with the ESSA does not appear to be a real departure from the NCLB era of sanctioning low-performing schools.[78]

The neoliberal state's efforts to restructure K-12 education especially for class-disadvantaged Black and Latinx youth is based in new programs branded as market-centric but that also represent a controlling and harmful redeployment of coercive governance that I frame as state carcerality. Much of this is done through a shift toward punitive policy structures where the key federal funding source for schools serving many low-income students is converted into a policing apparatus by which access to essential funds became contingent on states punishing low-performing schools. The schools experiencing high levels of this treatment serve mainly Black and Latinx students from class-disadvantaged backgrounds. Both critics and supporters branded this approach as "neoliberal," because it induced a larger role for markets in public education. Yet, in practice the state did not shrink; instead, it has changed into an (unevenly applied) disciplinary apparatus. The audit culture of NCLB-style policy is about transitioning leadership from local officials to public sector political elites, claiming to have superior knowledge to solve educational inequities. State elites think that the reason schools are struggling is "poor leadership" and hence they should lead, and then, in the name of improvement, demand conditions that engender a punishing type of education for the children in low-performing schools that they would never agree to for their own children.

3

"What Are We, Test Monkeys?"

The Testing Regime Complex

Sandview High School students were acutely aware that the state was threatening their school with closure if their state exam scores did not improve. As student named Martín observed, "The state will get us" if the "state's test scores" did not go up. "They will actually shut the school down; that's what the school is trying to avoid." And like most Sandview High students, Martín saw that state pressure on the school had put intense stress on students to produce state-valued achievement metrics through arduous test drills. As he put it, "The school's just focused on getting the test scores passing so that the state doesn't take their jobs and hire new people," continuing, "They [the test drills] take time out of actually learning the subject." Students like Martín adversely perceived "the state" as the entity responsible for the school's under-threat status and the resulting endless test drills that took the place of a meaningful education. Students like Martín saw that the purpose of school was to satisfy state mandates and keep the school from shutting down. They seemed to share a collective sense that their chances at gaining an effective education were sharply undermined because of Sandview High's need to improve their state exam scores.

Feeling entitled to good public resources in the community where you live is a key element of full political membership.[1] And the learning conditions at Sandview High that I describe as a testing regime seemed to undermine students' sense of political rights by teaching them they were not entitled to a good public education. Educational systems can, however unintentionally, undermine youth political incorporation, as listening to what Sandview High students had to say about their education illustrates. My focus on centering students' perspectives builds on a large critical youth and education scholarship that recognizes youth as knowledgeable social actors navigating school settings.[2]

The understanding of one's rights and value as imparted by school reaches beyond academic instruction and prepares youth for adulthood. And putting this self-perception into focus with concerns about youth political incorporation in mind raises important questions about how school structures can prepare youth to *feel entitled* to make claims on the state, including for better services. Conversely, students at Sandview High got the message that they were undeserving of these rights. They felt cynical about their education in large part because they wanted a good education but instead were put through a "testing regime." They were also often aware that they could be pushed out of school early if they were too "low-performing" and that they had no right to voice their grievances. As such, school structures like the testing regime can deleteriously shape this important area of youth development.

The messages that Sandview High students learned about their political membership is another element of what sociologists call the *hidden curriculum*, how school practices beyond formal lessons also include informal (i.e., largely unintentional) lessons, which prepare students for their adult roles.[3] Scholars recognize that this hidden curriculum subtly trains children for jobs that correspond with their social class of origin.[4] Analyzing students' perspectives through the lens of political incorporation explains how this type of school system reproduces social stratification beyond work and prison outcomes, clarifying how schools can prepare youth for unequal adult futures in political terms. As it is mainly African American and Latinx student populations from modest income families navigating this type of school structure, they are the ones learning to feel discredited from political engagement, through undermining students' sense of entitlement to good public services, like education. This engenders cynicism among them about the role of the state in their lives, and also teaches them they have limited rights, such as speaking up for yourself when you have a grievance.[5]

"School Isn't about Education Anymore"

Raul, a senior, was a self-described laid-back person who got "along with everyone." But his tone turned dark when he talked about the increasing pressure to improve students' state test scores. He asserted, "At some point, it just became about getting good scores on the state tests instead of trying to get the kids a good education." He continued, "School isn't about education anymore. Because they're not trying to give us a good education, they're just trying to get us to get [pause] I wouldn't say good, but the right score on the state tests so they don't look bad." Like his peers, Raul found the state exams, and the preparation for them, to be disconnected from his academic development. He thought the goal of the testing regime was not designed to effectively support his education.

Students like Raul learned that the school needed to produce certain data for the state *instead* of educating him and his peers. Like a number of states across the United States, all students in New York State public high schools had to pass certain state exams to graduate.[6] Yet, many youth are attending specific schools like Sandview High that must abide state improvement orders under the credible threat of school closure for unsatisfactory performance, largely based on the state's standardized exams. Even though state auditors ceremoniously decried Sandview High for "teaching-to-the-test," the threat of increasing sanctions sharply incentivized overtesting students in order to meet state expectations.[7] And the resulting "testing regime," as I call it, communicated to Sandview High students that their tasks in school were not for their education, but instead largely to be compliant with state orders they found meaningless.

Students, alongside their teachers, seemed to be learning to perform academic rituals because the state compelled them to; they also came to perceive school professionals simply as enforcers of state demands. For instance, while I was in a study hall assisting students working on an essay for an English class, the instructor arrived with a stack of multiple-choice practice tests for the state's US history exam for everyone to practice instead. Visibly uncomfortable, the instructor stammered uneasily, "There's a lot of pressure to get those history exam scores up." As ordered, students stopped their other tasks and started doing practice questions for the state's global history exam instead. Later on, a student named Marisol explained, "Their focus is only getting you ready for the Regents [state exams]. They constantly bring it up, 'you need to know this for the Regents,' . . . Or 'make sure you know this formula for Regents,' or 'hurry up so we can finish this, so we can practice for the Regents.' . . . So that's really bad, and it's not going to help the kids, say my generation gets to college, we're gonna realize that we don't actually know anything." Another student named Paola added in agreement, "They don't prepare us for the future, they just prepare us for the test . . . more and more tests that don't really apply to the students and then students get frustrated and they just give up on the tests."

Students also believed that the state exam board was actively trying to undermine them. In a school context where "everything" was about improving on the state's exams, "the state" itself, its role in society as it relates to them individually and their classmates, took on negative connotations. As another student, Aisha, stated, "The Regents [the state exam board], they want you to fail, they want you to fail, the way they rewrite their questions . . . like they tried to make it very difficult for you." She continued, "So is just it's just stupid, very stupid . . . I hate it, I think it's unnecessary." Students also made these types of statements when I worked with them on practice state exams. As one student visibly distressed, explained, "They tried to trick you." We looked at the first question in the state practice test; it read, "Why did plantations thrive in the South?" "Slavery," the student fittingly retorted. This sharp student further explained that rich White men wanted to exploit Black people for their financial gain. We discussed these political and economic reasons in detail. Yet, none of what we discussed was one of the possible answers to her practice question. Though it was a history exam, all of the possible answers had to do with ecology; "cotton grew well in the wetlands" was one of the options. Yet, that couldn't be the answer, as the chapter was mostly a technical lesson in tobacco farming and there was hardly anything about cotton. Together the student and I pored over the textbook and finally found one caption in a picture in the textbook referencing ecology, indicating the position of the plantations on hills allowed them to organize territory around and below them with everything they needed. This was the answer. The student huffed justifiably; this was exactly the type of question she had called "tricky."

Learning You Are Undeserving through New Test Prep Tools

New test prep tools were a key component of the school's testing regime and also a central way students learned that they were undeserving of a good education. Both the "Writing Project" and MAP were part of Sandview High's state funding because of the school's required improvement program.[8] The MAP is a standardized test Sandview High purchased to evaluate students' progress toward preparation for state exams and also to evaluate teachers.[9] Because it was designed to measure student growth, students took this test in most of their classes at the beginning of the semester and then again at the end. Sandview High used students' MAP scores to evaluate teachers based on how much students improved over the semester. The MAP was also a high-stakes test for teachers because they could be more easily fired based on students' MAP exam scores than under other (nonthreat) school conditions.[10] The "Writing Project" was an auxiliary test that Sandview High purchased as a result of its low-performing status with the state. Sandview High contracted with a private company to purchase it as well as to train the teachers to teach and grade it. This was a rote training practice test for the essay part of the state exams in which students wrote the same essay based on a short article. There was one right answer to all of the boxes and teachers normally told students what to write into each of these boxes. Thus, no analytic learning went into the writing.

Students knew that these standardized auxiliary exams were *supposed* to help boost students' state exam scores but doubted that either of these exams were meaningful to their education. As a student named Robert put it regarding the MAP test, "It is useless . . . I bet a bunch of students already told you this. It's useless. It doesn't do anything for us." He explained, "It's supposed to boost our [state exam] scores, but I don't believe it . . . it takes away from my class time," continuing, "It's taking away from our education, honestly." Students like Rocio often made similar comments: "Honestly, I just [randomly] click." She continued, "[The MAP tests], they don't help at all." Like Rocio, students reported arbitrarily "clicking" through the MAP exam. This was a problem for their teachers because they were evaluated on their students' performance on these tests.[11] Many students expressed similar opinions about the Writing Project. As a student named Chloe stated, "It takes a lot of time out of the regular curriculum and it doesn't help." She continued, "There's already just so many tests." Chloe was dumbfounded that Sandview High was adding even more standardized tests, like the Writing Project, to improve students' state exam scores, further undermining her education. Students' critical take on MAPs and the Writing Project was similar across the academic achievement spectrum. Rocio was a struggling student, while Chloe and Robert were both high-achieving students, but for all of them the new test prep tools limited the time they needed for learning and sent the message that their education could be taken from them to meet "useless" state obligations.

For students like Felicity, the new test prep tools impacted their view of Sandview High as a whole. I asked Felicity in our interview, "How do you feel about your school?" To this question, she first replied decisively, "I don't like it." So, I asked her, "Can you tell me what you don't like about it?" Felicity responded, "The education system is what I don't like about it. *Because of the scores*, they give us extra stuff; [like] MAPs testing, . . . [and] the Writing Project" (emphasis added). Felicity described herself as struggling academically, but she blamed the school's focus on test-training for worsening her education and thus blocking her opportunity to be successful. Felicity later quipped, "They tend to think we're pretty dumb in this school, that's why they give us all this extra stuff." Felicity explained that everything there was "all about" practicing for the state exams to get students' scores higher. Fortunately, Felicity did not think she and her classmates were "dumb." She did think that if she went to a different school, would be learning "a lot more stuff" because they would not be "rushing you" and focused on all of this state test training.

The MAP tests had no legitimacy with either students or teachers. Both groups also viewed "the state" as culpable for stealing their education. As Raul put it, "We'd be complaining to each other [about the MAP test] and the teachers would be like, "we don't want to do this either." [But] Everybody just did it . . . it's like a state requirement." A student named Keon shared similar statements about the Writing Project: "The kids did not want to do it nor did the teachers; it took away from instruction time." He clarified this was not just a little time, "It took a whole week in each subject to do." Keon continued, "I think the [school] administration tries to enforce the things but it's unpopular at the school." Keon saw that these "unpopular" things, like the Writing Project, were aimed at improving the state exam scores. "Here everything is about the Regents [state exams]." Crucially, statements like this highlight that students saw a certain negative form of education specific to their school due to its sanctioned status with the state.

Students also understood that they learned less course material and did more poorly in their classes as a direct result of the time spent on these new auxiliary tests. As a student named Ranyinudo described, "I failed trig because of that [the Writing Project] . . . I didn't have enough time . . . It wouldn't even increase the scores." Thus, in addition to seeing the extra test prep as worsening their "real" education, students also saw that it would not improve student outcomes on its own terms. Students like Ranyinudo observed that these new supplementary tests worsened their education instead of improving it.

I saw firsthand how test prep negatively affected students' education. I observed school personnel removing small groups of students from their regular classes for MAP testing without notifying their teacher. That kind of interruption understandably made it hard for teachers to effectively run their classes. And, as students like Ranyinudo made clear, these additional tests replaced even more instructional time that they needed to learn course material.

Students developed a deep sense of loss as their access to a good public education vanished. As a student named Claudia aptly put it, "*What are we, test monkeys?*" Like her fellow students, Claudia felt that the new state-mandated test prep regime was a digression from actual learning. "It wasted weeks of work," Claudia explained, speaking about the "Writing Project."[12] She continued, "I really feel like there was no need for it." The "work" Claudia referred to was coursework. In contrast, she saw the extra test prep programming as detached from "real" schoolwork, like reading a play in her English class. "We were reading a Shakespeare play and we had to stop it . . . instead of classwork that the teachers planned for the week, we had to work on the Writing Project for each class in *all* the classes." When I asked her where the "dumb" test she mentioned was coming from, she replied, "the state." Claudia's perspective was characteristic of Sandview High students' experiences with standardized test drills. Like her peers, Claudia was frustrated with the seemingly endless time spent on new state test prep tools and it made her feel cynical about her education. In this way, the school's testing regime, stemming from Sandview High being "under threat," sharply undermined youth development as political subjects for students like Claudia.

Adolescents in this school learned harmful messages about themselves and their place in society. Students' experiences with these testing tools were a key means by which they were receiving marginalizing messages about their entitlement to good public services in their own community. These are informal socializing messages, thus constituting an additional pattern of hidden curriculum transmission.

Learning You Are Undeserving through School Pushout

The worst result for students subjected to Sandview High's testing regime was likely the outright exclusion of some students, as it created extra student pushout (aka dropout) incentives. Exploring this issue, together with the embedded lessons of disentitlement through the testing regime itself, is a way of understanding how schools help make (or unmake) citizenship for many Latinx and African American youth.

The state pressed Sandview High to produce higher test scores, and in response the school appeared to be excluding some students as prospective poor test-takers. Excluding the most "low-performing" students has been an incentive for schools since states began sanctioning schools using their standardized exam scores in the early 2000s.[13] The structural conditions of schooling under threat reveals the worst case of how amplified (and explicit) these pushout measures can be.

Just before the state testing period, the school administration counseled some students with poor academic performance to drop out of Sandview High and pursue a High School Equivalency, GED (at age 16, once New York State law no longer requires them to attend school).[14] I learned about this from multiple school professionals and students at Sandview High. School administrators reportedly told these students they had no chance of graduating because they were too low-performing, so they should drop out. Most students who the school counseled to leave did ultimately drop out. By the end of my fieldwork, nearly all of the students that I knew who had been pressured to leave school had stopped coming.

The school pushed out more Latinx students than African American students. Sandview High needed to improve test scores for the Latinx immigrant students, and getting the vulnerable among them to leave was a strategy the school seemed to actively pursue. This was an unintended consequence of the testing pressures as a school under threat of closure. As Jane, a school professional, explained, Latinx immigrant students experienced pressure to leave the school as a result of the testing demands, stating, "The school can't figure it out [how to get the test scores up] and they are looking for a scapegoat.... they are really looking for somebody to blame for the struggles of the school." She added, "There was a document on the district website that the ELL [English Language Learner] population is a target population and their struggles were bringing down the school." A great many of the Latinx students were enrolled in English for Speakers of Other Languages (ESOL) courses and were labeled "English Language Learners" (ELL) by the school. These students also got the message the school wanted them to leave. As Jane put it, "I think they definitely feel there are negative feelings toward them from people within the school as immigrant students. I've had students say, 'they want me to leave, they think I'm not going to finish and that I'm going to drop out, they don't see the point of me being here.'"

A lot of the Latinx students struggled with the state exams because they were still learning English. The state's solution was to provide the exam in Spanish. However, most of these students were not literate in academic Spanish and the quality of the Spanish version of the exam was poor. As a Spanish teacher at Sandview High stated, "There are some words there [in the Spanish version of the state exam] that even I don't use." This solution seemed more about maintaining the production of state data than any real effort to include language-diverse students.

Many Latinx students also struggled with school at Sandview High in part because of their immigration history. A great number of these students had been out of school for a while, lacked school credits, their school records, and/or other forms that the school wanted. They tended to be older than their African American peers for their grade level. Lucia was one of these students. She was a sixteen-year-old student from Nicaragua. I met her in the advanced ESOL class and an after-school tutoring program. Due to her immigration background, she started at Sandview High with no credits. She had no school transcripts and had been out of school for more than four years. I learned from Lucia's teacher that Sandview High administrators told her that she had no chance of graduating and had been pressuring her to drop out. Essentially, Sandview High had indicated to her that her commitment to school did not matter. During my informal conversations with Lucia, she described how she cared deeply about her education, that she had worked hard to learn English, and was trying her best to get good grades so that she could get into college. One afternoon during after-school tutoring, she expressed that she was "proud" of me and another tutor, "because you are college students and I want to be like you someday."

Sandview High's efforts to persuade students like Lucia to leave the school illustrates unmaking youth citizenship. Like all young people in the United States, Lucia was entitled to a public education. However, her immigrant experience presented a challenge for the school and how best to teach her. Sandview High did not work with Lucia to fulfill her right to an education, and the state testing pressures for the school incentivized losing students like Lucia. Schools can work to accommodate students like Lucia, but it is unsurprising (though offensive) that Sandview High decided to push her out instead.

Rubén, a senior, was also being pressured by the Sandview High administration to drop out, right before the testing season began. I learned much of Rubén's story from his teachers, who explained that although he had all of his credits, he had not passed any of his state exams, and therefore he would not graduate.[15] His teachers explained that the school administration had counseled Rubén to drop out, but at the time I met him he was still attending. It was common among students who were pushed out, like Rubén was, to keep attending school for a while before withdrawing. This lag period demonstrated these students' hesitancy to leave, the benefits they saw in continuing to attend school, and, I believe, also acted as a small form of resistance to being pushed out.

Rubén had come to New York in order to escape violence and poverty in Tegucigalpa, Honduras. He had fled from there, alone, when he was just twelve years old. Because Rubén made the journey to the United States alone as a youth, he is what immigration specialists today call an "unaccompanied minor."[16] This struggling young man made it all the way through high school, learned English, and passed all of his classes, but was denied a diploma because he could not pass the state exams.[17] Now, Sandview High reportedly wanted him to drop out before his test scores would negatively impact the school's average.

African American and Latinx students both struggled with being pushed out of Sandview High, but the specific methods of exclusion were different. African American students were largely counseled individually to leave school. In contrast, Latinx immigrant youth were mainly counseled in large group meetings at school. This approach created an intersectional pathway in the type of treatment students received from the school, in terms of this most punitive aspect of the testing regime. These different methods of pushout also seemed to send different kinds of harmful messages to students: African American students tended to blame themselves for dropping out of school, whereas Latinx students tended to fault the school for denying them their rights to an education.

Deron (African American) was one such student who described being individually pressured to drop out of Sandview High. As he explained, the principal met with him individually during his junior year and told him that he had no chance of graduating. In that meeting he was told that he "had no choice but to drop out instead of taking the year over again . . . There was no way in the world I could recover [academically]." He concluded, "I was forcefully dropped out." Deron saw that he was pushed out of Sandview High for low achievement. Yet, Deron blamed himself for this outcome, attributing his academic struggles to a lack of focus and effort. This was in stark contrast to many Latinx students' experiences.

Latinx students' experiences with school pushout seemed to communicate a shared identity with their peers as being part of an undeserving racialized group. Sandview High counseled Latinx immigrant students to leave the school so often that these students described it as something that "just happened" to Latinx students when they were about to become juniors. As a Latino student named Hector described it, immigrant Latinx students were told to drop out at meetings that were held in the school library, "There were like fifty kids there . . . they tell them that they should stop coming, that they have to stop coming . . . mostly Latinos . . . most of them were not born in the United States." He highlighted his classmate Isabel, who had left Sandview High as persuaded by the school: "She got told that she needs to leave too." He stressed, "She was smart . . . I think she could do it, but they didn't give her a chance."

Two school professionals working with recently immigrated Latinx students provided more context for Hector's observations. As they each separately explained it, the ELL student population particularly struggled to pass the state tests and were thus a major subgroup of students for whom the state pressured Sandview High to improve test scores. So, right before the exams, the school held an administration-led meeting of Latinx students, in which these students were told that they had no chance of graduating and that they should drop out so they wouldn't fail the state tests.

Felipe was one of the Latino students who was told during one of the school's group meetings that he needed to leave Sandview High. The school administration had also told him to leave several times, but he continued attending. He wanted to stay in school for several reasons: He wanted to improve his English, and he also knew that he would need a high school diploma for the career he wanted to pursue. Felipe was undocumented and hoped to join the military if he got his immigration papers. Additionally, his immigration lawyer told him that if he were still enrolled in school, it would improve his immigration case to regularize his status.

Felipe recalled that coming to school had made him feel encouraged about his future, but the school administration took that away from him when they told him not to come to school anymore. He was critical of the fact that there were only "Latinos" and no "Americanos" at these meetings. Felipe stated that this experience of being pushed out of school along with other Latinx immigrants taught him "El país es de los gringos y de los que nacen aquí." (*This country is for White people and people who are born here.*) Experiences of students like Felipe illustrate how being pushed out of school taught lessons in racialized citizenship and led new Latinx immigrant youth like Felipe to become disillusioned about their rights.

The difference in methods of exclusion experienced by African American students and Latinx students seemed to impact the students differently. African American students expressed individual-level harm and failure, whereas Latinx students indicated their experiences were ones of collective marginalization resulting from Sandview High's efforts to push them out. Both situations create harm, but of different forms. African American students experienced messages of individual self-blame when they were pushed out of school, whereas the Latinx immigrant students experienced ethno-racial group-based exclusion. But patterns of student exclusion for both groups of students were related to the institutional racism that was the testing regime itself, incentivized by state sanctions to the school.

Being a school "under threat" of closure created strong incentives for Sandview High's testing regime, and the cost of this regime reveals yet another form of systemic racism in public education. Students enduring schooling-under-threat testing schemes are mainly African American and Latinx, and these student populations are also those whom these "school improvement" practices are aimed to assist. Thus, the adverse effects on youth political incorporation are heavily racialized and that process is the result of public policies. The concept of "substantive citizenship" is especially useful here.[18] Race scholars studying citizenship argue that people of color regularly have experiences that marginalize their social citizenship.[19] Focusing on the features of citizenship as lived, this substantive citizenship theory stresses how citizenship is created through daily social interactions; that is, it is made real by people to people. Being a full member of society is something that individuals learn through their everyday experiences. My critical examination of the testing regime reveals how the social citizenship of African American and Latinx youth is undermined in school and how this is an element of youth political (under) development.

Learning You Are Undeserving through Silenced Voices

Students had a lot of criticism about their schooling experiences, so I asked them, "What can students do if something is not right at school?" Most of them said, "Nothing." They did not believe they could make demands that would be heard. One student named Chloe exclaimed, "Just do whatever they throw at you." "I don't have any rights as a student," Another student named Tara expressed.

Students' discontent was a collective experience that engendered a sense of shared struggle with the school, increasing mutual social citizenship among each other. They saw their experiences as caught up with the experiences of their peers. But they also felt trapped. As Paola, another student, put it, "They don't listen to us . . . All the school cares about is the [test] numbers." Pedro, another student, directly compared the situation to a lack of political voice, explaining, "Because the school is failing state tests, the state wants a radical change to the school," and, as a result, the administrators respond to students "with an iron hand" which "makes the students hate them . . . maybe I'm comparing it to politics but you want to be able to talk to your elected officials, feel like they're protecting and not oppressing you, but I feel like that's not what happens at the school."

Students' perceptions of Sandview High's focus on raising their state exam scores seemed to contribute to their sense of having no "voice," even when describing aspects of their school that they believed "weren't right." Students saw that they experienced a rigid testing regime in ways the state incentivized by putting the school at risk of being shuttered. This stressed organizational context communicated to students that they had no right to a voice. On one hand, students had a critical analysis and despised the testing regime collectively as a form of mistreatment, but they also did not feel they could do anything about it. They did not feel entitled to make demands or formally challenge the kinds of school services they received.

Damage to Youth Power for Navigating Structural Disadvantages

Schools can foster a sense of entitlement to good government resources for marginalized youth and encourage them to see the role of the state as a potential source of help or support, or even an establishment that they could change for the better.[20] Unfortunately, the dominant state-led remedies given to "failing" schools create incentives that erode their power to navigate their structural disadvantages. Students' narratives about their school experiences at Sandview High illustrate how they learned to form cynical views about the state and its role in their lives. Barriers to political development for already disenfranchised adolescents do not bode well for their political participation as adults.[21] Successful political incorporation of marginalized youth is crucial to their ability to combat an unjust society, such as through activism or membership in political organizations that advocate on their behalf. The importance of this group's political incorporation is clearly underscored by the fact that this group has much to fight for in order to achieve full membership in the communities in which they live.

Awareness of injustice can be a powerful tool to build solidarity. As sociologist of youth Jessica Taft demonstrated in her work on youth participation in social movements, the possibilities for youth organizing from disenfranchised communities start with strong political consciousness.[22] But the voices of class-disadvantaged and minoritized youth are undermined through this widespread school structure, which I call "schooling under threat of closure." Children from disenfranchised communities believe in the value of a good education and want that for themselves.²³

This chapter speaks to a problem of limited access to good public resources and resulting disillusionment about the role of the state. The students saw the state as illegitimate; they resented it. Though an individual public high school is certainly part of the state, it is the elite state that is the target of critique. As the recurring community uprisings against the state over the poor quality of public education around the country keep illustrating, there is plenty that people like about their public schools; they just want their state and the federal government to do a better job of both funding them and reforming them in effective ways, truly informed by local school professionals and the communities they serve.²⁴ And, as we learned in chapter 2, even in Sandview High's politically fragile school context, none of its local school professionals directly serving the students thought the state's improvement schemes were good ideas, and most of these professionals also recognized that state-led improvements created new harms for the students.

4

"Bad" Kids

The Stigma of a School under Threat

"Are you here because we're so bad?" a student named Andre asked with downcast eyes. Andre knew nothing about me except that I was a researcher. Like Andre, most students at Sandview High had gotten the message that they were "bad." When asked to clarify *why* they thought they were "bad," they always offered a reply similar to what Keon said: "Have you seen the test scores?" As Zoe, a school professional, put it, "The students here are really aware that it's a 'low-performing' school . . . they're aware that they are ranked in the bottom 5 percent of the state." It seemed that the students had learned the following: Sandview High had a bad reputation due to *their* average "too-low" test scores; this represented them as students; it was a huge problem for the school; and all of it meant that they were very "bad."

Sandview High's status as a school under threat of state closure, and school practices related to that status, engendered a fierce stigma to the student population. Students learned (however unintended) through regular school communications that they were to blame for the state's sanctioning of their school. In turn, this stigma seemed to incentivize students to turn on their peers in hopes of salvaging their dignity. Students tended to shift the rebuke they faced away from themselves by blaming each other for the school's challenges, focusing on their classmates' "poor culture." This is harmful on several levels; but in this chapter I stress how it undermined Latinx and Black youths' identities as well as their relationships to each other.

Like many sociology of education scholars, I find that examining how schools foster youth racialization reveals important truths about Black and Latinx students' commitment to their education. Sociology of education scholars like Prudence Carter have thoroughly debunked the racist "poor culture" arguments used to explain the "too-low" academic attainment of many working-class Black and Latinx youth.[1] Studies show that Black and Latinx youth value education as much or more than their White peers.[2] And there is no evidence of the popular claims that these student groups "reject" academic achievement on the cultural grounds that it will undesirably mark them as "acting White."[3]

None of the students at Sandview High rejected academic achievement, which is consistent with the academic literature. Moreover, all students blamed themselves for failure, including those who dropped out of school. Students clung to the ideal of meritocracy, understanding that in school this meant obedience to the testing regime. They blamed each other for the struggles in their school in ways that retold "poor culture" myths, asserting broad rejections of their Black and Latinx peers and the popular youth cultures associated with them.

Like everyone in American society, Sandview High students were subjected to the deeply rooted dominant American cultural view that there are two sources of and suitable answers to poverty: misfortune and bad morals. In other words, the *deserving* and *undeserving poor*.[4] Sandview High students wanted to be the "deserving poor." Most of the students were from families struggling to get by and they strived for social mobility. To be the deserving poor, they distanced themselves from and disparaged their peers. This helped them to feel less anxious about their future. It was also alienating, stressful, and bolstered the racialized stereotype that places youth cultures at the root of obstructions for the social mobility of disenfranchised groups. Students spoke of their peers as stereotypical Black and Latinx youth with "poor culture" from whom they needed to isolate themselves. They saw their peers as the chief problem with the school's broad challenges, indicating that their peers could contaminate them and ruin their own chance of prosperity.

Crucially, I argue that the coerced neoliberal orientation of Sandview High incentivized this survival strategy. In this milieu, students tried to make sense of the strict emphasis on compliance to the testing regime and shaming of students in ways that relied on racialized tropes, such as Black and Latinx youth being "apathetic" about their education.[5]

"I Don't Want to Be the Group That Is Disrespected"

Because Sandview High was under threat of closure, the school leadership created new practices, which, in effect, framed students as problems to solve. One example of this was the massive "Sandview High Data Wall" posted across a full side of the main hallway. This Data Wall was a state-sponsored strategy, the logic being that drilling students with this data would compel them to work harder. A dark blue paper background with a border composed of little books, the Data Wall displayed students' average state test scores in each of the five state testing areas. The first oversized-font headline read, "Where we are"; a second heading displayed, "Where we will go," presenting much higher scores. Students were labeled like a set of data points and a work in progress, statistics for the school's survival.

Knowing the score averages did not improve exam results, but it did humiliate the students. As a student named Lucas said, "I don't want to be considered a bad student just because of where I go anymore." He explained that students' test score average "makes us look bad." Lucas went on to describe school assemblies as another space where students learned that they were bad. As he saw it, assemblies were "normally" just about shaming students into "working harder" because most students were "failing" the state tests. Thus, students like Lucas had learned in multiple ways that students' fortitude was lacking for the purpose of meeting the state's testing targets.

Students also tended to be like Alan, who emphasized that attending this school threatened his desired identity as a good student. As Alan put it, "The other students' scores stereotype me, and I don't want to be part of that stereotype . . . I don't want to be part of that stereotype that no one can make it from Sandview . . . I don't want to be the group that is disrespected." Understandably, students like Alan did not want to be considered "bad," and they aimed to achieve some degree of personal dignity.

There have long been racialized stigmas attached to Latinx and Black students regarding their academic abilities, as well as to schools themselves when they serve mainly working-class minoritized youth.[6] But Latinx and Black students' experiences with a school under threat added new layers of meaning to how they faced this type of stigma. The school managed the state's neoliberal imperative to raise students' test scores not only by overtesting students, but also by pressuring students to work harder to get higher scores, then assigning the blame to students for unsatisfactory outcomes on their own poor efforts. These are high-stakes tests, and not only for students: Failure to meet state benchmarks would mean more sanctions for the school. And although Alan was a "good student" in the traditional sense of making good grades, Lupe's story below illustrates that anxiety about being stereotyped as a "bad student" because of the school they attended was by no means limited to students making good grades, and also just how hard it is to navigate the stigma of being "bad" as a Sandview High student, especially if you are struggling academically.

Lupe sipped the coffee she ordered at the café where we met. She was tired from balancing school with work, a financial necessity for her family (as is the case for many Sandview High students). Lupe worked as a laundromat cashier, a job she had held for the last three years. Her parents were from Mexico; her mother worked in the home and spoke little English, while her dad spoke a bit more English and worked at a restaurant.

"Everybody talks bad about Sandview High," Lupe stated openly. She continued, "I mean, I can see why they talk bad because a lot of people don't got respect in that school and they need to get themselves together." Lupe positioned herself in contrast to most Sandview High students: she saw herself as "respectful"; she "cared" about her education and "worked hard" to achieve academic success in order to move ahead in life. Yet later in our conversation, Lupe confessed "I struggle," repeating, "I'm struggling," her eyes downcast in humiliation. Lupe revealed that she had failed all her state exams that year, despite taking them three times, and was not passing most of her classes. She stammered, "I just can't handle school sometimes," explaining, "I wake up every day and I'm ready to study, to get an education, but sometimes, I just, I can't take that day anymore." Lupe clarified that this happened often, particularly on days that she had "a test" or "a rough day at work." On these days, Lupe felt overwhelmed and shut down in school. Lupe tried to have little chats with herself to pump herself up to *work even harder*. In these chats, she often told herself, "I *have* to be something in life, I *have* to."

The stigma of people talking "bad" about Sandview High because of students' flaws was clearly the most harmful for struggling students like

Lupe. Lupe appeared to feel even more ashamed about the stigma she already felt about her school when her narrative of self-reliance came face-to-face with her own personal educational struggles. Like the majority of Sandview High students, Lupe was not on track to graduate. For that, she blamed herself, for not working hard enough, as well as her peers, for "not getting themselves together." Lupe struggled academically but also tried to believe that she would advance through continued hard work, juxtaposing herself against her peers in similarly stressed situations. Even though she was facing academic failure, she was not going to be like her peers. Assigning some of the blame to her classmates allowed Lupe both to recover her dignity and to explain why she would escape poverty through education.

Trying to Change Test Scores through Authoritarian Education

The authoritarian education style at Sandview High also sent the message to students that they were "bad kids." As a sharp student named Pablo observed, "The way they're trying to do education here, to change the way the school works, to change the test scores, is through a very authoritarian type of education . . . it makes the students hate them." Pablo's account exemplifies students' views on Sandview High's tactics.

Students like Raul also observed that the strain between students and school professionals was related to rigid expectations of students' compliance to classwork. As Raul put it, "Teachers try to put students on a leash and act hostile toward them when they do not obey in class." To explain, Raul recalled an incident in which a teacher responded to students' defiance "right off the bat" by "kicking out" the student from the classroom. He explained that this was precisely "how arguments start" between teachers and students. According to Raul, if teachers wanted to avoid disobedient student behavior, they needed "to treat students with respect, you have to try to be their friend." Students tended to be like Raul, who reported that for school professionals, respect was about students' obedience irrespective of the adults' behavior.

State auditors agreed with Raul's point of view; their critiques of Sandview High classes concluded that most teachers had an authoritarian style.[7] I described these state auditor observations in chapter 2. There

I also argued that the burden of being a school under threat of closure seemed to encourage an exacting teaching style which, in turn, undermined students' relationships with their teachers, how they saw themselves, and their learning. Here I am focusing on students' perceptions of this dynamic, how it made them feel defamed, and thus why this regime undermined students' relationships with their teachers, with their own learning, and with their positive sense of self.

Ironically, "respect" was also what students desired most. Students' utmost desire in school was to be treated like full members of the school community, valued and worthy of consideration—in other words, to have *substantive citizenship*. Of course, students wanted to be academically successful, but they considered how the adults treated them most of all. As a student named Kiara described regarding her favorite teacher, "She doesn't give you attitude, she treats you like good student." Teachers spoke about students' desire for respect too, but as a critique of students, arguing that students needed to push past their feelings focused on their desire for respect.

Austere educational practices are normally associated with "no excuses" charter schools serving disenfranchised student populations; they are often seen as positive by many education practitioners due to the link with some gains in standardized testing outcomes.[8] What these different school contexts share is the goal of meeting state testing targets. As such, this parallel key element of neoliberal orientation suggests that this type of education reform is at least as much about punishment as it is about privatization. Felicity's story below illustrates students' experiences with this rigid education model.

Felicity was a small girl of 16 with long black braids. She self-described as a "really goofy" kid and liked dancing. She was also "in trouble a lot" with her teachers. To explain, Felicity narrated a day in class that ended with the teacher having security remove her from the classroom. Felicity said she was having "a *really* bad day," so she put her "head down on the desk" instead of doing the coursework along with the rest of the students. In response, the teacher told her, "'Pick your head up or you're getting kicked out.'" Felicity defended herself to me, stating that she "was quiet" and "didn't talk back," but picked her head up "slowly." The teacher then had security remove her for "disrespect," which seemed to mean not compliant enough.

Felicity's narrative reveals how students observed school professionals using "respect" to justify pushing a controlling education style. Teachers labeled students disrespectful when they disobeyed classroom demands or were not hard-working enough. Felicity acknowledged to me that she was unable to bring herself to meet the prescriptive demand that she "respect the teachers no matter what," when she felt like the teacher disrespected her too. Felicity felt she was "sticking up" for herself, which I took to imply her trying to save some self-respect in a demoralizing situation. In Felicity's view, she was just having a bad day and did not need to be humiliated in front of the entire class. Whereas it seemed the teacher subscribed to the "authoritarian" teaching style.

Accounts from teachers popular with students help to clarify why the school's pressurized "testing regime" fostered students' frustrations with school adults, especially their teachers. To these teachers, the obligatory focus on test drills fostered students' "troublemaking" behavior in the classroom, where students did or said inappropriate or defiant things out of frustration. As I described in chapter 2, I also observed this behavior. These teachers overall felt that the requisite testing regime made it more difficult for their students to tolerate school. Many Sandview High students were so worn out from practicing, taking, and re-taking the state exams that some students just gave up. As one teacher explained, "Some students take even just *one* of those five exams eight or nine times." Thus, the teachers also perceived that the state testing pressures made students want to give up on school, and ahead of pushing many students out of school, it was also a key source of what seemed to undermine student-teacher relationships.

The structural context at Sandview High encouraged school professionals to put intense stress on students to apply themselves, painstakingly, to a type of education that no one—even the teachers—seemed to believe in. Ms. Turner, who self-described as "snapping" at her students when they stopped doing their assigned worksheets, directly cited the pressure on her to raise students' state tests scores as the driving force for her sharp behavior toward her students.[9]

In an educational milieu saturated with test prep, there was a strong incentive on the part of teachers and administrators to pressure students into compliance. If students did not improve on state tests, teachers and administrators could lose their jobs or the school could be shut down.

In this setting, teachers often harshly pressured students to be diligent with a constant stream of repetitive worksheets tied to state tests. As one teacher put it, "We come in with our great lessons but instead we've got to prepare them for the state exams."

Grit and Character

School programs and professionals, including caring, popular teachers, revealed strong underlying narratives in which students' lack of "grit" was the key ingredient for their academic struggles. These critiques of the students came from Black, White, and Latinx professionals, including those in top leadership positions, such as the superintendent and school board members. The school's leadership at the time were all African American. School professionals' specific critiques of students ranged from the lack of a good work ethic (termed by multiple school professionals as a need to "pull up their pants") to broad critiques about students' poor cultural backgrounds and need to "change their mentality to be college-oriented" (as described by another school professional) and thus academically successful.

Schools shaped as austere spaces where "no excuses" grit ideology rules the day serve mostly class-disadvantaged Black and Latinx youth from segregated neighborhoods, promoting the idea that access to social mobility is open if they work hard enough and behave politely toward authority figures.[10] Grit narratives argue that poverty is not so bad because it can be overcome with enough individual effort.[11] The grit narrative is harmful, in part, because it minimizes the impact of students' direct experiences with structural challenges. Certainly, students from disadvantaged backgrounds are forced to work hard to have academic success. But focusing on grit closes off the political space necessary to recognize the underlying inequalities that undermine students.

School professionals tended to reduce students' obstacles to an issue of character improvement and hard work. Mr. Robertson was a teacher who clearly cared deeply and devoted extra time to his students, including offering a range of after-school extra support. But Mr. Robertson, too, framed students' problems as a lack of work ethic, insisting they should make "no excuses" for their personal struggles. In my interview with him, he stressed that when students faced life challenges that made it hard to participate in school, he told students, "Don't let that be your excuse for why you can't get here on time and be successful." For example, students attributed their tardiness in winter to the 45-minute walk to school from the public housing buildings they lived in (often in the freezing snow). There was no school bus service and students told Mr. Robertson that they had no money for the public bus. But Mr. Robertson instructed them, "It's not an excuse you can use." His lesson to students was that there was no excuse for failure.

With little control over the testing regime, it seemed that all teachers like Mr. Robertson could do was push students to work harder. As previously described, the state's sanctioning of Sandview High put additional pressure on school professionals to coerce students to work harder at test prep. Students fully received the denigrating message that the only thing preventing them from success at school was themselves, no matter how hard they struggled.

School leaders at Sandview High encouraged students to participate in a summer program entitled "From Ghetto to Success."[12] It aimed to "destroy the 'ghetto' mentality" troubling them, producing in the students "a new heart and mindset." The message of this program seemed to be that the school would correct students' poor attitudes and this would unlock their opportunities for social mobility. The program's flyer on the school website showed a crouching person in silhouette, wearing a hooded sweatshirt on the left. To the right were the silhouettes of a woman and a man both wearing suits and standing up straight. The flier sent the message that all students had to do was change their attitude and they could go from being poor and ill-mannered to respectful middle-class professionals. This program's approach minimized any structural disadvantages, stigmatized students, and stressed the need to make over their presentation of self.

Sandview High's focus on students' self-presentation is one way the school in effect repeats the long-standing "respectability" frame, stressing that soft skills, such as improving their self-presentation, would translate into social mobility in the absence of material resources. The goal of this self-presentation focus is racial uplift and improving the public perception of Black and Latinx communities. Both goals are set and motivated by Black middle-class members of these communities, who are invested in their communities and want to minimize the racial stigma that they also experience.[13]

Sandview High made efforts to cultivate students' appearance and demeanor to be more "respectable" for jobs. For example, there was an after-school mentoring program at Sandview High for the school's Latino and Black boys, which stressed improving their self-presentation. In other words, they aimed to support Black and Latino boys' social mobility by improving their soft skills. Several Black professional men at Sandview High ran this program. As one of the program leaders put it, "There is a negative perception of the Black and Latino males here, that our pants are down, that we are not interested in our education, we are disrespectful, and we aim to change that." He explained that they worked on improving the students' "character," illustrating that on Thursdays, the boys had to wear a professional outfit and tie. The logic was that this would help them to "change their walk" to be more professional.

In this way too it appears this traditional public school "under threat" of closure shares similarities to its privatized school counterparts, with similar neoliberal priorities focused on reforming working-class Black and Latinx youth. As others have argued, neoliberal imperatives for school reform encourage school practices that cultivate "grit" and "character" in disadvantaged students as the primary means to resolve the social inequalities these students face.[14] The recent literature on grit-focused schooling models tends to focus on certain specialized charter and other privatized school models serving working-class Black youth.[15] However, this traditional public school operated similarly.

The parallel across school types—traditional public and charter—suggests there is something about the neoliberal turn broadly that has changed schooling, and done so with a sharp effect along racialized class lines. Beyond reorganizing schools using market principals, these new structures expand state carcerality. Grit narratives are *punishing*. They bully students to submit themselves to strict training. These regimes are also like welfare-to-work programs, which coerce marginalized populations into stigmatizing treatment using the language of uplift.[16]

"Bad Kids"

Sandview High students tended to juxtapose themselves as "good" and their fellow students at Sandview High as generally "bad." They wanted to be considered good students, even the ones who had already been pushed out of school or were on the verge of doing so. Good students, they told me, were obedient, polite, and tried hard in school. In contrast, they described bad students as not listening, talking back to the teacher, and being overly interested in popular youth culture at the expense of their education. Given the school's situation, this also meant that bad kids did not acquiesce to test prep. As a student named Alfredo explained, kids here were bad because "they don't listen in class." Similarly, Righteous described how his peers were bad for "not doing the [teacher's course] work." He individualized himself as compliant to the teachers in class, stating for contrast, "I do my [course] work." Jamar felt that Sandview High students "just act like they didn't know better . . . if you were told to do something by the teacher, you not allowed to talk back and be rude . . . you don't have the authority to disrespect that person."

Students like Alfredo, Righteous, and Jamar clearly received the message of normative obedience to authority. Yet, like all students criticizing "bad kids," they also shared stories where they too did all of the things they disparaged about their peers: talking back, skipping class, or goofing off. Righteous got into an argument with his teacher who he thought was "being rude" to him, Alfredo was eventually pushed out of Sandview High, and Jamar was already pushed out of Sandview High by the time I met him. Jamar disclosed that he had a "bad attitude" toward school, routinely got "angry" with school professionals out of frustration, "cut school" and was ultimately pushed out of Sandview High chiefly because he could not pass the state exams.

Blaming peers seemed to be the available discourse for students to mitigate their anxiety about their opportunities. For instance, a student named Robert condemned his peers for having "poor character," which meant being disruptive in the classroom and refusing a teacher's coursework, explaining that compliance was required regardless. "You do it [follow the teacher's instructions] regardless of how you feel: *character*." Yet, like his peers described above, I learned in a later conversation with

Robert that he too also refused to do in-class assignments for a teacher with whom he had issues.

Sandview High students also expressed fear of being associated with bad kids, focusing on myths of contamination. This meant staying away from bad students with poor character who could pull you away from schooling into "bad things." As a student named Tashauna clarified, seeking isolation from peers was a way to prevent contamination: "I keep myself away from people I know doesn't do good in school." Like her fellow student Lupe, Tashauna expressed that most of her peers "don't care about their education as much as I do." Tashauna explained that bad kids skipped their classes, which she felt reflected their disregard for their education. However, she mentioned separately that she also skipped many of her classes because she thought her teachers disrespected her. She contrasted her individual behavior with the rest of her peers, justifying that she was "respectful" to school professionals no matter what. Tashauna positioned herself as committed to her education in contrast with most of her peers. This was the case even though she also indicated that she was struggling academically in ways comparable to those of her peers. She explained that her peers made similar choices for different reasons than she did; her peers were uncommitted to school, but she cared about her education.

Students like Tashauna also reported that they aimed to isolate socially at Sandview High because they feared that "bad kids" would corrupt them, thereby ruining their chance to escape poverty through advancement in school. As a student named Esteban explained, it is not good to have lots of friends, as "They could drive you into bad things." Another student, Isabella, was concerned that hanging out with her friends would lead to poverty as an adult. "Sometimes I do hang out with the wrong crowd," she told me. "I don't want to be in a position where I can't do the things that I want to do in life." Isabella worried that if she enjoyed her friends, they would prevent her from her goals of "going to school and stuff and getting a job and stuff." Isabella placed the blame for the challenges she faced in advancing in life on her peers and their culture.

Anxiety about contamination from "bad kids" seemed to mean that students viewed most of their peers as too undisciplined to make it through school. These students did not have the right cultural attributes to work hard enough. In other words, students acquired "poor culture" myths as explanations for structural inequalities. Sandview High students wanted to isolate themselves from their peers in order to be cultural exceptions to what they *perceived* to be the rule: that Latinx and Black youth were unproductive citizens.

Students specifically criticized their peers for being overly materialistic and suggested that materialism would cause their peers to fail. As Jumaane explained, "Kids around here are really thinking about material things more than actual academics, or anything else." He continued, "The general consensus of the school really seems, do you have the latest shoes, do you have the latest clothes, to have the latest rap album, those type of things." He explained that the graduation rates were "Pretty bad around here." Only about half of Sandview High students graduated, and for him that reflected students not caring. Yet, Jumaane admitted that he also did like getting clothes and music albums. But he was careful to contrast his materialism with that of others. As Jumaane put it, "Oh I'm a little bit driven by materials but not exactly the same type or to the same degree as some students." And while other students "flaunted" the stuff they had, he did not.

Thus, as Jumaane's account above shows, students got the message that it was culture and not structure that limited their upward mobility. They learned that enjoying popular youth culture—fashion, hip-hop music, and relationships with peers—would lead them into poverty. The message they received was that it did not matter that your school was under duress, under-resourced, and consequently ineffective; the problem was that students devalued school and were not working hard enough. Thus, because they wanted to exit poverty, they had to prove they did not fit "the stereotype." This message insulted students while seducing them into some degree of compliance.

Strikingly, students attributed the school's budget issues to the students' "bad" test scores. As one student, Sofía, put it, "I feel like if the kids paid more attention to school and stayed more focused instead of socializing, then maybe we would have more stuff in the school." She explained, "At our school the budget is really low, but that's mainly because the kids, the majority are failing." For Sofía, her peers did not care about school, and that was why there was an insufficient school budget. Students seemed to think that if the students' test scores went up, the school's overall budget would increase. I never learned where they got that idea, and they did not know, so I can only assume it was a rumor that floated around the school and could have potentially been sourced from school officials.

Sandview High students restated the narrative that if they were obedient (i.e., kept participating in test prep), they would pass the exams and advance toward a middle-class life, and that their peers were less acquiescent to school than they were, all the while struggling with the school's demands for docility, deference, and a resolute approach to schoolwork composed largely of standardized test drills.

Overall, students appeared to struggle to be what I term "super minorities." This effort involved creating as much cultural distance as possible from their ethno-racial group as they worked to prove how different they were from their peers. This is not to be confused with the "model minority" stereotype, which is applied to an entire racial group in order to shame less successful racial minority groups and create a wedge between these groups, the classic example being the comparison of Asians ("the model") with Blacks ("the unsuccessful"). Both the model minority myth and the super minority idea minimize the role that structural racism plays in creating and sustaining racial inequalities. But the super minority ideology is a reaction to racism, shaped by but not imposed by the dominant US public. In this way, it is a form of respectability politics, which pressures disadvantaged groups to be the best version of themselves, specifically as members of their stigmatized group. It represents a strategy by members of disenfranchised groups to deflect racism. This is critically important to understand in this school context, because school adults used respectability politics to navigate the testing regime. And, while students rejected how this politics insulted and undermined them, it was also something they took to heart as a means of social mobility. Students knew they were perceived as members of a racialized population due to their low test scores, and they felt ashamed of their situation. They believed they had to prove they were not like their peers and decided the best path to social mobility was to alienate themselves from their peers. They wanted to be the extraordinary members of their social group.

Most students were like Jamar. Jamar explained to me that he was "the opposite of the youth today," they were all into "street life." By youth today, he meant Black youth. He also explained that his being "different" from "youth today" also involved *fashion*. As he put it, "If everybody likes a certain pair of sneakers, like a pair of Jordans, I'm gonna get a different pair of Jordans. *I'm different*" (emphasis added). He continued to say that when he got some money and started dressing nicer, "a lot of people were like 'oh, he's fly, he's fresh dressed.'" He stressed that while this was unimportant to him, his peers were fixated on the nicer clothes he had.

Other students also told stories like Jamar, describing their peers as overly materialistic at the expense of their education. As Righteous put it, his peers were usually "worrying about a pair of shoes." In contrast, he was "worrying about my education." Righteous stressed, "I'm not going to be like all these kids . . . I just want to get my education, so I don't have to worry about all the other stuff." He described himself as having dissimilar cultural values to his peers. Righteous explained the difference between himself and his peers in terms of how they managed the "struggle" for upward mobility, focusing on their divergent cultural consumption of rap music. He disparaged the "turn up party" songs he thought that "most kids here" liked, which were meant for "gangsters." In contrast, he liked rappers who "might talk about gangster music" but also act as "guides" who have "been through the struggle." To Righteous, his classmates were uninterested in education, as demonstrated by their cultural consumption choices, which was connected to their limited potential for success. Even while he could simultaneously care about his nice shoes and his education, his peers could not. And, he believed his peers were listening to the wrong rap music to help them advance. Most importantly, he framed himself as unique from his peers because he *did* care, which was also demonstrated by his choice in distinct cultural consumption.

There were incentives for students to distance themselves from their peers in this type of school, and they wrestled with the contradictions of the school's meritocracy ethos and their own struggles as students. They resisted racialized devaluation by asserting themselves as super minorities and blaming their peers as typical members of racialized populations with poor culture. They also tried to distance themselves from stigma by blaming their peers, "bad kids," who did not care about their education, as the reason test scores were so low.

Salvaging Dignity

Students used the "culture of poverty" narrative to explain that *they* would exit poverty, in contrast to their peers. Students bought into the idea that their own youth culture was a negative influence on their education. They framed their peers as uncommitted to school, with bad attitudes, and described themselves in contrast: They were good students who cared about school, were polite and submissive to their teachers, and attended class. They also used cultural explanations to assert why they would be successful and their peers would not. The students criticized their peers for being overly materialistic and minimized their own consumption of the same goods and activities. They also identified popular youth cultural interests and behaviors with being disrespectful to the adults and disobedient with the schools' academic expectations. Nonetheless, these students also struggled academically.

The students' ethos of meritocracy led to demeaning each other as a survival strategy to manage the daily attacks on their dignity from the institution. Thus, no matter how much they were struggling, life and school would get better for them because they were not like the others in their predicament. They saw themselves as having character and grit. "Rebellion" in these students' minds was explicitly tied to being a nonstereotypical low-income Black or Latinx youth, positioning themselves against their peers. "Bad" meant lazy and defiant, which was connected to the explanations for why achievement levels, measured by standardized test scores, were too low. Students learned from the school professionals that lack of respect was their primary barrier to social mobility. However, while students distanced themselves from their peers for being disrespectful, they also admitted they engaged in all of the same behaviors and comportments, which they rationalized differently. Students indicated they only skipped classes that were less important; they did their work in class but not the homework; or the teacher did not like them and found them disrespectful when they were not. Some students described behavior that was certainly more oppositional than their peers, but still described themselves as wanting to do well in school.

Youth were pitted against each other in their fight to be seen as respectful, and thus different than their peers. In a school under threat, "respectful" translated into being compliant with the testing regime. The notion was that if you could not be successful in the testing regime, then it was your personal failure for which you should feel ashamed. And since Sandview High encouraged the students to see themselves as members of a stigmatized group that they needed to distance themselves from, the racialization that Black and Latinx students experienced at Sandview High undercut their ability to be resources to each other.[17]

Navigating Stigma in a School under Threat of Closure

Different school structures shape the types of ethos that children develop about school, and more broadly, society as a whole. Sandview High's orientation informed children's ethos in ways that revealed shocking consequences for self-esteem and the perception of racialized group identities. The students faced pressure from the school to be exceptional among their peers in ways that fostered narratives of grit, docility to authority, and a business-oriented presentation of self. Students learned these neoliberal individualizing messages through their experiences with school practices.[18] These messages were also racialized because they stressed that students should aspire to avoid culturally being "typical" Black and Latinx youth with poor character. Students largely navigated the onslaught of these types of demands reinforced in school by drawing on the survival strategy of peer distancing.

Punitive schooling regime systems under neoliberalism pit students against each other, destroying community, creating isolation, and damaging youth self-esteem. The children were systematically isolated, fearful of contamination from youth they perceived as dragging down their opportunities for a life without poverty. Moreover, students' narratives revealed a marked loss of enjoyment in being youthful and having fun at school. As such, these findings also contribute to the literature on the loss or limited access to childhood for Black and Latinx youth.[19] These outcomes facilitate the remaking of the existing racial structure in ways that persons most negatively impacted by those structures are incentivized, through the schooling process, to denigrate their co-ethnics. This is a critical corrective in the academic literature, which does not aim to unpack how students' views relate to their interpretations of neoliberal school policies. This chapter shows how schools undermine students' ability to be resources to each other.

This chapter also extends the critical education theory on hegemony. Education scholars draw from Gramsci's notion of hegemony, that dominance happens in part by getting those subordinated to consent to unequal relationships.[20] On the one hand, the students were critical of the testing regime and how the school adults treated them. But, on the other hand, they also believed that compliance to test prep and the development of soft skills would lead to social mobility. Yet, most students could not pass state exams and became frustrated with the constant test preparation. Students at Sandview High described how their teachers demanded unconditional respect from them while simultaneously being disrespectful to students. Navigating the testing regime left students feeling trapped and disrespected. This undercut students' potential for collective opposition to an ineffective education because it damaged their ability to respect themselves on their own terms and to respect their peers.

Entitlement to respect is a key component of substantive citizenship. The school's position as "under threat" fostered alienation from, and even antagonisms toward, their peers. This chapter uncovered the motivations behind these behaviors and, relatedly, where they learned the idea that they and their peers were "bad kids." Students echoed what the school officials told them: tales of grit, meritocracy, and a condemnation of investments in popular youth cultures. This was amplified by students' strong fear of future lives struggling with poverty. It was an acceptable sacrifice to isolate themselves from their peers.

5

On (Not) Fixing Racialized Policing through Neoliberal Accountability

Intensifying Pervasive Social Control beyond a Formal Suspension

Two administrators sat in front of a camera for a public web video address. "We are working toward a positive rather than punitive environment," one of them summarized.[1] They explained that Sandview High was working hard, in particular, to reduce student suspensions. Yet they also acknowledged that the school had not yet been able to lower the suspension rate.[2] Notably, efforts to reduce student punishment were not only up to the school administration. As the principal explained, because Sandview High had been a low-performing school since the early 2010s, lowering the rate of student suspensions was a key factor for getting the school out of its purgatory with the state.

Schools are generally under pressure to lower exclusionary punishment, and being under threat of closure amplifies this pressure.[3] State sanctions had been intensifying at Sandview High because of its ongoing poor scores on state evaluations, so it faced the very real possibility of the state shutting it down. Besides needing to demonstrate improvement on academic achievement, the state required Sandview High to improve "school culture and climate," largely because that, in turn, would bolster academic achievement. So, along with achievement gains, creating a less punitive school environment was essential for Sandview High to remain open.

As with academic achievement, Sandview High needed to use standardized, state-approved metrics to show improvement in its school culture, and lowering the rate of out-of-school suspensions was the crucial measure. Reducing the number of "serious" misbehavior incidents (where someone could have or did sustain an injury) and chronic absences was also important. A low score on these indicators would count negatively on the school's evaluation. These expectations were in the school's state improvement plans as a low-performing school and then amplified when the state put Sandview High into receivership for ongoing underperformance.

But despite the rising state pressure to foster a more positive school culture, the punitive environment seemed to be getting worse. As students like Claudia observed, security had become "tighter" and "stricter" since the prior year. If students were still in the hallways once classes had begun, school staff used to just urge them to get to class, saying things like, "Where you going? Get to class," she recounted. "And now, it's like, if you don't have a pass, you going to the principal's office, or in-school suspension, that strict."

High school senior Raul described this shift as school administrators "trying to assert authority" over students, characterizing them as "hunting" students down. Though they wouldn't use such a depiction, hyper-controlling student behavior to lower instances of misbehavior is what the school leadership intended to do. As one representative affirmed in a press statement, they planned to "ratchet up" their practices to lower disciplinary infractions and attendance rates. As emphasized in one schoolwide memo, the pressure was on to have "deliberate excellence" in academics, attendance, and discipline, as these were key factors to the school being removed from its precarious status with the state. This memo was followed with reminders about school rules and the threat of detention for not obeying orders. Other school memos defined a positive school climate as commitment to respect, accountability, and grit. These were the cultural values Sandview High aimed to instill in students, a set of "high expectations" that they related to improving academic achievement. Sandview High summarized its expectations to students with the declarative, "commit to graduate!" But in daily practice, all of this looked a lot like an anxious preoccupation with social control.

The omnipresent social control over students' movement through the school hallways was in part felt through sound. The school had recently begun playing the theme song for the TV show *Jeopardy* between classes, reminding students that "the clock was ticking" so they had better hurry to their classes. This use of the *Jeopardy* jingle was intended to instill anxiety within participants. A progressive series of loud bells also alerted students to hustle to class as the start time became closer. After the final bell, security guards stopped tardy students in the hallways. I would hear them shout to various students: "*You*, ISS. *You*, ISS. *You*, ISS." (ISS stands for in-school suspension.) Sandview High required teachers to lock their doors and bar late students from entering unless they had a "late pass" from the security desk, which was rarely given out. As a result, tardy students were often in detention for the entire class period.

Lowering suspensions is different than raising test scores. However, for both, neoliberal accountability is focused on threatening schools to (quickly) have better outcomes, which incentivizes unethical practices. As I find, this "holding schools accountable" also incentivizes hyperstrict behavioral expectations in hopes that it will both improve academic performance on standardized exams as well as help avoid serious behavior incidents.

Growing Surveillance through School Improvement Mandates

Students' sense that Sandview High treated them increasingly punitively was related to the growing presence of security personnel. As a student named Pablo described it, "There's security guards everywhere in the frickin' school, and police officers. I really feel like they don't trust us in the sense there has to be so much security." Pablo was correct: The school's newly updated code of conduct manual stated that these off-duty police officers were there to "defuse and de-escalate situations" with students. It also warned that students' "violent behavior," or "other criminal behavior in school . . . may result in a student's arrest" by these police officers.[4] Sandview High's focus on increasing security was well-known to school professionals. As Jane, a longtime school professional, put it, "Everything in this school is organized around security." She continued, "There's double doors where there used to be single doors last year; they search everyone's backpacks now . . . There's pretty much always police officers on campus and there's a large number of security officers."

In the conditions the state set up for school improvement, Sandview High was supposed to lower student suspensions but also increase security personnel and equipment. The types of school securitization measures Sandview High described above were an approved state option for the school to show what steps it was taking toward improvement. One of Sandview High's state reform programs was the "whole school reform model." In this program, one of the central means to improve academic achievement was to enhance "school climate," defined as improving "safety and discipline," and then measured by reducing the number of suspensions and "serious" incidents. This reform model was based on a federal guide that New York State used to select a restructuring plan for Sandview High's district.[5] Notably, the state's guides for improvement mainly consisted of adding new security technology and personnel. At this time, Sandview High also utilized federal grant money to acquire new student monitoring technology and metal detectors as part of their state improvement plan. In one self-assessment of their progress record to the state, the school highlighted new monitoring systems as a way to "track" interventions with students for more data analysis.

Thus, the state's improvement mandate related to Sandview High's status as an underperforming school was a key part of what ushered in greater securitization. This is a technical fix with temporary money the school could use to show it was improving the school climate. Yet, rising securitization tends to increase records and cases of student disobedience.[6] Still, rising securitization remains the leading approach for school safety improvement despite the chronically punitive outcomes for students of color.[7] And to students like Raul and Pablo, it just felt like more surveillance.

Reorganizing Punishment

Beyond the rising general social control throughout the school, Sandview High also seemed to be reorganizing punishment to keep punitive measures off the official record. As a student named Destiny stated, "It won't get counted as a suspension but you still get sent home." Destiny continued that she and her peers would "try to go to the principal for a pass, but they'll still send you home for the rest of the day." Reportedly, "a pass" would have allowed a student to stay in school that day even though they had broken a rule, in her case the dress code.

Like Destiny, students continually reported that the school began giving out "informal suspensions" for minor issues. In her statement above, Destiny was referring to her recurring experiences with informal suspensions for breaking the dress code. As she explained, "They won't let you even enter the school if you have sandals on in the summertime . . . there's a lot of stuff that you can't wear."

Students also described informal suspensions where they were sent to ISS (in-school suspension) for the remainder of the class period. As a student named Aisha declared, she was often "suspended" for being late to class. Like many of her peers, Aisha reported her frustration as she tried in vain to get a "pass" to attend her classes when she was caught coming in late. Since Aisha was sent to ISS, she was forced to miss the entire class. School staff, Aisha clarified, assumed that late students were just trying to skip class. Students were glad it did not count on their disciplinary record but were still frustrated that they were being suspended. Thus, instead of decreasing instances of punishment, state policies created incentives for Sandview High to simply move its punishments off the record.

As with the emphasis on students' test scores, the state's increasing pressure on Sandview High to rapidly improve disciplinary incidents and attendance overall seemed to exacerbate a punitive schooling environment: Sandview High adopted a growing securitization and an increase in the use of exacting behavior rules for fear of a "serious" incident (which would negatively impact their evaluation). The school also reorganized exclusionary punishments to be assigned off-the-record/informally. The types of hyper-socially controlling school elements found at Sandview High are notoriously central in "no excuses charter schools" (NECS), which studies have also linked to those organizations being under extreme pressure to quickly get children to produce higher test scores because the survival of those schools too depends on it.[8] The receivership threat especially lowered the school's stability, making it more vulnerable, as are charter schools, to the pressure to efficiently achieve certain student outcomes.

Neoliberal School Reform and School Discipline in Low-Performing Schools

The neoliberal revisions to the 1965 Elementary and Secondary Education Act (ESEA) in the twenty-first century—i.e., its transformation into the No Child Left Behind Act (NCLB) in 2002, and then into the Every Student Succeeds Act (ESSA) in 2015—use explicitly *market-centered* approaches to improving K-12 academic achievement. Undertaking a business-oriented logic to improving schools has meant focusing on specific accountability measures to evaluate and sanction public schools based on "low-performance." The key data sources for the determination of "performance" have been students' test scores, but increasingly the state also uses non-academic metrics—mainly attendance and disciplinary infractions.

Since the beginning of the neoliberal era of school reform, schools that states classify as low-performing for academic reasons must undergo comprehensive state-led reforms. This includes a focus on improving non-academic "student behavior metrics," which in practice largely means evaluating schools like Sandview High based on attendance and disciplinary infractions.[9] In part, this is because these data points can be standardized across the state (as with academic achievement metrics). For instance, in Sandview High's required state-led improvement plan for the 2014–2015 academic year, "Goal #2" was to enhance "Safety and Security." Sandview High needed to raise student attendance and lower their suspension rates. If Sandview High did not participate, the state could shutter the school. Then, in 2015, the new state receivership education law in New York State (NYS) deepened these conditions.

Like other state receivership laws, the 2015 NYS receivership law further reinforced ESEA school improvement programs because it broadened the state's power to restructure, take over, and shutter low-performing schools.[10] New York State placed Sandview High into receivership for the 2015–2016 academic year under this new corresponding state law because Sandview High was still not meeting state expectations, as defined by the ESEA. Under the receivership, improving student attendance and disciplinary infractions was part of Sandview High's state reform program. The school had to focus on lowering long- and short-term suspensions, student absenteeism, and the number of "serious incidents" (student behavior Sandview High documented as violent or possibly violent). The use of "serious incidents" as a metric for Sandview High was striking because Sandview High reported *zero* "serious incidents" for that year, which was the norm.[11] All of these were available indicators for Sandview High's improvement program with the state: Under this law, New York State specifies which indicators are available for selection and then chooses the majority of the metrics for the school. These metrics are then weighted into an index to calculate school improvement.[12]

Importantly, like most stressed schools, formal widespread discussions of restorative justice and "positive behavior" program alternatives to exclusionary disciplinary practices remain largely symbolic.[13] These items were listed in the school's documents without elaboration. I did not see any evidence of their presence in the school, and there was no mention of them by students or staff. The challenge of implementing these alternative programs pertains to the fact that exclusionary disciplinary practices remain central to schools' security procedures.[14] Even recent analyses of the now widespread Positive Behavior Interventions and Supports (PBIS) systems suggest that these systems also repeat the patterns of hyper-surveillance, hyper-punishment, and hyper-labeling that education scholar Subini Annamma argues constitute the deficit approach schools tend to take toward social behaviors of students of color, treating these students as problems to be fixed.[15]

Given the incentives of the neoliberal school improvement orders, it is not surprising that widespread punishment of students persisted and even seemed to increase as some punishments moved off the record at Sandview High. Such an approach includes even more student surveillance as a strategy to prevent any serious behavior incidents, because serious incidents count negatively in their state evaluation. Thus, like the focus on test metrics, the neoliberal policy context at Sandview High created conditions that were unlikely to lead to reducing a punitive school environment.

Significantly, the use of non-academic metrics (like suspensions or attendance) as school performance indicators has only been expanding, with new regulations in the ESSA and the growing state receivership programs under this same period.[16] The ESSA's increased use of non-academic metrics in the school accountability evaluation process was partly a response to NCLB critics that school assessments were based on overly narrow metrics.[17] Some scholars think that the ESSA's addition of new non-test measures might lead to schools just *recategorizing* disciplinary incidents, and there is evidence already that other schools under state scrutiny have wholly altered their records.[18] This is not unlike how the pressure to improve test scores resulted in schools cheating en masse to stave off state inspectors when they could not meet the expectations under their current conditions.[19] But this problem was already relevant prior to the ESSA for schools like Sandview High (under threat of closure by the state for low academic performance) who previously had to use non-test measures in addition to test scores.

Thus, the ESSA has now widened the use of non-academic metrics that schools at risk of closure had already been required to improve. As had already been the case at Sandview High, the ESSA expansion of "holding schools accountable" to non-academic metrics, like suspension and attendance, can largely be expected to result in even more system gaming because they continue the focus on trying to discipline public schools into performance rather than addressing root causes for a poor school climate, such as chronic under-funding.[20] The appeal of neoliberal accountability is that it continues to focus on imposing greater social control as a means to social mobility.[21] This requires no major deep-seated societal changes and can also be exhaustively documented and tracked for accountability purposes.

"Instilling a Culture of High Expectations"

Strategic, focused, and intentional: This is how the leadership at Sandview High described its planned approach to meeting the state's expectations for improved disciplinary infractions and attendance metrics. They stressed the importance of "excellence in discipline and attendance" to meet state expectations and cited the promotion of behavioral expectations as a strategy for meeting state expectations. And as Sandview High's situation became more dire under state receivership, they redoubled their efforts. They wanted to change students' "mentality" and "instill a pro-college mindset," in order to meet both test score and disciplinary goals. Overall, they aimed to "instill a culture of high expectations among the students."

School rules disallowed students from standing in the hallways, insisting that they move to class with efficiency. To enforce this rule (and others), there were usually eight school security guards posted in various sites across the school's main hall. "No standing in the hallways," I would hear school security guards shout at students. The guards wore brightly colored jackets with the word "SECURITY" printed in large green lettering on the back. School administrators and teachers were also posted in the hall. They stood near the guards, and I would often see all of them together watching students pass through the hallways between classes, reminding me of why students characterized school administrators as little more than extra security guards. As a student named Raul explained, "They all just do the same thing; roam the hall harassing students," referring to school administrators and guards. As another student, Jumaane, suggested, this harassment included harsh scrutiny: "Some are really the type to *stare you down*, making sure that you aren't doing anything."

The lunchroom, like the hallways, was another school space where students navigated intensified social control. As a student named Chloe explained, in the lunchroom students could not even stand up to talk to their friends—they must sit the entire time—nor could they use their phone. Chloe exclaimed, "It's 'free time,' we're supposed to be happy, but they are like, 'No.'" "They are just like, 'No phones!' and, 'Don't do this.' 'Don't stand up to talk to your friends at another table.'" The surveillance by school personnel during lunch exasperated Chloe. Like her peers, Chloe felt that at the very least students should have some of the freedom during their lunchtime that was ordinarily prohibited during the rest of the day.

Beyond the lunchroom and the hallway, one of the most disputed spaces in the school for students was the bathroom. For one, the school kept the bathroom doors locked for most of the school day. As Aisha explained, "Our school locks the doors for kids; they lock the bathroom door." She described that there were multiple bells during each period that marked when the bathrooms were locked: ten minutes before class started; when class started; ten minutes before class ended, when class ended. These ten-minute bells were a practice to keep students from skipping class by "hiding" in the bathrooms. This also infuriated students, as Aisha exclaimed, "I find it stupid, you have to use the bathroom, and you can't because they won't let you use the bathroom." Tightly controlling students in ways that did not include a formal punishment (i.e., suspension) coerced students like Aisha to tolerate authority figures controlling her basic bodily functions.

Under state pressure to quickly improve student discipline outcomes, Sandview High appeared to resort to techniques that were supposedly about "instilling a culture of high expectations," but in actuality were just coercive and in practice simply denied students agency. In fact, this approach looked a lot like another leading neoliberal school reform project, No Excuses Charter Schools. NECSs are characterized by wide-ranging schoolwide strictness, the explicit expectation of re-socializing students, uniformity of systematic rules that all professional staff must follow and major consequences if they do not, all because of the belief that culturally changing students would lead to higher academic achievement.[22] All of these elements were present at Sandview High. From hallways to bathrooms to the lunchroom, to teachers being unable to allow late students to enter class, centralized hyper-control under conditions of urgency seemed to propel the school's shift toward a "culture of high expectations" in order to "correct" student behavior.

In fact, both school types faced organizational survival mode. Beyond being privately run, the market-led NECS is also under pressure to raise test scores or face failure and shut-down. This resulted in the use of dubious disciplinary strategies in hopes of fulfilling academic achievement even though educators disagree with them.[23] As urban education scholar Beth Sondel found, the school leadership in NECS stressed strict student behavior rules, which educators followed even when they opposed the approach, both because of the pressure they were under to extract more from the children to meet testing outcomes and also because of their own vulnerability as employees hired at-will and being threatened with dismissal if their students' scores were too low.[24]

As such, the neoliberal idea of crafting market conditions where school organizations are exposed to pressure to "get results" or face closure seems like a probable blueprint for ensuring intensifying pervasive social controls over Black and Latinx students beyond a formal suspension.

"You Get Used to It," Surviving Learning to Be Policed

The school's use of formal controls often made students feel policed, stressed, and mistrusted. However, students also demonstrated that they were learning to normalize mistreatment through heavy school securitization. Students' efforts to normalize the social control they faced at Sandview High was also evident in the matter-of-fact way they spoke about discipline's function at the school, often telling their stories of harsh discipline with a casual air, implying that this was simply the way it was. A student named Righteous discussed incidents where he struggled with school authority figures punishing him excessively for minor transgressions; but in our conversation about school security guards' conduct toward students, he justified their punitive behavior. "They just do their job . . . I would do that too, because if I'm getting money for it, I have to listen to my boss." In this way, Righteous tried to normalize the intensity of social controls school personnel enacted upon him. Likewise, a student named José claimed that school personnel were "not strict," with his illustrations of "not strict" being anything but. He went on to explain, "If you're out in the hall, they'll send you straight to ISS. . . . And if you're destructive and rough housing, all a teacher has to do is call them up and send you up to ISS, or the assistant principal."

Jumaane, a Sandview High senior, was strikingly nonchalant when telling stories of harsh discipline, describing teachers, guards, and administrators as all "hard strung [strict] on the rules." In our conversation, he was wary of school authority figures "getting on you" for having a phone out in the hallway, "making a big deal out of taking it away" and "straight up suspending you on the spot"; at the same time, he felt pressured to accept this level of control. During my interview with Jumaane, the intercom came on several times to loudly to remind students they had to be in "designated areas" after school. When I flinched from the jarring sound, Jumaane said flatly, "You get used to it."

Tight control of students' behavior in the hallways, bathrooms, and lunchroom highlights the everyday punishments that students endured beyond informal suspensions. These punishments contributed to a disciplinary atmosphere, which students had to learn to navigate, often through a process of normalization. In part, students' efforts to manage their situation by trying to normalize it seemed to be about mitigating the pain of being treated as a population in need of control. Exposure to chronic social control delivered the message that these students can expect the state to be punitive toward them in all contexts. And none of these core elements of a punitive school climate can be remedied by counting the number of suspensions, in accordance with the state's school improvement plan.

Below I offer an updated framework for thinking about the social consequences of ubiquitous policing in school. It focuses on the harm produced when students are learning to manage routine social control from the state that does not result in an official punishment.

Social Costs of Hyper-Social Control, Off the Record

Socialization for prison is a key concern when it comes to the consequences of overpolicing of youth in school.[25] Punitive school discipline criminalizes youth, and schoolwide securitization and programs that "crack down" on low-level nonviolent student noncompliance criminalizes entire school student populations.[26] Yet, there is an even broader impact. These experiences can also harmfully shape youth socialization for citizenship. Like the watchful eyes and stops-and-searches of street patrols in neighborhoods, students' school experiences bolstered the development of what political scientists Amy Lerman and Vesla Weaver have called "custodial citizenship." I borrow and extend this term from Lerman and Weaver's examination of the political consequences of crime control.[27] As they describe it, "lessons learned through contact with social programs are lessons learned about the government writ large."[28]

Indeed, one way many young people learn they do not have full citizenship rights is through navigating surveillance in school.[29] For many youth, their primary contact with the state is school. And, instead of learning to be clients of the state, Black and Latinx students in highly securitized schools learn that the state thinks they are a risky or threatening population in need of surveillance and punishment. This analysis refines what we know from existing studies, like those of sociologist Carla Shedd, who argues that these experiences lead students to distrust authority. I extend this argument to also recognize how navigating surveillance in school undermines a sense of clientism, or what sociologists like Evelyn Nakano Glenn frame as entitlement to the state supporting or acting on their behalf.[30] This is a transferable lesson that has the power to shape not just how students deal with "authorities" in the future, but also how they deal with and relate to public institutions as a whole. This is a critical problem because marginalized youth populations need their schools to teach them to feel entitled to ask more of their public institutions, not less.

Learning to tolerate injustice from authority figures in school fosters a negative political message about one's citizenship prospects.[31] And while all students reported conflicts with the school's disciplinary system resulting in off-the-record punishment, students also experienced additional layers of punishment related to their race, gender, and immigration backgrounds.[32] This is an important observation, as prior analysis of harsh school punishment systems generally groups Black and Latinx youth experiences together.[33] One gendered way these intersectional lessons were imparted was through the school's approach to enforcing its strict dress code.

Girls and (Off-the-Record) Dress Code Policing

The dress code was a central aspect of off-the-record discipline at Sandview High.[34] When you walk through the second security door into Sandview High, there is a large diagram of a body in the door at eye level. The figure has many lines directed toward different items of clothing the person is wearing to show the dress code. For example, you cannot wear flip-flops; you must not wear your pants low; you must not wear clothes that are too tight, nor clothes that are too short, or too low cut. The student code of conduct explains, "Students who violate the student dress code shall be required to modify their appearance by covering or removing the offending item." "Any student who refuses to do so shall be subject to discipline, up to and including in-school suspension for the day."

The dress code rules appear to be gender-neutral, but in practice were largely only enforced for girls. As sixteen-year-old Felicity emphasized, the dress code was a "100% girl issue . . . [the boys] don't get punished, they just say 'take off your hat,' or 'pull up your pants.' We get ISS, we get kicked out of school." Both boys and girls explained that the dress code was "mostly for the girls." Like Felicity, another student, Paula, explained that boys were not supposed to "sag" and were told to "pull up" low-hanging pants, but that "The boys do it anyways, they pull them up for a second, they leave, and they pull them back down. And that's it." The girls contrasted their experiences with those of the boys. Sandview High examined, criticized, and often removed girls from their classes for transgressions to the school's dress code, such as a hole in their pants, a "low" shirt that was "overly revealing," and wearing sandals.

The basis of the scrutiny was generally about girls showing "too much" of their bodies—that they were "too adult," in their dress, indicating that staff did not want the girls presenting themselves as sexual. As one school professional explained, the dress code enforcement focused on what female students shouldn't be wearing because it was "distracting to the other students." In this way, the school deemed some girls disruptive to the academic process and consequently gave them an exclusionary punishment for it, off-the-record.

The school's ostensive goal was to teach students to "dress for success," which was related to the school's push to change students' culture to be one of "high expectations."[35] Instead, the girls (and their mothers) felt the school was overcontrolling children who wanted to be just that: children, wearing their latest fashions and feeling good about their personal style. A student named Rocio described her experience running afoul of the dress code: "You have to wear something long if you wearing leggings to school. And I wasn't wearing no long shirts or nothing, cuz I don't like long shirts." Rocio described how she tried to get away with wearing leggings without a long shirt anyway as dressing in her own style made her feel comfortable in her own skin. "I tried to walk in and they say '*You*, stop right there.'" Rocio described with exasperation that she was then excluded from school that day unless she changed her clothes. As another student pointed out to me, this was often not a viable option, as no one was at home to bring them different clothes.

Mothers criticized the school's dress code policies and the enforcement of them in a school blog (now discontinued). As one mother asked, "How is my daughter supposed to be successful if she is not in the classroom to begin with?" as her child had been sent home for breaking the dress code. Another mother wrote that "the school was too focused on a female wearing a pair of jeans with holes in them." A different mother condemned the school for using its scant resources to hire "people to stand in the halls to monitor dress code." In response, the school reminded these mothers that "dressing for success" was an important part of practicing a culture of high expectations.

From the school's point of view, they implemented strict dress code rules (and other forms of social control) in order to change students' culture to one that was college-oriented. The school further justified punishment for dress code violations as being necessary to enforce the college mentality that they were trying to inculcate in students as part of the school's state improvement plan. Sandview High's position was as a highly securitized school that was also under pressure to reduce student incidents, and they policed students off-the-record in ways that added an extra layer of punishment for Black and Latina girls through the school's approach to managing dress code violations.

Dress code policing sends a sweeping message about the girls' custodial citizenship, visible as racial and gender policing. Girls had to struggle to survive daily scrutiny from authority figures who evaluate whether they pass the moral code expressed in dress code regulations. This substantial emphasis on policing girls' appearance is racially discriminatory and humiliating. The policing of girls' attire draws on the imperative and license to control female sexualized and gendered bodies. In this way, the school used a "scandalous" frame to discipline the girls. Girls were told that the way they chose to present their bodies at school was improper and disrupted their peers' learning.

The beliefs at Sandview High about girls' morality replicate dominant stereotypes about Black and Latina girls as being sexually aggressive, which is also used to justify controlling them.[36] Other studies, like those of sociologist Edward Morris and education scholar Monique Morris, have also described racialized and gendered biases in schools' approach to dress code rules.[37] Yet here we also see how the practices at Sandview High reveal generally harsher consequences for girls than they did for boys. As students like Felicity described above, the boys were chastised to pull up their pants, but the girls were taken out of school. Dress code rules were also recognized across the Sandview High student community as a "girl issue." This is a layer of meaning-making across the student population about who the dress code was really for. Thus, while dress code can and does often police boys of color, it can also be a bright line of assault for girls.

Immigrant Students and Extra Layer of Vulnerability in School Punishment

One day in school, a recently immigrated student named Jesus went to the bathroom during a class I was attending. After a very long time he returned to the classroom, extremely upset. Security had unwittingly locked Jesus in the bathroom. He did not understand that the guard was announcing that he was locking the bathroom door, as Sandview High routinely does to prevent students from skipping class. Jesus seemed frightened by the incident and had no idea when he was going to be let out of the bathroom.

Recently immigrated Latinx students like Jesus were facing extra layers of punishment related to the school's practices of hyper-intense social control. His experience that day highlights how the school's heavy social control could be especially oppressive for the many Latinx immigrant students still learning English. The practice of locking the bathrooms throughout the day was especially dangerous for these students because many of them were still learning English. This is an extra layer of vulnerability to even more punishment related to parts of their immigration experiences.[38]

Immigrant students minimized the injustices they faced at school by juxtaposing them with their harsh migration experiences. Jesus dismissed issues with the school by constantly comparing it to the horrifying journey he had to take to reach this point. Jesus explained that he had traveled to the United States alone from Guatemala and had been detained in various holding facilities along the way. He was seized by the immigration police and then put in a series of different places he described as prisons. In one particular holding facility he was locked up for four months and could not go outside or see daylight. His parents signed papers to grant custody to his uncle, who lived in Sandview, New York; eventually, Jesus was able to afford the ticket to join his uncle by borrowing money from his uncle and the "coyote" who had been hired to bring Jesus to the United States. For his first year in Sandview, Jesus worked to pay this money back and did not attend school. Now that Jesus was finally in school, he simultaneously struggled with Sandview High's security regime and compared it favorably to his past experiences.

Carlos, another recently immigrated Latinx student still learning English, also struggled through a harsh migration pathway, in his case from Honduras. Carlos recounted his routine confrontations with security guards who refused to believe he did not speak English. "Aquí hay unos de seguridad que me gritan. Así, de repente me gritan." (*There are several security guards that yell at me, suddenly they start yelling at me.*) In relating these encounters, Carlos expressed that he does not understand what he has done wrong, or what it is that they want from him. He described with emotion that he tells them over and over, "No sé inglés." (*I don't speak English.*) He was visibly distressed in his account. "'No hablo inglés'; Ella dice, 'No, tú hablas inglés!'" (*I say, "I don't speak English," and then they say, "No you do speak English!"*). Carlos' story of dealing with school security guards visibly stressed him; but, like Jesus, Carlos minimized it by speaking about his journey here alone as a fourteen-year-old from Honduras. As he stated bluntly, "Es la vida, sufres" (*In life you suffer*). What he faced at Sandview High was, in contrast, "un jardín" (*a garden*).

Students' immigration experiences shaped how they perceived securitization-related injustices they faced in school. These students are exposed to a variation of the "carceral continuum" described by sociologist Carla Shedd.[39] Shedd's original formulation reveals that students' views about their exposure to school security systems can vary by school type: racially segregated or integrated. At Sandview High, there are some differences between students in the same school in ways related to their contact with carceral systems outside of school, clarifying different perceptions of injustice among students navigating a hyper-securitized school.

The fact that students often tried to accept the securitization of their school as normal also reveals how permeating social control in school undermines the cultivation of social citizenship. As we saw earlier with non-immigrant students like Jumaane, effort to normalize punishment generally was certainly not limited to immigrant students. However, for recently immigrated students like Carlos, immigration backgrounds were a specific way that these students constructed normalization; both by comparing it to their harsh migration background but related by minimizing school harm with the harm they faced even getting to school here. Thus, their immigration background not only shaped students' extra layer of vulnerability in terms of exposure to punishment related to school securitization, but also seemed to play a role in making it even harder for them to defend themselves when they faced injustice in school.

Punitive Attendance Tactics: Threatening CPS

Sandview High routinely called students' parents to threaten that they would send Child Protective Services (CPS) to their house to investigate them if their child continued to miss school. I learned about the practice of threatening CPS as an unofficial school policy from multiple Sandview High professionals. In their separate accounts, they indicated that the school had discovered that a CPS threat would compel students to either attend or formally drop out of school. The person overseeing these calls described "getting a drop date" for students in a way that made it actually sound like an achievement. They explained that they told the parents their child needs to come to school tomorrow and either start attending regularly or formally drop out; otherwise the school was going to send CPS to their house. They further explained that this was a "threat" designed to "scare them, it was a scare tactic" and it was "the only thing that works."[40] This practice was thus yet another off-the-record punishment: directed to intimidate students with the goal of protecting the school's state compliance with student attendance. Being a school under threat incentivized this perverse behavior because student attendance was a key metric for Sandview High's improvement programs. The school either needed students to miss few days or to drop out of school so they did not have to count them as a chronically absent student on the school's evaluation for the state.

During a discussion of the CPS issue with a school counselor in their office, I saw the list of students who were flagged as "chronically" missing school. Several students I knew to be undocumented. One of these students was a quiet fourteen-year-old from Guatemala named Eduardo. A few weeks after the school called Eduardo's home I saw him back in school. The warning of bringing in CPS was a scare tactic, intended to incite fear in families that the state would tear their families apart if the kids had excessive school absences without officially dropping out. The school did not in fact plan to call CPS, it was just a scare tactic.[41] But it worked because people believed it and felt frightened. And immigrant students with vulnerable immigration statuses like Eduardo faced a drastic raising of the stakes: It sparked fears of potential deportation.[42]

Importantly, threats of legal action have become a major approach to the way schools have been managing chronic absenteeism as attendance is now a widespread school accountability indicator under the ESSA.[43] This is an extra weight for schools under threat for low student test scores because those same schools already struggled with poor attendance.[44] Driven by these accountability pressures, the practice of threatening CPS has occurred alongside more extensive monitoring and an increased categorization of students as at risk of being chronically absent, and both extend school surveillance practices toward disenfranchised student populations and their families.[45] Unfortunately, this suggests the "measure and punish" strategies of the post-NCLB ESEA seem to be further motivating schools into more forms of policing Black and Latinx students, and doing so in intersectional ways as it created greater vulnerability for some students, here related to their immigration status.

Extreme Punishment and Administrator Fear of Black Youth

"I seen a lot of stuff," a student named Claudia recounted. Claudia was referring to the common view among students that school administrators "started problems" with students. She described a recent case in which an administrator told a Black male student to remove his hat (per the school's "no hats" policy) in the hallway. Claudia recounted that the boy complied but did so "slowly," and "smirked" at the administrator. She reflected, the boy's attitude was like, "'yeah, yeah, I got you'; and headed to class." But the administrator approached the boy and reached toward him take his hat. The boy recoiled. A "physical altercation" ensued between them. The boy stated, "don't touch me," and backed away, but the administrator advanced on him, likely to display authority. The official story was that the boy had "attacked" the administrator. The boy was then "put in a side school" (alternative school) which Claudia thought was unfair. For her, "a student was just trying to go to class." He was not "dumb" so he, like the rest of the students, would never "start something" with a school administrator. "Nothing would happen," Claudia stated. The trivial issue of a hat spiraled because an administrator overreacted to a student's noncompliance over a minor issue.

Raul (another student) told a similar story. A different school administrator was "telling some girl to get out of the cafeteria and the girl was not paying attention so they grabbed her by the collar, by the back of her shirt and started dragging her out, and the girl turned around and started hitting them." Like his peers, Raul stated that students often discussed these episodes and agreed that school administrators "deserved" being hit back by students in these types of situations.

Zoe, a young school professional who had established a close connection with Sandview High students for several years, was especially empathetic to their concerns. As a youthful-looking Black woman, she had been mistaken by school administrators for a student on more than one occasion and felt alarmed by the hostility they exhibited toward her. Zoe reported that administrators initiated problems by grabbing students physically when they refused to be deferential upon request; if students then fought back, the situation would escalate, with administrators getting into physical altercations with them. Zoe summarized, "There is a lot of mistrust and there is definitely hostility of school administrators toward students." When I asked her where administrators' mistrust toward students came from, she replied, "I think that lack of trust comes in a lot of ways from the fear the administration has of students, mostly that." So, I asked Zoe, "Are you afraid of the students?" "No, not at all," she replied. I think it is important to remind readers that most of the administrators, as well as the security guards, are Black. That is to say, as others have noted, Black guards and administrators are not excluded from being implicitly biased in their fear of Black youth.[46]

Like most schools "under threat," the majority of students at Sandview High are African American. Black youth, both boys and girls, were the targets of administrators' overreactions, thus illustrating yet another layer of vulnerability for overpunishment in a school fixated on social control. In these cases, it was always Black students who were overly punished, both boys and girls.

The theory of "racial threat" suggests that schools with more Latinx and Black youth are more punitive because of racist fears (however implicit) school personnel hold about these students as likely to act hostile.[47] Quantitative studies suggest that while schools with a greater number of Latinx and/or Black students are associated with more punitive treatment, this is more consistently the case for Black students than it is for Latinx students.[48] As this qualitative analysis shows, an underlying school cultural context emphasizing social control and entrenched racist hostility persisted even when the school was under state pressure to be less punitive.

Putting school leaders under intense pressure to perform was unlikely to help diminish the fear of Black youth. As other scholars, like sociologist Simone Ipsa-Landa, have noted, implicit racial biases continue to be a key force driving excessive school punishments even during efforts to improve.[49] And other scholars of school discipline, like Aaron Kupchik, have also stressed the role of the now dominant rise of school securitization, from new surveillance technologies to security guards, as associated with intensified harsh punishment toward students of color.[50]

In a context of state pressure to lower the suspension rate and absenteeism, and avoid serious misbehavior incidents, the school leadership doubled down on social control. As part of its school improvement plan, Sandview High brought in new school administrators to help develop a positive school culture; but students referred to these new administrators as "the punishment." As one student, Felicity, explained, "They don't care what's going on with you, they just give you a not appropriate punishment for your situation." As Jumaane pointed out, these administrators acted like extra security guards. The new administrators' efforts exemplified both the widespread method of being punitive for minor infractions in order to avoid major incidents in schools with a large Black student population and the fixation on official school discipline metrics like suspensions; these efforts also did not remedy the occurrence of extreme punishment.[51] Even the state auditors, in one of their notes related to the school's improvement efforts, remarked that it was unclear what the new administrators added besides more discipline. This punitive stance taken by the new administrators was systematic, as nearly all of the school administrators (of which there were about ten in all) were new every year.

The leadership of Sandview High had decided to focus on changing the students' culture, as they consistently stated across various school improvement documents and both written and oral commentary to the public. As the superintendent receiver stated, the students needed to have their "mentality changed" to have a "culture of high expectations." This was restated by the principal, as well as generally in their school's improvement plans as a key part of how they would improve student discipline metrics. As education scholars like Terrienda White have noted regarding no excuses charter schools, this largely puts students in the position of being told that they are deficient in ways that reproduce long-standing racialized "culture of poverty" ethos that minimize social inequalities.[52] In short, the neoliberal ethos justifies recycled racist rhetoric, reframed as instilling culture that Black and Latinx children lack.[53]

Time to Rethink Neoliberal Accountability

Since NCLB, schools under threat of closure by the state have been tasked with working to meet non-academic student behavior metrics, in addition to academic ones. State receivership laws—enacted to sanction "low-performing" schools into ESEA compliance—are also a means toward this end, as New York State's 2015 receivership law illustrates. State receiverships in particular are a growing state tool in the ESSA era of ESEA.[54] And even beyond schools like Sandview High that are threatened with closure through state receivership programs, the ESSA mandates that states use a non-academic standard to assess and rank their schools for potential intervention.[55]

But the neoliberal policy of school improvement, implemented through increasing pressure on schools, did not reduce Sandview High's punitive environment. If anything, it incentivized the school's harsh school security regime to get worse. The state required Sandview High to demonstrate it was improving culture and climate using suspension rates, attendance, and "serious incidents" to measure school improvement. However, under the threat of school closure to quickly meet these targets, Sandview High heavily policed students' basic social behavior and increasingly punished them in off-the-record ways. The pressure on the school to meet certain student behavior metrics (like suspensions) incentivizes "gaming" the system, just as it does with test scores. Reorganizing disciplinary incidents to be off-the-record is a key example. The school also used draconian state-sanctioned securitization methods to safeguard against serious incidents, which could have devastating effects on their state evaluation. This pressure also undermined the capacity for good relationships among all members of the school community.

The school administration's security and discipline practices criminalized the student population, but this did not stem entirely from the school district's leadership. Rather, the school had to make significant changes for its improvement program, following state and federal guidelines to enact those reforms. The school leadership implemented an increasingly prison-like school environment, where school professionals and security technology heavily patrolled, punished, and constricted student movement.

Importantly, schooling under threat of closure at Sandview High mirrored key elements of the context and strategies for no excuses charter schools. The conditions of threat at Sandview High were very much like the vulnerability of both NECS and the professional staff hired to work in them. In NECS, school culture is synonymous with social control and the belief that the benefits of this control outweigh the concerns.[56] NECS also aim to change the culture of working-class students of color and do so through an emphasis on discipline.[57] Sandview High seemed to be taking the lead from NECS to figure out how to make students perform well. Yet, the focus in NECS has largely been on test scores as the key motivating factor for harsh "no excuses" disciplinary practices for the "normalization of unethical practices."[58] In contrast, as this case study, and the supplementary data on the ESSA presented early in this chapter reveal, adding non-test student behavior data to the ongoing neoliberal accountability focus of "measuring and punishing" schools worsens punitive schooling, just as a focus on test scores degrades academic lessons.

The pervasive social control at Sandview High, or what I call the school security regime, shaped students in ways that undermined their socialization for citizenship. Students felt mistreated, under surveillance, and contained, and often created narratives that normalized this treatment; all of which taught them that they were "custodial citizens." That is, they were learning to tolerate an adulthood where they could expect the state to surveil them widely, even when such surveillance did not result in a formal arrest. This models the "custodial class" that Lerman and Weaver emphasize is created in the midst of wide-ranging neighborhood police patrol practices that include routine stop-and-frisks.[59] As they note, if state surveillance is one's only exposure to the state, there is little room to see the state as something you can make demands on as a democratic citizen entitled to make claims on their government. The intersectional analysis in this chapter also underscores the extra layers of vulnerability in students' experiences with off-the-record punishment shaped by gender, race, and immigration. Their experiences reflect further social consequences of highly securitized schools, which create additional harms. I expand on these social consequences in the next and final chapter.

6

Go Get Them (and Not Me)

Fostering Peer Antagonisms through School Policing Practices

Like most Sandview High students, Janel navigated problems with school authority figures and felt particularly distressed about her interactions with the school's new administrators who had been hired recently as part of the school's state plan to improve its social climate. While the new administrators' job was to supervise student behavior, Janel and other students called them "the punishment." Janel thought these new administrators were "rude" because they suspended her for breaking even minor school rules and refused to consider extenuating circumstances. For example, Janel explained, the prior week she was late for class because of a problem at home, but one of these new administrators still assigned her to detention instead of allowing her to attend her class. At the same time, Janel was adamant that she was different from other students in the school. Janel maintained that while she sometimes broke the rules, she always had "a good reason." She contrasted her behavior with that of other Sandview High students, whom she labeled "bad." As she explained, "The bad kids at the school, they mess it up for everyone," maintaining that "bad kids" broke the rules "for no reason" at all, and *those* kids needed to be punished.

Many students shared Janel's view: The bad kids at Sandview High were the reason for the increasingly harsh discipline system, and they deserved to be punished. As Righteous stated, "If they're being bad, just kick them out." He explained, "Some kids yell or say all of this crazy stuff." It was his sense that the school professionals did not suspend students quickly enough for being disruptive. But, like Janel, Righteous was critical of how he himself experienced harsh punishment in school. Righteous recounted that his teacher had sent him to one of the school's administrators for arguing with them. As he put it, "[I said to the teacher] don't talk about a good student that does your work." He told her, "You're not gonna walk over me like that because I'll be the one doing the work." Thus, while he saw his own resistance as warranted, he saw his peers as deserving punishment.

Students like Janel and Righteous were both trying to make sense of their experiences with the rising social control in their school. In their struggle to maintain dignity under these conditions, students seemed to accept the neoliberal idea of disciplining "the bad." Under this logic, badly behaved individuals cannot self-regulate and therefore must face punishment in order to resocialize them into acceptable social behavior.

Students' distancing behavior (to differentiate themselves from their "bad" peers) was related to navigating criminalization in a highly punitive school environment. That is, students were competing with each other to avoid punishment in a context where punishment was ubiquitous. As a student named Chloe explained, she should not have to face the same harsh social control that her peers did because she tried to be compliant. "If you're doing the right thing you should be able to do what you want to do." She sensed that she deserved less restrictive rules, for example she should be permitted to "go to the bathroom when you need to, have your phone out at lunch, stand up and talk to your friends in lunch," all of which she had been firmly disciplined for. Like her peers, Chloe was, in practice, learning to support a punitive environment by justifying it for others. Similarly, another student, Lucas, described struggling with the security guards overdisciplining him for minor issues like being late to class, and he emphasized the guards' "condescending attitude" toward him. Yet, he also felt that the strict discipline system was the consequence of having students "who actually need the disciplining who actually need to be talked to in that manner." Thus, even though he felt that he did not need the discipline he experienced from the security guards, he thought that other students did.

Learning to Punish the "Bad" under Neoliberal Accountability

As we saw in earlier chapters, Sandview High School increased surveillance and punishment of students in an effort to quickly meet state performance expectations for both students' academic achievement and disciplinary infractions. In practice, the school's tight social control of students contributed to reproducing racial and gendered stereotypes of their students. In the neoliberal socialization of youth, school structures teach students to compete for resources in an insecure society. In this school context, students were learning to compete to avoid the pain of criminalization.[1]

The school securitization that Sandview High expanded under its neoliberal school improvement plans expanded what counted as unlawful student behavior and heightened the scope of student surveillance through added security measures. In this school context, with ubiquitous social control, youth tried their best to not be the "criminal." Therefore, while the school personnel and the increasing number of strict school rules reminded students every day of their criminality, students understandably strived to be less criminal than their peers. This punitive state model encouraged students to see punishment as the mechanism for improving student behavior and suggested there would be no need for criminalization if there were no criminals. From their experiences, they learned the state was punitive, and in order to be a legitimate participant in the state, youth also had to think punitively. Criticizing each other was a survival strategy to manage rising state surveillance and stigma in this type of schooling process.

The social costs of criminalizing Black and Latinx youth in school include undermining children's relationships with each other; these injured relationships, in turn, contribute to recreating racial and gendered inequalities. I explore how the school's treatment of students reproduced three dominant criminal frames: scandalous, illegal, and violent. These frames pitted students against each other: Students then used these frames on each other as a strategy to reduce the marginalization they faced from punitive school discipline practices. Consequently, fostering antagonisms among Black and Latinx students is a significant (and often overlooked) harm of hyper-policing youth of color in school.

My analysis expands the race relations scholarship that explores the impact of social contexts on interracial group relations and the particular role of school policies in shaping these relations. Although not in a school context, analysis by sociologist of race Jennifer Jones shows how specific social contexts can positively shape the intergroup relations between Latinx and African American individuals.[2] In my case, I argue that the school context negatively shaped those intergroup relations via the disciplinary regime. As sociologist of education and race and ethnicity

Gilda Ochoa found in a school with mainly Asian and Latinx students, I suggest that *school discipline regimes* can fortify Latinx and African American students' stereotypical thinking about each other, which has been seeded by other interactions such as with media and at home.[3]

My analysis here also extends Angela Valenzuela's sociological case study, which focused on how *school structures* can negatively influence intragroup relations (among a student population that was largely either Mexican American or Mexican immigrants).[4] I add that the intergroup relations of Black- and Latinx-identified youth are also harmed through school policies and practices, consequently undermining students' ability to see each other as resources and likewise build social solidarity among their peers as minoritized youth facing criminalization in school.[5]

Fear of "Violent" Youth

In addition to routine security practices, Sandview High held special assemblies to address the risk of the violence they feared from their students, specifically the fear that their students would engage in gun violence at school. Notably, Sandview High had no history of gun violence; the school's records showed zero incidents of violence with weapons.[6] No one had ever been shot at Sandview High, and the "school violence index" there was moderate.[7] When I asked students and school professionals about weapon incidents, I heard the same two stories over and over again: One student had brought brass knuckles to school, and another student hit someone with a screwdriver. Teachers stated that none of the weapons reported at Sandview High were guns, and guns were not a problem at Sandview High. One teacher I spoke to had been working at Sandview High for more than decade. In that time, they had "heard reports of students having weapons in the school, but no one had ever used it." Students likewise had no knowledge of guns being used at school. Official Sandview records indicated a similar story: *Zero* youth had been arrested for killing anyone.[8] Sandview violent crime was unremarkable and had been in a steady decline for at least the last decade.[9] According to the last ten years of violent crime cases prior to this research, an average of two people were killed by gun violence annually. Violent crime happened in spikes, such as a shooting at 2 or 3 am in a bar among men in their twenties and thirties, not among teenagers.[10]

Sandview High's special anti-gun assembly, part of its intensifying efforts to improve school climate, sent students the message that the school administration feared they would bring a gun to school.[11] Sitting on the school auditorium's metal bleachers along with school staff, students recited the superintendent's anti-gun pledge during the school's special rally: "I will never bring a gun to school. I will use my influence to stop any friends from bringing a gun to school or using a gun to settle a dispute." The kids all swore at the end. When I asked a Black student named Kevin what he thought the event was about, he replied with shame, "It's so we stop killing each other." Other Black students felt the same way, and Sandview High encouraged them to feel responsible for potential gun violence in school. My subsequent conversation with Ruby (a veteran after-school program youth educator) confirmed that Sandview High students took a lot of responsibility for problems for which they were not liable. Ruby shared with me that she told her students, "If that's not your experience then don't own it, don't own the stereotype." Sandview High undermined students' ability to get away from the criminal frame of being violent youth.

Although Sandview High encouraged students to see themselves as liable to engage in gun violence at school, Black students did *not* actually fear the prospect of gun violence in school. As a Black student named Alan stated, "I wouldn't come to school if I thought there were guns." He explained, "I mean there are fights but I don't think that I'm going to get like stabbed or shot; there are fights, that's it." Deron (another Black student) described the fighting at Sandview High as "slap fights" between girls, or "punching and kicking" among boys. Teachers had similar stories, adding that school fights were mostly between girls. According to students (and teachers), these "girl fights" were started because one girl allegedly took another girl's boyfriend. Fights can certainly alarm students, but girls slapping each other over a boyfriend is far removed from potential gun violence.

Latinx and African American students at Sandview High held divergent views about the school leadership team's safety strategies, differences that seemed to be about the survival strategies available to deflect the pain of criminalization. Like Black students, Latinx youth also had to deal with being heavily policed at school, strict disciplining, watchful eyes of security, being questioned as gang members, illicit drug users, and instigating fights. But Latinx students at Sandview High also seemed to be trying not to be seen as violence-prone, the way they knew their Black peers were perceived.

In contrast to Black students' views, Latinx students did not feel the anti-gun message or event was for them. For one, few Latinx students even *attended* this anti-gun school event.[12] And, when I asked the Latinx students why they thought few Latinx students attended, many responded as Marisol did, "Latino students are less involved in that stuff." And, in contrast to their Black peers, Latinx students also repeatedly stated that they worried about guns at Sandview High. As Alfredo (Latino student) put it, "Guns are a problem here." I learned that this was related to rumors among Latinxs and that none of them knew of any actual incidents of gun violence in the school. As Pablo, another Latino student, reported, his friends told him, "you're gonna get killed, you're gonna get shot" at this school.

Latinx students' narratives also described the presence of heavy school security policies as a signal that their school was dangerous, which they blamed on their Black peers—linking them to the stereotype that Black youth are violent. As a Latina student named Lupe stated, "Our school's pretty dangerous, we're having lockdowns." Latinx students also reported wanting Sandview High to add more security guards for increased safety, with one Latino student even suggesting that guards should carry bats. They also described guards as incapable of doing their jobs. "Say there's a fight," said Martín, a Latino student, "they're not at the age or physical physique to actually separate the kids." Latinx students also cited the use of guards to break up basic fights among students as proof that Sandview High was out of control. As a Latino student named Hector put it, "When they see students fighting they call security."

Contrary to their Latinx peers, Black students did not report perceiving their school as dangerous. In fact, Black students cited the same elements of school security practices Latinx students did as evidence of school safety, rather than signs of insecurity. Regarding school lockdowns, a Black student named Chloe explained, "When there is a problem they put you in a lockdown situation; they take control of the situation."[13] This was similar to how Black students portrayed security guards. In contrast to their Latinx peers, Black students reported they felt the security guards were capable and did not have much to do because nothing serious ever happened. Black students also believed that security staff strictly controlled student fights. As a Black student named Aisha explained, "You can't get one hit in without security breaking it up. Nothing big happens here." When I asked Melissa (another Black student) if she felt safe in school, she replied, "There are tons of security guards, there's no reason not to feel safe. And the other adults might as well be called security guards because they do the same thing, they're just not wearing the uniform. So, I feel pretty safe here."

There were some exceptions to Latinx students feeling the school was dangerous. Raul was one of these students. He said plainly, "I feel like if a student was gonna shoot someone at school, it would've already happened." Raul also mentioned he did not hang out with other Latinx students at the school, which may have shaped his views on race; his friends were Black. "I don't really talk to Latino people at school, they kind of shove themselves apart," Raul explained. He later stated candidly, "If they [Mexicans] see a Black person, they be like he's probably up to no good, I've known a lot of people like that." Janel, a Latina student, felt similarly. When I asked her about weapons and safety at school, Janel replied, "No, never, kids aren't dumb to just bring them to school, the main thing I think the school should worry about is weed, it's always the same three boys that have it but not like a lot." Janel explained with a sigh, "People make it seem like it's a bad school but there's not much that happens here." Like Raul, Janel's friends were Black.

The divergent views about school safety between the two groups also likely reflects the practice of widespread punishment for minor nonviolent acts ("zero-tolerance" discipline) *and* the fact that much of the student population was Black. Latinx and Black students were suspended at similar rates (as a percentage of each group's overall population in the school). But because Black students made up *most* of the student population, on a regular basis students saw school professionals punishing Black youth for having "done something." Student misconduct was mostly for nonviolent acts. During my fieldwork, there was a yearly average of nearly 800 student incidents Sandview High categorized as "Miscellaneous Disruptive."[14] Students and professional staff reports indicated that these "miscellaneous" actions reflected discipline for minor disobedience. Thus, Sandview High had a very high rate of addressing issues where, in the school's view, students had done something minor that was otherwise uncategorizable.

The zero-tolerance discipline policies, security guards, police officers, and anti-gun campaigns at school all seemed to send the message to Latinx students that they attended a dangerous school, which they tended to blame on their Black peers. The town of Sandview itself was considered a dangerous place, a view that seemed embedded in the dominant idea that local Black youth were the problem. Latinx youth felt less self-identification, responsibility, and shame with the stigma of the local area. Latinx students commonly espoused anti-Black views of their Black peers as "violent." And the way the school organized violence prevention programming and hyper-policed students also communicated to Latinx students that their Black peers could become violent.

Latinx students' interpretations of their Black peers' behavior also directly expressed the anti-Black stereotype of them being prone to violence. "The Black kids, they like to get into fights," said Sofía, a Latina student. Marisol, another Latina student, characterized most of the Black girls at Sandview High as "crazy," explaining she saw them "scratching each other's faces off." Martín (Latino) explained that the Black kids were violent and the Latinx students were not. "I've seen three different girls get hit by a guy." He stressed that "it was Black, African American students, I've never seen a Latino student hit another girl." It is quite likely that Latinx students' collective embrace of anti-Black stereotyping may have been to distance themselves from, and assign blame for, the stigma that Sandview High students were violent: These were survival tactics to recoup dignity.

Beyond efforts to avoid the stigma of being seen as a dangerous population, Latinx students also felt in competition with their Black peers to avoid school punishment—and saw themselves as losing. Latinx students explained that they were disciplined more than Black students because of their race, which they identified as "Latino" or "Spanish," indicating that some of the Black administrators and security guards were prejudiced and discriminated against Latinxs. Latinx students generally stated they were marginalized in relation to Black Sandview High students but, when asked to explain, their stories were about racially biased (anti-Latinx) treatment in school *discipline*. As a Latino student named Martín explained, he felt hyper- surveilled and punished by the school guards and administrators. He chalked it up to being Latino (and not Black). To illustrate, he described that at lunchtime, he was punished for having his phone out in the lunchroom. He felt he was being "picked on" because of his Latino race, noting that he saw Black students nearby also doing similar things that were against the rules. Because he was Latino he believed he was "judged more harshly" than Black students. Similarly, a Latino student named Felipe explained that the security guards held Latinxs back at the security gate but let the Black kids ahead of them even though they were there first when he and his friends were late for class. And when Marisol (Latina student) raised the issue of anti-Latinx discipline bias, her example was that she had heard there were only Latinx students in detention sometimes even though Black students also skipped class.

I cannot identify whether Latinx students were punished more than Black students informally. School records indicated that Latinx and Black students were suspended at similar rates, with Black students slightly overrepresented.[15] All students, Black and Latinx, reported individually facing widespread punishment routinely. This is also what I observed in the hallway.[16] These data suggest that both groups of students, Black and Latinx, were being extensively punished at Sandview High.

Black students did not report anything to indicate that they saw themselves as powerful or receiving preferential treatment in school discipline. And, as I describe later this chapter, when it came to punishment for dress code violations, Black girls reported that they received more stringent punishment than the Latina students. All students struggled to manage the pain of criminalization by distancing themselves from their peers in different ways. For Latinx students, one key way this occurred was through a frame that presented as a collective anti-Black ethos.

"Not All of Us Are Like That"

Black students also tried to distance themselves from this criminalizing "violent" racial stereotype, by redeploying it toward their Black peers. "We're the stereotypical high school, that's what everybody says," stated Chloe, a Black student. "Because they're like, 'that's all the Black kids and they're gang violent,' and I'm like, 'not all of us are like that . . . There are people here that are bad but not all of us.'" Black students like Chloe distanced themselves from their peers to navigate the pain of being criminalized and pegged as violent.

I particularly observed Black students distancing themselves from others in their racial group to avoid the "violent" criminal frame when navigating a school program explicitly for Black male Sandview High students. As one Black student in the program, Robert, stated, "They tell us stories about real life events, gangsters, gangsters who died, just warning us about life." He continued, "I have nothing to do with that lifestyle, but those kids need it."

This self-distancing did not shield Robert from being framed as threatening at Sandview High. After interviewing Robert one day, I ran into a school professional who coordinated various school programs. Within earshot of Robert, she spoke in a stage whisper: "Be careful with him, we kicked him out of our program and we don't kick out many students." She looked intently worried about my safety. Robert was a regularly enrolled student at Sandview High; it stands to reason that if he was in serious trouble for being "violent," he would not have been allowed to remain in the school. Later, Robert told me that he was kicked out of the program for stealing an ice cream bar from another student, explaining, "I guess for her the ice cream incident was really bad." He continued grimly, "maybe it's because I'm Black, I don't know, it doesn't affect me," and sunk into his seat.

"If I Want, I Can Call Immigration to Take You Guys"

In this section, I turn to the "illegal immigrant" criminal frame that Latinx students experienced.

Latinx students faced being seen through this criminal frame, but also used it on each other to suggest that their Latinx peers were the *truly* "illegal" ones. Scholars have already suggested that in schools with authoritarian discipline practices, students are more likely to model a domineering approach with each other.[17] Unfortunately, this can also be extended to the use of specific racial criminal frames where students try to weaponize criminal frames to limit the pain of criminalization they face.

Latinx students dealt with direct and indirect exchanges where school professionals and students weaponized "illegality," framing Latinx students as unlawful and unwelcome immigrants. I call this *illegal talk*. This illegal talk reinforced the marginalization of undocumented immigrants and also accused all Latinx students of being undocumented, chastising them as undeserving citizens in the school community. As a Latino student named Pablo put it, "They [his peers] put all of us in a category, all you guys are Mexican, all you guys are undocumented . . . you guys are taking our jobs, you illegals." Pablo was from Costa Rica and had immigration papers, but he too experienced this type of criminalization in school. This frame was extra-punishing for the many undocumented students like Rubén, from Honduras. Rubén illustrated his experience by stating, "When I go to school programs, they say, 'Latino; they doesn't have papers,'" imitating his peers' mocking tone. Alan, a Black student, offered his assessment of students' illegal talk in Sandview High: "I think in our school we can make jokes like you're an immigrant, you ran across the border." He asserted, "Sometimes they can take offense, but I don't see it really being a problem." Although Black students did not tend to share anti-Latinx views with me, Alan's view of illegal talk suggested it was a common practice.

As an important note, the small number of Black immigrant students at Sandview High did not experienced the illegal frame, even though some of them were also undocumented.[18] These students reported discrimination related to language (e.g., speaking Jamaican Patois), or being from Africa (e.g., "Africa boy"), but never "illegal talk." This is consistent with the literature that this racialized criminal stereotype is not similarly deployed for persons racialized as Black.[19]

Sandview High did not invent the "illegal" racial criminal frame toward Latinxs.[20] Yet, the school's disciplinary practices tacitly reinforced this practice by students. As a Latina student named Rocio explained, it was common for teachers to ignore illegal talk. "I guess teachers don't hear it, and if they hear, I guess they don't say nothing," Rocio concluded. Rocio recounted a day in her economics class where another Latina student asked the teacher if government-housing subsidies (the topic) were available to students without immigration papers. In Rocio's narrative, several Black students chimed in to confirm that it was a "Mexican" student who had asked the question and then started laughing. Rocio explained, "They were like, 'Oh yeah, because she needs help, but she don't have papers,' and everybody started laughing. And that's not funny." I asked Rocio what the teacher did, and Rocio replied that the teacher did not seem to hear it happen. To students like Rocio, teachers' silence affirmed racializing and shaming Latinx students as acceptable. As with selective discipline, inaction informs students' conceptions of the boundaries between normal and offensive. In this case, the teacher has tacitly affirmed that Latinx students belonged to a class of transgressive people.

Black students' use of illegal talk can also be seen as a strategy to minimize the stigma they faced. For instance, Black students like those in Rocio's story mocked undocumented Latinxs for needing government support while being unable to access it and labeled Mexicans undocumented, including their classmate. This is in a school where a great number of Black students' families relied on government support, something that remains socially stigmatizing for Black families.[21] In a direct conversation about welfare, Black students engaged in illegal talk toward their Latinx peers, likely because it helped them to negotiate their social position in ways that did not leave their group on the "bottom shelf," as sociologist Vilna Bashi puts it.[22] Students' use of racialized insults seemed to be deployed in ways that helped them solidify their social standing.

Importantly, illegal talk by school professionals included using this language, ignoring when others were using it, and also employing it as a method of discipline. When it came to disciplining Latinx students with illegal talk, there were extreme instances of staff both using and tolerating it. One teacher close to the Latinx student population described the issue candidly, stating, "They [the school administrators] think all Latinos are illegal. To them, all of the students are illegal, just because they look like Latinos." To illustrate, the teacher described a time when a Latino student was in trouble for an offensive social media posting. In a meeting with the school administration team, one administrator reportedly told him that he was "lucky the administration did not call immigration on him . . . If we had gone to the police probably at this time you would have been deported already."

A Latino student named Felipe repeated a typical taunt he and his friends heard during lunch time: "Si yo quiero, llamo a la Migración para que la venga a traer ustedes" (*If I want, I can call Immigration to take you guys*). Felipe described how Mexican students at school called him and his Central Americans friends "ilegales" and threatened to call immigration on them as a common intimidation tactic. I observed a soft version of this in class one day when I was assisting a Dominican student named Alma with her assignment. Diego (Mexican) strutted by Alma's desk and said, "You swam here." In response, Alma glared and rolled her eyes at him, then returned to her assignment. Diego grinned and walked away, looking for someone else to pester. As Rocio (Latina student) also explained, illegal talk among Latinxs was common, stating, "Even though we all Spanish, they say comments like that too . . . like 'Ha, he don't got papers.'"

Latinx students' use of illegal talk toward each other was a way to navigate the criminal frame of their racial-ethnic group as "illegal" lawbreakers. As Karen Pyke and Tran Dang found, minoritized youth have often leveraged racialized insults among their own group members about one's relative degree of "foreignness" to navigate their own experiences with racism.[23] This study shows how intragroup redeployment of racialized insults can use the specific criminal framing of a racial-ethnic group, not just as foreign but also as "illegal" lawbreakers.

Importantly, school context matters: Sandview High's punishing disciplinary regime treated students in everyday school life as criminals, and in response, they appeared to be striving to be seen as less criminal than their peers.[24] Like the other dominant criminal frames fortified at Sandview High, Latinx students confronted with illegal talk also used it on each other to seemingly feel less defamed themselves. All students seemed to be fighting to declare themselves innocent relative to their peers; this involved identifying someone else as guilty and therefore more deserving of punishment.

"I'm Not That Bad, Look at What *She's* Wearing"

The girls at Sandview High, who were subject to most of the dress code policing, aimed to distance themselves from other girls to lessen the criminalization pain they felt. As explained in the last chapter, working-class Latina and Black girls faced regular scrutiny over their chosen dress, often pleading unsuccessfully with school officials not to send them home. And yet, even as girls at Sandview High struggled with the dress code, they justified these rules by applying them to their "scandalous" female peers.[25] Unknowingly, the girls were participating in fortifying Sandview High's discipline regime, and more broadly, dominant raced and classed expectations for feminine gender performance.

When girls at Sandview High were punished for dress code violations, they responded by saying things like, "I'm not that bad, look at what *she's* wearing." Lupe, who was suspended multiple times for breaking the dress code for issues like her shirt being "too low" cut, objected to her disciplinary treatment. "They [Sandview High administrators] have been *really* rough on clothes." At the same time, Lupe stated that "it is good that they have the dress code because of the way some of the girls dress; some girls who be wearing short shorts." Responses like Lupe's illustrate students distancing themselves from female peers to detach individually from the shame the school put on them personally. For her, a "low" shirt was okay but "short shorts" were indecent. This was similar to what another student named Kiyana stated: "I wear ripped jeans, and they will be like 'I'm sending you home,' but they didn't say it to a girl who just walked in wearing leggings, I am dressed appropriately but she is not." Overpolicing motivated girls to reclaim their dignity by disparaging other girls as the *truly* scandalous ones.

Girls' narratives about Sandview High's dress code system revealed that they criticized each other as a survival strategy to cope with being policed in school. Here, in a school that heavily policed students, avoiding additional punishments was a highly valued resource: There was a lot of school punishment to go around. At schools like Sandview High, the number of potential violations due to the strict rules and the highly punitive mode of their enforcement intensifies the school's engagement with selectively punishing students for minor infractions like breaking the dress code. With such extensive rules and policing of students' behavior for minor issues (like breaking the dress code or being late to class), it was unfeasible for the school to apprehend everybody because the bar for potential punishment was so low. As sociologists of education and race Amanda Lewis and John Diamond note, schools generally do not have the capacity to punish all students for each observed violation of school rules; consequently, school professionals selectively discipline individual students.[26] This is exacerbated in schools like Sandview High, where the rules are strict and surveillance is high; having such a wide net for potential punishment also means that students will observe even more so that the rules are not applied to all: There was just far more potential for punishment than school professionals could enforce. Consequently, this school structure incentivized students to compete with each other to prevent individual mistreatment.

Competition over valued resources is also a key factor in the reproduction of antagonistic race relations.[27] Black girls reported that they were treated more harshly than Latina students for dress code violations. As Aisha explained with authority, "You know this is a majority Black school, right? Well, they have rules about what you can wear that apply particularly to Black girls, there's stuff we want to wear, and we can't; they send you home." She continued, "Black girls get targeted and sent home because we have a figure." A group of Black girls discussed this issue during break in a class I sat in on. One girl in the group asserted, "They target Black girls and send us home because we have a figure, White and Mexican girls can wear what they want; and it's 100 degrees outside." Thus, for the Black girls, Latinas (and White girls) were favored over them, and, in this way, received less punishment than they did.

Latina girls told the same story: They were overpunished for dress code compared to Black girls. Rocio (Latina), summarized this view: "We wear it to school and they [security or school administrators] say something. But Black people wear it to school, they don't say nothing." She described wearing "something short" or leggings without "something long" over them as key examples. Rubén (Latino) echoed this sentiment by stating, "With Latinas, cuando las vienen a la escuela con chores pegados, tienen que regresar a casa, pero when you see another like Black girl, no les dice nada. Eso se llama racismo." (*When Latinas come to school with short-shorts they get sent home, but they [school officials] don't say anything to the Black girls. That is called racism.*) With the exception of Rubén, male students were largely unsympathetic to the girls' critiques of the dress code policing.

These types of student observations also included Latina girls viewing the outfits worn by Black girls as inherently more scandalous. As Paola (Latina student) described, "Black girls can wear half shirts and belly button showing and spaghetti straps while they try to send me home for wearing leggings." For Latina students like Paola, not only did security pick on her because she was Latina and let the Black girls go by freely; she also saw her leggings as relatively less scandalous compared to half shirts and spaghetti straps that she observed Black girls wearing. All of the items Paola described were outlawed at school. In practice, all girls (Black and Latina) regularly wore them and only sometimes were punished for it.

Being caught for a dress code violation was a central way that both Black and Latina girls separated along clear racial divisions to explain their unjust experiences with school discipline. This analysis connects with Julie Bettie, who also found that girls framed their gender identities oppositionally to other girls, constructing different raced girl groups in the school.[28] This study expands on Bettie's research by identifying how the school's discipline structure incentivizes Latina and Black girls to see themselves and other girls negatively. Sandview High's use of raced and classed frames in its punishment system disciplined girls at Sandview High for acting outside of these boundaries. Girls then discursively negotiated in favor of themselves individually, and their racial group more broadly, as the ones who presented normatively acceptable femininity.

Emboldening Boys to Police the Girls

Boys at Sandview High generally condemned girls when it came to school dress code policing practices, even directly criticizing girls for having a scandalous style of dress. A male student named Jamar reported that he would scold his female friends for "wearing belly shirts," and would say things to them like, "Where's the rest of your shirt?" and, "Don't wear that around me." He felt the dress code was important to reinforce because girls should not try to "draw attention" to themselves by wearing skimpy clothing. Jamar felt that the school put those rules into place because girls dressed, in his words, "provocatively." Boys like Jamar felt emboldened not only to criticize their female peers, but also to police their dress in daily school life.

Like sociologist of youth and education C. J. Pascoe, my analysis demonstrates how school structure fosters hegemonic gendered and raced interactions among youth, fortifying these types of identities for youth and their understandings of each other.[29] Boys tended to proclaim, as one male student named Martín did, that dress code rules were mostly "just for the girls." Boys like Martín felt this was a good social control on the girls. He explained, smiling, that the school dress code prevented the girls from wearing "most of the stuff that they wanted to." Seemingly amused at this social control on the girls, Martín stated, "Girls don't want to wear anything to school at all; every girl just wants to show her stuff in school." Like his other male peers, Martín felt that the girls' protests for dress code–related discipline were unwarranted, while also indicating they were judgmental of the girls' choices of lewd clothing. As Martín stated with an air of superiority, "The girls are like, 'Why don't you let me wear that shirt?' Maybe it's because you're not wearing a shirt at all."

Accounts like these were typical of male Sandview High students. These same boys, all Black or Latino, suffered extensively from racialized and gendered overpolicing at school, but not usually in ways related to the dress code. To the extent boys faced dress code policing, they had to remove a hat or pull up their pants, to which students (boys and girls) reported that the boys would just pull them back down after the school officials walked by. The boys echoed the school professionals' enforcement of the dress code. This perhaps made them feel less defamed in the overpolicing they did experience at the hands of school officials.

The school's regulation of girls' presentation of self engendered in the boys an entitlement to criticize their female classmates. In this way, Sandview High strengthened boys' sense of authority to criticize girls for "immoral" presentations of self, according to dominant standards of femininity. As such, the school, in effect, reinforced boys' efforts to inflate their projections of hegemonic masculinity.

The Social Costs of Hyper-Policing Black and Latinx Youth

School discipline and security practices pit students against each other, fueling antagonisms among students. Students faced different racialized and gendered criminal frames through school discipline, and to navigate these frames, they commonly applied these descriptions to each other. Latinx students often blamed the highly securitized school structure on their Black peers, and Black students used the "illegal" frame for their Latinx peers to feel less defamed themselves. And the "scandalous" criminal frame Latina and Black girls faced in terms of dress code policing was also a motivation for girls to shift the criminality onto each other, and for boys to shift blame onto the girls. Students used these stereotypes against peers in their own racial groups as well.

Importantly, all of the students' distancing acts are related. The distancing from the criminalizing Black stereotype is parallel to Black and Latina girls separating from each other through using the "scandalous" frame; likewise, it was also similar to Latinx students distancing themselves from each other by disparaging one another as "illegals."

Students' perceptions are useful guides to understanding the implications of school securitization and the corresponding harsh discipline regime.[30] This chapter's analysis illustrates how avoiding the pain of criminalization in this school context is an example of perceived resource competition, which remains a key ingredient to reproducing racial stratification.[31] Students struggled against each other for access to this resource. Thus, one result of school criminalization was reinforcing racial tensions among Black and Latinx youth, undermining students' sense of social citizenship to each other and consequently damaging the potential for interracial solidarity among students of color to combat racial injustice in school and in the future as adults.

The school discipline regime's criminalization of the students promoted racial and gendered stereotypes about Black and Latinx youth, from which students then tried to isolate themselves, and in the process, redeployed these same criminal frames onto each other. Thus, students tried to survive this difficult situation not only by normalizing school practices (chapter 5), but also by turning on each other. Their reactions are understandable, as students observed how even minor acts of insurgence resulted in stark punishment. Nevertheless, through no fault of their own, students' responses largely supported the maintenance of an oppressive regime.

Conclusion

We Can't "Measure and Punish" Our Way Out of This

The stark pressure on school professionals that reoriented the schooling process strained relationships among everyone. Some people also just left. As one Sandview High student named Aisha put it, "The kids just give up on the state tests and leave." Teachers and school administrators also responded to the stress by leaving. Sandview local news stories continue to report on the ongoing, immense state pressure to rapidly improve without sufficient resources and its role as the key reason for turnover among school administrators. Sandview High incessantly being threatened with a state takeover continues to make working there untenable for teachers. Many teachers continue to cite state threats as the main reason they leave, often taking the first opportunity available to move to a different school. Thus, beyond weaponizing metrics like standardized test scores, schooling under threat of closure induces teachers and administrators to quit, with the result being that kids are taught by inexperienced teachers and face erratic school leadership from recurrently new administrators.[1] Teacher and administrator turnover is a national issue but is most acutely felt in stressed schools like Sandview High.[2] Consequently, state discipline toward school professionals to produce state-desired results drives people away from serving the most vulnerable students.

Spending time talking to students and their allies at a school long targeted by state pressure to improve or face school closure suggests that the neoliberalism of K-12 schools is more than market orientation; it is also about growing state carcerality. State scrutiny reoriented schooling practices at Sandview High to be more authoritarian, surveillance-oriented, stressful, and punishing as school professionals doubled down on their efforts to coerce students to perform in ways that would produce desirable state metrics. And this state pressure did not end with the federal NCLB's (No Child Left Behind) transition into the ESSA (the Every Student Succeeds Act).[3]

Punishment and threat are cornerstones of neoliberal experimentation and will persist as long as these types of experiments remain the prevailing option for school improvement. The ESSA and state receiverships have expanded the state's tools for what they continue to style as holding schools accountable. This is framed as a helping hand from the state, but in practice is a form of punitive governance as it grows surveillance, stigma, and control. Especially through the ESSA and state receiverships, the state increasingly seizes control of schools using methods beyond testing, with audits widened to include students' attendance and discipline records. The results are programs and practices that expand hyper-social control of students of color, which replicate the ethos of the No Excuses Charter Schools (NECS) model.

The types of popular programs, such as PBIS (Positive Behavioral Interventions and Supports) that the ESSA specifically encourages and funds for low-performing schools to improve their students' discipline and attendance rates tend to create new mechanisms of hyper-surveillance, stigma, and punishment for Black and Latinx students.[4] As part of the ESSA, low-performing schools can hire education consulting companies to help them meet their ESSA accountability expectations for student discipline and attendance. Popular education consulting companies continue to focus on "character" education, emphasizing student accountability and "grit." Seemingly, this is just one more way to inject No Excuses Charter School ethos into traditional public schools serving mainly Black and Latinx youth from modest income families.[5]

Neoliberal accountability forcing underperforming schools like Sandview High to face the threat of school closure for poor performance is a key part of the federal government's business approach to school improvement, explicitly as an equity effort for socially disadvantaged children. The threat of increasing sanctions leading up to school closure are supposed to impel people into performance. Under this logic, structural and managerial changes would improve performance and "schools that did not perform would be closed just like businesses."[6] The idea is that low-performing schools aren't sufficiently disciplined in how they are managed to efficiently provide educational services to children. This lens justifies the state's interventions into the school.

The punitive nature of neoliberal governance toward working-class people and the organizations that serve them can mean various things depending on context. This can help us think more deeply about what actually underlies official rhetoric about a "business approach" to improving education for socially disadvantaged student populations. According to this rhetoric, the missing ingredients to success are pressure, guidance, and competition. This is what the state means when it operates using an "accountability" approach to reforming low-performing schools. Facing rising state sanctions with school closure pending, Sandview High participated in state-led restructuring. This was done under the auspice that state pressure would oblige school professionals to perform better, with the state increasingly overseeing the school's shifting reform efforts if they "fail." In this view, failure is easily rated using standardized tests and other student behavior data. Yet, these data are dubious and the pressure to meet particular metrics incentivized dreadful schooling conditions.[7]

Increases in state oversight is a hallmark of neoliberal governance: If you fail, it is because you haven't properly managed your situation. State social control is for one's own good and provides a temporary path that will lead to success if followed properly. In this way, state oversight of schooling is structured similarly to other programs that target disenfranchised populations, like foster care and welfare-to-work.[8] With school accountability, failure is organizational rather than individual, but is remedied with the same state strategies. Struggling schools are subjected to corrective oversight, justified on the basis of presumed failure. The notion is that organizations, like individuals, have unsuccessfully disciplined themselves, and so the state will do it for them.

The threat of school closure endures as the key element of state efforts to enact the school accountability mandates of the federal government.[9] With the states now having more influence in how they enforce federal neoliberal accountability policies, they continue the "big stick" approach, in part by increasing state receivership laws that expand their ability to threaten low-performing public schools with closure. Recently, under public pressure, state auditors have begun to denounce teaching-to-the-test and the overpolicing of youth of color, while the dominant school improvement policies continue to incentivize these practices.[10] These recent shifts are reminiscent of earlier criminal justice reform policies that proclaimed to be kinder and gentler even as the basic infrastructure criminalizing poverty largely remained in place.[11]

Sandview High and the Threat of School Closure Nationally: Trends by Region

In order to think more about where the case of Sandview High sits in the national picture, we have to consider the role that gentrification has played in tandem with the interrelationship between the school accountability and "choice" elements of neoliberal school reform. Specifically, it seems that if Sandview gentrifies (as many inner-ring suburbs are starting to be), it is likely that Sandview High will finally close.

Gentrification has been a key factor in school closures throughout the neoliberal accountability era.[12] School closures occur in divested urban spaces serving a large number of Black students from working-class families.[13] These are the places most vulnerable to gentrification.[14] Alongside that fact, the threat of school closure has only deepened in recent years, with actual school closures on the rise and expected to grow as the ESSA continues to be implemented, as well as state receivership laws that are designed to implement the federal ESSA mandates related to neoliberal accountability.[15]

Part of the role gentrification plays in driving school closures is how it shapes enrollment. Importantly, gentrification's driving force on student enrollment mainly occurs alongside the presence of charter school options (an important feature of neoliberal experimentation for school improvement). In these cases, under-enrollment occurs for several related reasons. For one, the new affluent White residents generally do not send their children to the local public schools, and the presence of charter school options makes this an easy option.[16] In addition, many long-term residents are priced out due to the rising costs of living and are forced to leave the area.[17]

When state or district leaders justify a public school's closure for low performance, they also typically cite "efficiency," that is, the financial necessity to cut costs due to under-enrollment; but in practice, a large number of Black students, a city center location, and the presence of charter schools are actually what statistically predict an urban school's closure.[18] Moreover, the efficiency argument used as the reason for most school closures feels especially hollow to long-term residents when the city sells the closed school building to private developers to build high-end condos (as has happened in Washington, DC) or even subsequently builds a new public school in a different area of the same district with wealthier residents (as in California).[19]

During the neoliberal school reform era (the twenty-first century onward), rising school closures for low performance have largely been an urban school phenomenon.[20] But suburban school closures also happen, and when they do, it is in schools where most of the students are Black and Latinx.[21] This is related to the new patterns of suburban racial segregation that have also been followed by early gentrification.[22] As segregation and education scholars Erica Frankenberg and Genevieve Siegel-Hawley report, the suburbs surrounding our largest major cities now serve nearly a third of all US students, and the majority of those students are Black and Latinx. As they put it, "We are a metropolitan society dominated by vast suburban rings."[23] As their 2024 report illustrates, there are vast inequalities between districts among the various suburban rings that largely mirror long-standing urban segregation patterns. These are places where, for many affluent White families, commuting to the city part-time is more appealing, a trend intensified by the post-pandemic shift toward remote work. In this way, the inner-ring suburban small towns to which many working-class people of color have relocated as they have been priced out of the city centers are now places that affluent White residents want for themselves.[24]

As of this writing, gentrification is not currently an issue for Sandview. Decline and demographic shifts in student enrollment are the key indicators.[25] Sandview High's current student enrollment is both stable (not declining) and unchanged in their students' demographics by race and class. If Sandview becomes one of these new gentrifying inner-ring suburban communities, then it is likely that the threat of closure will become definite, and the school will be closed.

Schooling under threat of closure appears to be growing in rural communities too, though under slightly different neoliberal experiments. In a rural context, the population is low enough that any drop in student enrollment has a severe impact on public schools' funding.[26] There, the growth of homeschooling has resulted in growing financial anxiety and a sense of schooling under threat of closure.[27] The rise of homeschooling can be seen partly as an outgrowth of neoliberal "choice" policies, with these policies facilitating this growth.[28] Because of their small populations and therefore lower funding, budget constraints have always been the main reasoning for rural school closures.[29] Importantly, rural communities of color are growing, and as such, we should be additionally concerned about how schooling under threat of closure will likely harm this population of students in particular.[30]

Many rural communities are now facing a new layer of school closure threats beyond homeschooling, as school voucher programs, mainly in Republican-led states, have diverted critical public school funding, even as these areas have no nearby private school options.[31] Few students actually leave public schools for a private school through voucher programs, but the latest versions of voucher programs dramatically drain public school budgets because they are available to affluent families, who are more likely to take advantage of them.[32] Even a number of Republicans have become concerned about the burden of voucher programs on rural schools' viability.[33] Those leading the party have continued the pressure on reluctant Republicans, especially, and effectively, through instigating moral panics, such as around book bans. These political moves drum up Republican political support for vouchers and thus defund and destabilize public schools.[34]

As long as neoliberal experiments are the only available governing route for improving public schools serving socially disadvantaged students, there will be more schooling under threat of closure. The neoliberal experimentation at play varies by context, but the effect is largely the same. And neoliberal experimentation nationwide persists whether or not one specific neoliberal choice experiment remains. Neoliberal experiments create schooling under threat of closure, which generates chaos, putting schools into deep crisis. This crisis is by design; it is supposed to "motivate" educators and school administrators to overcome their supposed laziness, thus improving school performance.

From the start of the neoliberal education reform era to the present, it is still considered good public policy to threaten public schools with losses, from straightforward funding cuts to losses in student enrollment that result in funding cuts, because the threat of funding loss from competition with various other private school options "may compel small improvements in at-risk public schools."[35] In reality, the persistent threat of school closure worsens the experience of schooling, reorienting the schooling process toward one with greater surveillance, stigma, and hyper-social controls that contribute to the subordination, racialization, and criminalization of youth.

Youth Citizenship and Neoliberal Socialization

I have also argued that a key effect of schooling under threat for students is undermining citizenship development for Black and Latinx youth. I elaborate on this idea to include efficacy in making societal claims, dignity, peer solidarity, and entitlement to challenging unjust schooling. Minoritized youth have and will in the future organize against poor social conditions, but most of the time, this does not happen.[36] A look into these students' school experiences helps to clarify how socialization in school contributes to this problem. In this book, I have focused on student experiences and views in relation to schooling practices shaped by neoliberal accountability. The children that I met during my research were all critical of their schooling, expressing a desire for a much better education. They wanted their school to facilitate their growth, provide understanding of the world, and nurture their leadership skills. At the same time, they felt voiceless and tended to blame their peers for the problems that undermined their educational opportunities, destroying potential solidarity between these students.

When struggling schools undergo neoliberal reforms, the experiences of already class-disadvantaged minoritized students within the educational system can have detrimental effects on their beliefs about their ability to demand improvements in school services, as well as other rights from the state. It is important to recognize that this sense of efficacy in making societal claims is crucial for both individual and collective efforts to challenge social injustices.[37]

Students' experiences with schooling under threat of closure harmfully shaped their political development, as they undermine students' belief in their capacity to make formal claims against the power structures they encounter. While youth socialization in K-12 schooling, as it relates to dealing with authority, is often associated with its effects on youth involvement in higher education, work, and prison, it also extends to students' ability to demand better from the state. Furthermore, the low sense of efficacy resulting from the lack of entitlement that I have documented can hinder personal growth and curtail young individuals' ability to view themselves as active participants in collective efforts for social change.

My analysis also describes, in a school context, how pressure on marginalized youth populations to be individually successful—i.e., "grit"—made it harder for them to see structural inequalities. As sociologist Michèle Lamont argues, neoliberalism ruins our sense of selves and our ability to imagine freedom from stigma and economic precarity.[38] Lamont argues that the diffusion of various neoliberal policies over time has generated "scripts" for social relations among groups, as well as with the self. This script offers normative tales of individual "grit" and competition, paired with greater stigmatization of those on the disadvantaged side of social inequalities. Schools are not alone in this dominant cultural frame of grit and competition, but understanding its transmission in a specific school context with attention to school practices reveals how this message is reinforced and what these ideas look like from children's point of view.

Youth at Sandview High learned to "rise above" their peers with "poor culture," who did not apply themselves enough. Class-disadvantaged Black and Latinx students at Sandview High wanted to be successful through hard work and felt alienated from their peers in the process, as well as ashamed of themselves when they did not see progress. They learned to work on their individual effort, which largely meant to face odious test drills that everyone hated but had to continue.

Students not only tended to internalize an ideology of grit; they also aimed to isolate themselves from peers who they learned may drag them down. They got the message that the majority of students who failed to complete school were responsible for their own shortcomings, were lazy, materialistic, and drawn to the streets. They learned they could not see themselves in line with their peers, or even individually enjoy popular youth culture among working-class Black and Latinx youth, without being deemed ripe for failure.

My analysis shows how neoliberalized education often prescribed to poor Black and Latinx youth challenged solidarity and their sense of self. This has a powerfully negative effect on these youth, who faced stigma of being "bad" (likely to fail) as part of their racialized class group membership, but to manage this stigma, they used dominant neoliberal scripts of grit, competition, and isolation from peers.

Challenges and Opportunities to Organizing for Just Schools

As education scholars such as Noliwe Rooks have pointed out, there is no apparent political willpower among top officials to shift priorities toward providing equitable education resources to all public schools, especially through school desegregation, which is the one thing that has historically been hugely effective in improving the public education resources for minoritized students.[39] Instead, these student groups face ongoing neoliberal experiments that follow accountability models, inducing punitive schooling experiences. The exact reform plans shift, but the general pattern persists. Like most low-performing schools, Sandview High remains under ongoing state interventions driven by this accountability logic.

The evident lack of political willpower becomes apparent when we consider the more than twenty years of "accountability" policies that began with NCLB (No Child Left Behind). This lack of willpower seems to stem from policymakers' reluctance to undertake the challenging task of fulfilling the civil rights promise of *Brown v. Board of Education* to end segregated, and thus unequal, schooling. Consequently, there are two simultaneous challenges to organize against: the older system of de facto segregation and the new one maintaining coercive school accountability policies for schools serving marginalized student groups.

The ongoing bipartisan commitment to neoliberal "accountability" restricts the consideration of other possibilities to improve public K-12 education, especially for marginalized and disadvantaged student groups. Existing policies prioritize standardized testing, securitization, and hyper-controlling student behavior. By abandoning these efforts, we can create more time and space to prioritize critical thinking, leadership, and relevant subjects that directly impact students' lives. However, there is currently no political determination at the federal level to change course and provide equal opportunities to all schools by adequately allocating resources. The federal ESSA (Every Student Succeeds Act) only makes minor adjustments to NCLB without fundamentally addressing the underlying conditions for struggling schools.

There is a wealth of high-quality research demonstrating the key factors for achieving positive educational outcomes. These factors include allocating more funding to hire highly trained educators, ensuring small class sizes, and granting teachers the flexibility and autonomy to be recognized as professionals.[40] These are qualities that the best public schools already possess.[41] Unfortunately, in places like Sandview High, the struggle is significantly more challenging.[42] Low-income suburban schools do not have the financial resources or the infrastructural support of either large central cities or affluent suburbs.[43] The community faces financial isolation and tends to perform low-wage labor for neighboring affluent communities in both central cities and neighboring suburbs. I refer to this phenomenon as "double free riding" because *both* adjacent communities (affluent central cities and suburbs) benefit from inexpensive labor from people in places like Sandview without having to support public services. Schools in these low-income suburban communities are particularly vulnerable to neoliberal reforms and struggle to address the needs of their students. Under present conditions, in which poverty continues to rise in suburban communities, this problem can be expected to grow.

The current "accountability" system under neoliberal governance necessitates more inclusive social movements to bring about genuine change. Without this element, history shows that political elites are incentivized to maintain lobbyist perspectives. Research by political scientists Benjamin Page and Martin Gilens reveals that public policies favored by the majority of regular Americans are not often implemented in legislation.[44] Instead, elected officials tend to support issues favored by the upper-class income brackets, irrespective of public opinion. This demonstrates why it has been necessary for regular people to achieve concessions from elites through their own collectivized efforts, employing confrontational politics beyond the expected channels of polite discourse.[45] Understanding how these collectivities are built is therefore crucial.

The practice of contentious politics, which necessitates solidarity, also stands in direct opposition to neoliberal principles of competition, zero-sum politics, lack of a safety net, and total self-regulation. As social movement scholars have observed, the risks associated with contentious politics are a key barrier to participation but, when trusting relationships exist, people are more willing to participate.[46] Solidarity also entails the need for coalitions. A recent instance of a successful statewide grassroots education reform in a particularly unreceptive political context can be seen in West Virginia, where teachers collaborated with students' families and classified workers to secure increased state resources for education.[47] This solidarity across different group interests served as the key ingredient for a successful strike.

Considering the effect of oppressive education reform on the most directly affected children, it is important for school professionals, particularly teachers, to envision collaborating with their students to make demands on the state. Teachers' unions and associations can serve as potential starting points for organizing such efforts. In 2014, Portland, Oregon, students organized with their teachers citywide, threatening to walk out of schools together. They won crucial new school supports, including smaller class sizes.[48] Portland modeled its efforts on earlier work in Chicago, which in turn linked their efforts with earlier-formed coalitions in Philadelphia.[49] As the late social and education policy professor Jean Anyon reminds us, youth leadership has always been central to building social movements.[50]

Research has demonstrated that this collaborative work involves treating youth as genuine leaders and actively involving them in decision-making processes.[51] While children possess valuable ideas, they require nurturing to believe in themselves, trust their ideas, and feel empowered to engage in creative political endeavors. Investing time in their political education will establish a strong foundation for young people to facilitate adults' willingness to step outside the box. This political education can create opportunities for young individuals to later play a more significant role in larger-scale fights for genuine bottom-up education reform.

Various examples already exist of young peoples' political involvement in different places and spaces. As sociologist Hava Gordon discovered, the primary challenge existing youth organizers face from marginalized communities is their peers' sense of disempowerment and helplessness.[52] Political education aimed at dispelling stereotypes proved effective in empowering and fostering collaboration among youth. Celina Su's analysis also highlights the improvement achieved in schools when parents and students collaborated with established grassroots organizations.[53] This kind of accountability stems from the bottom up rather than the top down. Establishing trust in coalitions is crucial to embolden youth to engage in confrontational politics.

Positive youth political socialization is vital to foster their ability to challenge an unjust economy. Mere compliance with school testing and discipline regimes is insufficient in the struggle for good jobs and freedom from state violence. Therefore, it is crucial to recognize how schooling under threat particularly undermines the power of Black and Latinx students to navigate an economy that inherently disadvantages them. Even if youth manage to meet schools' demands, this type of schooling erodes their ability to demand economic and administrative justice from the government or employers.

Neoliberal accountability policies set the conditions for schooling under threat of closure, undermining students' entitlement to government resources, their efforts for respect and rights, and creating divisions among students that hinder peer solidarity. Consequently, many marginalized youth internalize the belief that they lack substantive citizenship and are consequently disengaged from political participation. There is an urgent crisis in American schools, and the structure of schools like Sandview High and the lessons students learn about their role as political subjects will profoundly impact their development as political actors within their communities.

ACKNOWLEDGMENTS

This book has been more than a decade in the making. I have so much gratitude for all of the people who helped turn it into a reality. I am overwhelmed with emotion when I think of the vast number of individuals who supported me intellectually and emotionally over the years. I began this project when I was a graduate student at the CUNY Graduate Center, and I finished it while on the tenure track at the University of North Carolina, Wilmington.

First, I want to express my deepest gratitude to everyone at "Sandview High School" and the broader "Sandview" community for answering my questions and sharing their knowledge, experience, time, and space. My greatest thanks go to the students of Sandview High, as this project would not exist without these sharp and insightful young people. My analysis of the school is critical of social structures, practices, and ideologies that inform individual actions, and is not intended to criticize individuals themselves.

I received important mentorship from a number of people at the CUNY Graduate Center, especially Carolina Bank-Muñoz, Ruth Milkman, David Brotherton, and Phil Kasinitz. All of them provided me with excellent advice, critiques, and suggestions that helped me strengthen my ideas and map out what I wanted for the book. I also send a big thanks to Ruthie Gilmore—her encouragement and openness to my early ideas were essential. I am also thankful for the essential support I received from my community at the Inter-University Program for Latino Research Mellon Fellows Program: Jennifer Boles, Albert Laguna, Veronica Terriquez, Ramona Hernández, and Nena Torres; and especially the other Fellows: Kendy Rivera, Esther Díaz Martín, Nadiah Rivera Fellah, Roberto Rincon, Pablo García Gámez, and Omar Ramadan-Santiago. I am particularly grateful for the friendships built during those CUNY years, with Bronwyn Dobchuk-Land, Anna Gjika, Brenda Gambol, Sara Martucci, Dominique Nisperos, Marnie Brady, Jane McAlevey, and Sarah Tosh.

I am thankful for the support for this project from my wonderful colleagues at the University of North Carolina, Wilmington. From my first year on the tenure track, I was welcomed into writing groups, invited to share chapter drafts, and received advice on the book writing process, all of which were so valuable in my path to crafting this book. A special thank you to Jennifer Vanderminden and Jill Waity for our writing group, it was such a supportive and important space for me, particularly in those early days starting out as a new assistant professor. I also want to give another special thank you to Mike Maume, Ethan Higgins, Mary-Collier Wilks, Candice Robinson, and Julia Morris, all of whom read and commented on multiple chapter drafts.

In addition to my wonderful colleagues, I was also lucky to have mentorship on the book process from many other sociologists throughout my writing process. In particular, I benefited from thoughtful conversations with Jennifer Jones, Helen Marrow, and Joanne Golann. I also benefited greatly from the coaching at the National Center for Faculty Development and Diversity. I am also thankful to Jesse Maker for his wonderful assistance with copyediting.

At NYU Press, I want to express heartfelt appreciation to Ilene Kalish, whose enthusiasm, support, and feedback on this project from the start have been tremendous. I really appreciate the time and energy she has dedicated to helping me develop this book. I also want to give a huge thank you to the entire production team at NYU Press for all of their hard work to make this book happen. Additionally, I am enormously appreciative to the anonymous reviewers for their thoughtful feedback; their thorough reviews really helped me to strengthen my arguments.

I also want to thank my early mentors at Portland State University who introduced me to sociology and really inspired me to think that I could become an academic, and even write a book. In particular, I thank Johanna Brenner. Her guidance, support, and belief in me as a scholar since those early days has been a huge sustaining factor in my intellectual growth. Johanna's style of feminist mentorship helped me find my voice, and I can only hope I learned enough to pay it forward.

I am so lucky to have a far-reaching community whose support throughout this project made the work possible—through conversation, encouragement, laughter, and not more than a few tears. This network includes my parents, sister, grandparents, aunts and uncles, and cousins, as well as my friends from the way back, Lisa, Julie, and Jessica, and also more recently Brenda, Candice, Hikmet, Shannon, Christina, Aaron, and Julia. I also wish to thank Chae for our exchanges over the last few years, it really helped me learn to thrive and improve my focus both professionally and personally. I send an extra special shout of thanks to my friends Anna and Sara, who have been a constant bedrock of support for me, for which I am deeply grateful. Finally, I thank my husband Jeff, who has been with me since the start of this project, and supports me every day in everything I do; thank you for being my guy.

APPENDIX

Research Methods

When I made contact with Sandview High School through their tutoring center in the spring of 2013, I introduced myself as a (then) graduate student writing about students' experiences and perspectives on recent changes in schooling. I offered to volunteer at the school to help me with "getting into place" but also to provide some services to the school while I was doing my research.[1] Especially in the beginning, volunteering helped me get established at the school, develop a role for myself there, learn about people and get acquainted, and spend time explaining myself to people. My primary role at the school was as a tutor who also spoke Spanish. I tutored students during and after class, and I also attended various school events, student club meetings, special programs outside of school, and walked the halls.

My position as a White woman likely made it easy for me to move through the social space without inquiry. I was consistently able to move through the school without much oversight or questioning. I was trusted to be doing something appropriately, and no one ever interrogated me about my work there. It also related to how I likely blended in. Because of the school's duress, there was not only continual staff turnover, but also regular visitors from various organizations, and a great many of these people were also White women. The staff in particular likely viewed me as just another one of the various young White women coming in and out of the school in different professional and volunteer roles.

My Whiteness also unquestionably contributed to students' perceptions of me as a cultural outsider. The rapport I developed with many students was likely influenced by my helping with coursework and significant time in the field. My Spanish language skills were also helpful to connecting with Latinx students. My impression was that, overall, students thought of me as somewhere between a counselor, tutor, and older college student writing a book about them who liked to hang out and was interested in what they had to say.

ACCESS ISSUES

"Do you have any tattoos?" a student named Rocio asked. I was driving her home the evening after her formal interview in a tutoring room at the school. I confessed I did not and asked her the same question. She promptly described that when she was 18 she was going to get a long-stemmed red rose with thorns wrapped around her leg. Rocio had surprised me by even wanting to do the interview; she hadn't returned my phone call after filling out one of my student interest forms for the formal interviews. Yet there she was one day, walking toward me with her signed parent permission slip and child assent form.[2] When I indicated my surprise at her participation, Rocio stated that she no longer had access to the phone number she gave me, and that she had been having trouble getting time off from her restaurant job.

A lot of students were like Rocio, difficult to schedule for formal interviews, even when they stated an interest in doing so. This was at least partly because of their busy schedules. Many students had to work after school. Students' unreliable access to phones presented another obstacle—they had prepaid phones and ran out of money to refill them, or they had to buy a new one and their phone numbers changed. Students also lost the parent permission slips that I required. Some students simply forgot and did not show up. In fact, I got very comfortable with the fact that a not-insignificant amount of my time was consumed getting stood up by teenagers I was scheduled to interview.

"SHE'S HERE TO TALK TO ME"

I intentionally waited to recruit students for formal interviews until I had spent substantial time volunteering at the school. I wanted to build trust with students, as well as spend time learning about them and the school context before starting interviews so that I had a better sense of what questions I wanted to ask. When talking to students about why I wanted to speak with them, I told them I was writing a book about them because they were experts on being high school students. Students liked this explanation and were generally pleased someone wanted to hear their perspectives, often responding with a sense of pride that I was asking for their opinion.

I mainly recruited youth for interviews through tutoring, as these were students I knew would vouch for me to other students. This strategy allowed me to meet a range of students, both those who were involved in school programs and those who were not. I also went to additional after school programs to recruit students for interviews. I aimed for programs run by teachers who were popular with students.

I always offered to meet students wherever was convenient for them. As a result, I conducted interviews in a range of places, including fast food restaurants, on the grass in front of the school, and in their homes. Visiting students' neighborhoods, and in some cases their homes, illustrated the deep economic insecurity most of them were navigating. A student named Alfredo asked me to come to his home because neither he nor his family had phones and it would be hard to coordinate the interview otherwise. He also had trouble remembering his address because he had just moved and could not remember the street number. His family moved often; they were frequently evicted for not being able to pay the rent. His stepdad laid blacktop pavement, which Alfredo knew was "very hard and sometimes dangerous." Alfredo sometimes went to work with his stepdad and helped him by earning extra money. Alfredo liked seeing how much he could earn. When I arrived at his home, Alfredo's mother shyly answered the door. We spoke briefly in Spanish, then Alfredo burst into view, publicizing that I was there to speak to him. Before sitting down to do the interview, he showed me his exercise weights, arm muscles, and explained how he was refining his graffiti skills.

Another student, Hector, also requested that I come to his home for the interview. Hector was supposed to keep an eye on the place for his mom so no one stole anything, which he was doing until his mom could move the rest of their stuff into their new place with his little brother. When I arrived, Hector invited me into the living/dining room to sit with him on an old bare mattress, the only visible piece of furniture. As we sat and talked, Hector told me about the time he was briefly in jail, stressing it was "no place for kids," and disclosed that an older man had tried to assault him while he was incarcerated.

"YOU MADE ME FEEL SAFE"

My interviews were intentionally open-ended conversations led by guiding questions on the broad topics of schooling experiences, views related to the school's testing and discipline policies, and family and work life. I opened conversations with students by pointing out the many changes happening in the school and that I wanted to hear expert views from students about what was important to them. When inviting students to do the interview, I emphasized it was completely voluntary and confidential. The students sometimes asked why I selected this school, fully aware of the state scrutiny the school was under.

I asked students what they liked or disliked about school, how they managed school security measures, and how they felt about testing practices at their school. We talked about their migration stories, and I asked them if people respected each other at school and what respect meant to them. When feasible, I probed into how students negotiated schooling in relation to immigration status.

I was concerned that students would not want to speak with me, would not be candid with me, or would feel badly about what they shared given the sensitivity of the issues. These fears proved unwarranted. Overall, I had more students want to speak with me than I had time for and my interviews often went over time. Most students were pleased that someone had asked them to tell their stories.

Many of the students I met with wanted to talk about their aspirations or share traumatic stories from their lives.[3] Such encounters gave me the sense that some students viewed me as somewhat of a counselor. When I asked students who had shared a traumatic personal story whether they had any questions for me, their replies would often resemble this one, from a student named Jamar: "I got your number and your name. I think that's all. I might be hitting you up soon because you're very interesting." To which I replied, "What's interesting about me?" Jamar responded, "The questions you asked, you made me feel safe." Though not the purpose of the study, my sense was that Jamar had felt he had gained somewhat of a therapeutic benefit from our interview. For instance, when I asked him about his background (he had mentioned moving to the area a couple years ago), Jamar shared that he had escaped family violence and moved here to live with his older sister. This type of response from youth is not uncommon in interview and ethnographic research, such as that conducted by sociologist Julie Bettie.[4]

I came to know some of the students very well, and others I only met with once. The students I interviewed generally reported earning Cs and Bs but also struggled to pass some of their courses. Some students I interviewed reported either doing very well or very poorly in school, and several other students I interviewed no longer attended their classes but came to school to visit with their friends. A number of these latter students ultimately dropped out of school. I also spoke with students who had already been pushed out of school; I met these students through nonprofit organizations that were trying to help them earn their GED.

ON BEING "MISS"

As with many ethnographers of young people, I tried to establish myself with the students as a "least adult" figure.[5] This included assuring students I would not "tell on them" when I saw them skipping classes. I befriended many students and often just "hung out."[6] But trying to perform a non-authority role was challenging in ways that felt related to both gender and race.[7] For example, I initially tried to have students call me by my first name instead of "Miss," which was typically how students addressed female school professionals. I had hoped that being on a first-name basis would help students to not see me as an authority figure, especially as one that was formally associated with the school. This proved unrealistic. As one student, Martín, told me, "Miss, you're not my homegirl. When we go to the club together, then you're 'Erin,' until then you're 'Miss.'" I did not go clubbing with Martín. I also stopped trying to get students to call me Erin. Trying to be a "least adult" was not realistic. Attempting to act more like a peer also made some of the boys feel comfortable enough to make innocuous attempts at flirting, which also discouraged me from taking that approach.

Overall, being "Miss" to students proved adequate in giving me enough distance from the teachers at Sandview High. As mentioned earlier, students often seemed to want me to enact some version of a caring femme adult role, interacting with me like I was a therapist or wanting to confer with me about their future adult lives. I also received hugs, excited waves, and all kinds of stories—good and bad—from some students that had nothing to do with my research. I felt like I drifted somewhere between student and school professional. I had no formal authority (as I reminded students), but being an adult, an academic, and a White woman in this space surely brought a level of informal authority. Though I was a "helper" at the school, I tried to emphasize my student identity, given that I was a graduate student at the time.

"DO NOT DISTURB"

Though it is often the normative desire for ethnographers to be treated as an apprentice of sorts, I found that I was not going to have the opportunity to learn directly from school administrators about their work.[8] School administrators were indifferent to me. They directed me to talk to other people or simply slipped their business card in my hand, stalling until later. I tried multiple times to contact a particularly promising administrator, with no luck. There were real reasons that administrators were unable to be helpful. They were always busy and felt constantly under threat, and (perhaps as a result) none of the school administrators I met stayed longer than a year or two.

I also think that my status as a woman contributed to their sense of me as being inconsequential. At the same time, my "insignificance" had very important advantages. For one, it made me seem unthreatening to administrators, who were already under so much threat. In addition, because things were tense between school administrators and students, it was likely very positive for my relationships with students that they did not see me standing around talking to one of the school administrators who they largely associated with being arbiters of student discipline.[9]

BEING A "HELPER" AT THE SCHOOL

My role at the school did lead me to sometimes participate in ways that challenged my image as being outside of the school system. Sometimes, school professionals would ask me to translate their instructions to students into Spanish when the students were being noncompliant. I was usually able to rebuff these requests by reminding them that I did not want to participate in anything that was discipline related. Over time and related to the specifics of the situation at hand, teachers sometimes pushed back against my reluctance. On two occasions I relented but attempted to characterize the message in a softly sarcastic way. Such subversions of teachers' authority did make me feel uncomfortable. But my priority was fostering and keeping good relations with students.

"OH, I CAN TALK"

Though this was a project focused on understanding students' perspectives, I also talked, both informally and formally, with school professionals and community members who worked with youth. I regularly talked with a number of school professionals both to develop my analysis and to ask questions. I asked school professionals about their impressions of the testing and security reforms and if/how the reforms had affected their jobs and the students. I was especially interested in their thoughts on how these changes impacted the school climate for students, themselves, and other school staff.

My experience of scheduling and conducting an interview with a teacher named Mr. Robertson was typical of my experiences with school professionals. I had stopped by his classroom after school, told him about my research and my interest in talking to him. He was happy to talk with me but had after-school duties with students that day, evidenced by the large group of students still in his classroom waiting for him as we briefly spoke. I followed up by emailing him but got no reply. The next time I saw him face-to-face was a few weeks later, and he agreed to meet. We sat down in his classroom after school later that week. Though he initially seemed hesitant, he ended up continuing to talk even after I turned off the tape, so much so that I eventually turned the tape back on. He finally ended our conversation after an hour and a half (much longer than the 30 minutes we had agreed upon) when he had to pick up one of his children. "Oh, I can talk," he stated, amused with himself. In these last moments, he also shared that it was "great" that I was there and had the "perspective" that I did of the students and this place, explaining that "people who are not from here" have bad impressions about the students, that they are "crazy" and "bad." Although I probed, I never got a more straightforward answer about who he thought I was and what perspective he had assumed I had. Yet, it was clear to me that he was talking about my White race as much as about the fact that I was not from the geographic area. I had surprised him and that was a good thing.

Other school professionals I interviewed were like Mr. Robertson, hard to schedule but happy and interested once we talked. Being at the school for a long period of time allowed me to build trust with the school professionals that I worked with directly, and as with the students, I waited to do most of my formal interviews until I became a regular presence at the school. For those professionals who I did not get the chance to know well, it was casual encounters at school that led to them agreeing to share their sparse time with me.

I also met with various community members working with youth, most of whom also had adult children who had previously attended the school. Some of these community members worked in the nonprofit sector serving current or former Sandview High students. I met them by attending local community events, or through professional contacts and referrals. My questions for them varied depending on the phase of the study, but largely aimed to get a sense of their experiences working with the youth, as well as their perceptions of the school and the larger community, both present and past.

Table A.1 lists the interview subjects, with some basic details for each participant. It describes interview participants only and does not include the many other individuals who also contributed to this study through their informal conversations with me. In the list of school professionals (as well as any time professionals are mentioned throughout the book), I am intentionally vague about their roles at the school to help maintain their confidentiality.

TABLE A.1: List of Interview Subjects

Adults	
School Professional	Mr. Kemple
School Professional	Mr. Robertson
School Professional	Ms. Guzmán
School Professional	Ms. Turner
School Professional	Ms. Lamont
School Professional	Jane
School Professional	Barbara
School Professional	Zoe
Community	Ruby
Community	Ellen
Community	Michael
Community	Richard

Community	Pam
Community	Roger
Community	Dara
Community	Marta
Community	Mateo
Community	Mary

Total number of adult interviews=18

Students	Age	Place of Origen	Yrs. US	Parents
Hector	15	Texas		Mexico
Alfredo	15	Sandview		Mexico
Lupe	16	Sandview		Mexico
Fatima	16	Mexico	6	Mexico
Pablo	18	Costa Rica	10	
Isabella	14	The Bronx		Puerto Rico
Edgar	14	Honduras	1	
Eduardo	14	Guatemala	1	
Robert	17	Cameroon	10	
Keisha	17	Jamaica	5	
Esteban	15	Mexico	10	
Alma	16	Dominican Rep.	2	
Jamal	17	Sandview		Jamaica
Rocio	17	Puerto Rico	7	
Martín	17	Mexico	12	
Sofía	16	Mexico	7	
Marisol	17	Mexico	13	
Paola	17	Sandview		Mexico
Jesus	18	Guatemala	4	
Carlos	17	Honduras	1	
Felipe	18	Honduras	2	
Raul	17	Mexico	12	
Claudia	15	Mexico	10	
Rubén	17	Honduras	5	

Demaj	16	Brooklyn		Jamaica
Kiara	15	Tortola, VI	6	
Fatima	15	Mexico	11	
Ranyinudo	16	Nigeria	15	
Rita	14	Dominican Rep.	8	
Felicity	16	Sandview		Kenya
Destiny	17	Sandview		
Tashauna	16	Sandview		
Janel	15	Florida		Puerto Rico
Chloe	16	Sandview		
Melissa	16	Sandview		
Deron	18	The Bronx		
Terell	19	The Bronx		
Righteous	14	Brooklyn		
Keon	16	The Bronx		
Aisha	16	Sandview		
Tara	16	Sandview		
Eric	16	Sandview		
Jumaane	18	Sandview		
Jamar	18	Brooklyn		
Alan	16	Brooklyn		
José	16	The Bronx		Puerto Rico
Lucas	17	The Bronx		Dominican Rep.

Total number of student interviews=47
26 Latinx students; 21 Black students.

NOTES

PREFACE

1 Fighting for the city is related to the concept of "right to the city," contemporarily popularized by Harvey (2012) and also Smith (2005). Pauline Lipman (2011) has an excellent analysis of how state-sponsored gentrification motivates neoliberal education policy focusing on the case of Chicago. For a recent analysis of state-sponsored gentrification in a prominent New York City neighborhood, see Martucci (2024).
2 Fabricant and Fine 2013; see also Lipman 2011.
3 Han et al. 2017.
4 Ewing 2018.

INTRODUCTION

1 All names of people and places are pseudonyms.
2 See Ewing and Green 2022.
3 See Han et al. 2017.
4 For examples, see Carter 2005; Lewis 2003; Morris 2016; Ochoa 2013.
5 For examples, see Calarco 2018; Ferguson 2020; Thorne 1993; Willis 1981.
6 For examples, see Lopez 2003; Shedd 2015.
7 I first elaborated on the punitive nature of neoliberal accountability for struggling schools with a focus on the element of "conditionality" in a separate article for the journal *Critical Sociology* (Michaels 2021). In that article, I focused on the similarity of these types of school reforms to the state development programs of international governance organizations, namely the International Monetary Fund and the World Bank. I highlighted the parallels between these two very different arenas of neoliberal interventions to illustrate how neoliberal programming does not in practice inculcate an enfeebled state, instead it builds up a very different kind of governance that is not only less democratic but also more surveillant, and thus, punitive. Conditionality is a well-known key feature of neoliberal state development programs that were called "Structural Adjustment Programs." Like the reforms for struggling schools, these programs attached essential financial support with massive restrictions attached (Michaels 2021:1172). Thus, there I am also highlighting the role of growing elite state power in the context of critical conversations that overlook this as a key element of neoliberal governance. In short, there is too much focus on profit motivations alone.

8   Kozol 2012.
9   See Lewis-McCoy et al. 2023.
10 For examples, see Apple 2013; Au 2016; Fabricant and Fine 2013; Hursh 2007; Lipman 2011.
11 For examples, see Bettie 2014; MacLeod 2009; Pascoe 2011; Willis 1981.
12 For examples, see Carter 2005; Lewis and Diamond 2015; MacLeod 2009; Ochoa 2013.
13 Small portions from chapter 2 have appeared in an earlier version in Michaels 2020 and Michaels 2021.
14 Small portions from chapter 3 have appeared in an earlier version in Michaels 2020.

CHAPTER 1. THE CREATION OF A "BAD" SCHOOL

1 Struggling schools that mainly serve Black and Latinx students are increasingly located in high-poverty suburbs (Anyon 2014; Frankenberg and Orfield 2012).
2 In struggling traditional public schools, 85 percent of the student population is low-income and 83 percent is Latinx and Black (Han et al. 2017:40).
3 Diamond, Posey-Maddox, and Velázquez 2021.
4 For example, Lewis and Diamond 2015; Lewis-McCoy 2014.
5 See Frankenberg et al. 2019; Frankenberg and Orfield 2012.
6 In contrast to Sandview High, four out of five students graduate from high school in New York State overall. See New York State Education Department (2023) for this and more data on the state's high school graduation averages.
7 New York State Education Department (2016:5). The five largest cities are the exception.
8 de Graauw, Gleeson, and Bloemraad 2013.
9 As I later describe, low-income suburbs like Sandview just outside of rich cities are categorized in the literature on the changing suburbs as "inner-ring" suburbs (Kneebone and Berube 2013).
10 See Hannah-Jones 2015.
11 "Savage inequalities" refers to Jonathon Kozol's use of the term, the title of his 2012 book of the same title.
12 Nationwide school districts serving mostly White students receive more money than those serving mostly students of color. A recent report from the nonprofit EdBuild (2019) calculated the total difference to be about $23 billion per year, a number that includes serving the same number of students. This funding gap is especially striking when considering that in struggling traditional public schools, 85 percent of the student population is low-income and 83 percent is Latinx and Black (Han et al. 2017:40).
13 Frankenberg and Orfield 2012.
14 These poverty measures are based on New York State Education Department data for percentages of students in a given school or district qualifying for free or reduced lunches. The approximately 80 percent poverty rate for Sandview High

students is also much higher than the 50 percent statewide average of students living below the federal poverty line.
15 This research in part can be seen as a contribution to the recent calls for examining the political economy of education issues within a metropolitan framework (Diamond et al. 2021).
16 Frankenberg and Orfield 2012; Frankenberg and Siegel-Hawley 2024.
17 Lichter, Thiede, and Brooks 2023.
18 Owens and Rich 2023.
19 Affluent White parents took their tax base and other resources into a newly formed public district. Today, Sandview's property values are among the lowest in the region, while those of its now annexed neighbor, Trails, boast increasingly high property values.
20 Frankenberg 2009.
21 Massey and Denton 1993.
22 Gilmore 2007.
23 To be clear, one big district would not solve all of Sandview High's resource deprivation problems. Inequalities within districts are still an issue (Frankenberg et al. 2023). However, it would be easier to sustain resources, including fighting for them within a district.
24 See Frankenberg et al. 2019; Frankenberg and Orfield 2012. Broadly speaking, high-poverty suburbs have a much smaller nonprofit social services sector (Allard and Pelletier 2023).
25 Frankenberg and Siegel-Hawley 2024.
26 Ravitch 2016.
27 Reardon, Kalogrides, and Shores 2019.
28 Carter and Welner 2013:3.
29 Lewis-McCoy et al. 2023.
30 Allard and Pelletier 2023.

CHAPTER 2. SCHOOLING UNDER THREAT OF CLOSURE
1 Han et al. 2017.
2 As Ewing and Green (2022) note in their review of the last two decades of analysis on school closures, there were mass school closings in the mid-2010s.
3 For example, Ewing 2018; Pearman and Greene 2022.
4 Apple 2013; Ball 2016.
5 Hursh 2020.
6 Hursh 2007.
7 Ravitch 2016.
8 For examples, see Aldeman 2017; Karp 2016; Meyers, Brandt, and VanGronigen 2023. The US Department of Education promoted the Every Student Succeeds Act (ESSA) as giving states more control over restructuring their failing schools, stressing that "states will no longer be told exactly how to evaluate schools or how to hold failing schools accountable." See US Department of Education (2017).

9 Noguera 2016.
10 Meyers et al. 2023; Sunderman, Coghlan, and Mintrop 2017.
11 Black and Rea 2021:5.
12 Welsh 2019:311.
13 See Lipman (2011), especially chapter 3, for more on how federal leadership has framed shutting down "failing schools" as a model for neoliberal education reform in major cities like Detroit, Chicago, and New Orleans.
14 "Low academic performance" is often either the only factor or a central official reason schools are slated to close (Tieken and Auldridge-Reveles 2019).
15 Scott 2011.
16 Deeds and Pattillo 2015: 475.
17 Fabricant and Fine 2013.
18 Lipman 2011.
19 Buras 2014; Ewing 2018; Gordon 2021.
20 Wacquant 2009.
21 For examples, see Aggarwal, Mayorga, and Nevel 2012; Lipman 2017.
22 For examples, see Fabricant and Fine 2013; Hursh 2020; Lipman 2011.
23 Harvey 2007:79.
24 Fine and Saad-Filho 2017:690.
25 Apple 2007:111–12.
26 Welsh 2019.
27 For examples, see Lopez 2003; Nolan 2011.
28 Gilmore 2007.
29 Foucault 2012. The limited state role under neoliberalism is contested by scholars, but the explicitness in terms of what it says it is doing is based in limited governance.
30 Shedd 2015.
31 To be clear, some critical scholars have identified that there are social control aspects to restructuring "low-performing" schools (Apple 2013; Love 2023; Monahan and Torres 2009). My study builds on these types of analyses, arguing that these neoliberal school reforms are part of a growing transformation of the state into one more focused on punitive governance.
32 See Dumas (2014). Moreover, many critics frame the accountability focus as "carrot and stick"; see Gordon (2021) for an excellent summary. I aim to pull on this thread harder, arguing that it is mostly the stick.
33 This is an argument I also developed in Michaels (2021).
34 New York State Senate 2015.
35 To be clear, state receivership programs do close schools: Philadelphia and Chicago have closed schools en masse; and in the spring of 2017 alone, New York City closed five schools it deemed too low-performing (Zimmerman 2017). All of these school closures occurred through receiverships in large cities where the mayor, the governor, or a combination of the two appoints the local school governance boards (rather than being elected). These bodies decide to close schools they deem under-performing, often replacing them with charter schools. Yet, beyond

the very real harm of shuttering a public school (or a string of them), there is the threat of being closed, which also harmfully shapes the school's environment, and that threat is ongoing.
36 Black and Rea 2021.
37 Sunderman et al. 2017.
38 Klein 2018.
39 Noguera 2016.
40 Au 2016; Owens and Sunderman 2006; Ravitch 2016.
41 See also Michaels 2021.
42 These rankings are based largely on students' state test scores and graduation rates for high schools. New York State uses an index formula to identify schools, requiring increases in index points.
43 See New York State Education Department (2012).
44 Quote taken from a media interview on August 10, 2015, accessed by the author on March 6, 2018.
45 See New York State Senate (2015).
46 See New York State Education Department (2015d). See also New York State Education Department (2015a).
47 See also Michaels 2021.
48 See New York State Teacher's Union (2015).
49 For more details on this policy shift, see the New York State Education Department (2015b).
50 For more details on this policy, see the New York State Education Department (2015c). One can also reference important parts of this policy in New York State Education Department (2015b). This document, entitled "Making Demonstrable Improvement," describes how the state used a weighted "Demonstrable Improvement Index," for which schools need to achieve an index of 67 percent or higher to improve. Sandview High agreed to use two measures of the students' graduation rates, test scores and the number of "serious" incidents on their records. During the 2015–16 school year, requirements included a 1 percent increase in its regular and honors four-year graduation rate for all students, a 10 percent reduction in "serious incidents" of student misbehavior, and making "yearly progress" to move out of the "priority" (bottom five percent) ranking in the state.
51 Downey, von Hippel, and Hughes 2008.
52 See also Michaels 2021.
53 In this document, the Sandview High administrative team also demanded that the state provide "flexibility with grant allocation to support the diverse needs of each school," that the state "work directly with schools." All of this documentation was downloaded from the school's website in 2016 by the author. It has since been removed from the school's website.
54 Ravitch 2016.
55 Today, Sandview High is still in the bottom 5 percent, undergoing more state-led interventions in the lowest performance category under the Every Student

Succeeds Act (ESSA). As was the case during this research, just about half of the students graduated and the school remains in the lowest accountability status according to the New York State Education Department's most recent (2023) data.
56 See also Michaels 2021.
57 Author's review of Sandview High's 2014–2015 "District Comprehensive Improvement Plan."
58 According to Sandview High's "Violent and Disruptive Incident Reporting" records, there had been no student "altercations with a weapon," and the "school violence index" was moderate.
59 See also Michaels 2021.
60 US Department of Education 2004.
61 See New York State Education Department (2004).
62 See Ferrara (2004). The SAVE Act created a new "intermediary" level of punishment for nonviolent low-level offenses (e.g., any student the school finds "disruptive"). The state defined disruptive students as "substantially disruptive to the educational process or substantially interfere with the teachers' authority over the classroom" (Ferrara 2004:58). The SAVE Act granted schools the option to remove students without it contributing to the suspension data, an area "failing" schools needed to improve.
63 New York State still uses this "Diagnostic Tool for School and District Effectiveness" (New York State Education Department 2024b). Until recently, "low-performing" schools were called *focus* and *priority*; the names have since changed to "Comprehensive Support and Improvement" or "Targeted Support and Improvement" schools, but it is essentially the same thing, these are the "low-performing" schools the state is required to identify and restructure or close. See Meyers et al. (2023) for a full review of all state's ESSA plans for "low-performing" schools, currently labeled Comprehensive Support and Improvement (CSI) Status.
64 Specifically, "safety and discipline" are part of the improvement program because it is a "whole school reform model," which refers to comprehensive school restructuring, rather than only certain aspects. See New York State Education Department (2013).
65 Golann 2021; Oeur 2018.
66 See Ravitch (2016) for an overview of the problem of high-stakes testing.
67 Sandview High hired a corporation called K12Insight to administer the survey that New York State mandates for "low-performing" schools. K12Insight sells survey research to struggling schools nationally. I obtained the survey results from the district website in 2015. As of this writing, only the current-year survey results remain on the district website.
68 The average number of teachers in their first or second year of teaching at Sandview High was about 20 percent from 2011 to 2017. In New York State that number is at about 11 percent.
69 These are still used in New York State as of this writing (New York State Education Department 2024a).

70 See New York State Education Department (2015d). See also New York State Education Department (2018a).

The MAP test is a major example of these extra tests; it has been used in more than 5,000 school districts (Shaw 2013). The MAP test was a state "approved" product Sandview High purchased and implemented as part of a special federal grant because of its "low performance." One state-approved program Sandview High underwent was related to its receiving a "School Improvement Grant" (SIG). At the time of my fieldwork this was through Obama's "Race to the Top" program. These grants are specifically for raising "academic achievement" in public schools serving a high number of students living below the official poverty line. An explicitly market-oriented policy, it allowed states and local districts to compete for money if they implemented federal policies such as using student test scores to evaluate teachers; and states that did not comply were ineligible for these funds (McLaren 2015:5).

71 The teacher ratings created from students' MAP test scores have resulted in teachers' dismissals in several states, including New York. See New York State Education Department (2018a).

72 Shifrer 2022.

73 The Sandview High teachers described above had been punished for their students' "too low" scores on the MAP test. They had been put on "probation" because this test, like several others, was tied to teachers' performance evaluation, which could result in them being fired. All of the teachers I met shared comparable concerns about the MAP test. As earlier described, *even more* of the teachers' evaluations were based on "state-approved" student test scores than before because of added conditional federal funding at the time. In the case of Sandview High, that meant the MAP test. As stated earlier, this increased weight on student test scores was enacted through an agreed modification of the teachers' union contract.

74 See also Michaels 2020.

75 I did not "tell" on Carlos, and told him just that. As mentioned in the methods appendix, I tried diligently to avoid any action that I thought would lead students to view me as an authority figure from the school; I also took any opportunity to mention to students that I would not "tell on them" if I saw them doing anything that could get them into trouble at school.

76 The state's observations took place at the start of the fall 2014 school year. This was during the middle of my fieldwork.

77 Darling-Hammond 2007; Fabricant and Fine 2013; Michaels 2020; Michaels 2021.

78 Meyers et al. 2023:7.

CHAPTER 3. "WHAT ARE WE, TEST MONKEYS?"

1 Glenn 2004.

2 For example, Alonso et al. 2009; Bettie 2014; Calarco 2018; MacLeod 2009; Pascoe 2011; Pascoe 2023; Valenzuela 1999; Willis 1981. This approach overlaps with studies examining Latinx youth "belonging" but in a way that also includes African

American students, as well as one that takes a more specified approach; I am exploring a particular school context and school improvement policy measures as implemented. See Fernández (2021) and Flores-Gonzalez (2017) for examples of studies focusing on barriers to full citizenship and belonging for Latinx youth. See Terriquez (2017), as well as Terriquez and Kwon (2015), for examples of how Latinx youth from immigrant families are experiencing political development positively with the supportive role of certain community organizations.

3 Oakes 2005.
4 Anyon 1980; Bowles and Gintis 2002; Golann 2021.
5 For examples of other types of schoolwide structures fostering race and class reproduction, see Golann, (2021); Kozol (2012); and Oeur (2018).
6 As of this writing, New York State is poised to make passing the Regents optional for graduation; however students will still have to take these state exams and schools like Sandview will continue to face sanctions as long as their students' scores remain too low.
7 See chapter 2.
8 See New York State Education Department; for example, New York State Education Department (2015d). See also New York State Education Department (2018a). See also chapter 2 for more of my policy analysis.
9 The MAP test continues to be on the list of approved "local tests" for New York State teacher evaluations under Education Law §3012-d (NYS Education Department 2018a). This test has also been used to rate teachers and in some states like New York it has had the power to prompt their firing (2018a). The MAP test was also used as a way to comply with the federal education policy Race to the Top (RTTT). For this situation, if teachers received a low rating twice, they had to be removed from the classroom. It could also result in a more extreme impact if the school had a Title I School Improvement Grant (SIG), which necessitated an improvement plan, including a process for removing a significant number of teachers. This condition has often compelled local teachers' unions to agree to a contract change where students' test scores have an even greater impact on teachers' evaluations. There is change on the horizon in New York State however; as of July 2024, the state has amended education law §3012-d by establishing §3012-e, which is intended to give districts generally greater flexibility in teacher evaluation, ending the state's universal mandate that districts use student performance to evaluate teachers. Yet, the new law still stipulates that the teacher evaluation "plan may include student performance if agreed to through collective bargaining." See New York State Teacher's Union (2024:3). A modified union contract allowing additional use of students' performance on state-approved assessments for teacher evaluation is something that teachers' unions in low-performing schools, including Sandview, had previously agreed to. Districts will also have through the 2031–32 school year to submit modifications to their currently approved plan. See New York State Education Department (2024c).
10 This was possible in part because their teachers' union agreed to a modified union contract.

11 See chapter 2.
12 See chapter 2 for more of my policy analysis.
13 See Hursh 2007.
14 There is no High School Equivalency, GED program affiliated with the school, and Sandview High does not connect these students with such a program. Additionally, the school does not have to count these students toward their dropout rate because they are considered to be enrolled in an "alternative education program" even if the student does nothing.
15 As of this writing, while the state exams are still required for graduation in traditional public schools across New York State through this current academic year, New York State is now poised to make passing the Regents exams optional for graduation. However students will still have to take these state exams and schools like Sandview will continue to face sanctions as long as their students' scores remain too low.

   The recent trend is that fewer states have this requirement, in fact just about one out of five states have similar exit exam requirements to New York State. However, for schools like Sandview High nationwide, the pressure persists even without exit exam requirements to raise their students' average state exam scores under the threat of school closure.
16 See Kandel et al. (2014) for a brief introduction to and background on "unaccompanied minors." See Canizales (2024) for an in-depth analysis of the experiences of these youth.
17 As described in prior notes, New York State is poised to stop requiring passing the Regents for graduation, but students will still have to take them and schools like Sandview will continue to face sanctions as long as their students' scores remain too low.
18 This view draws on those developed by Marshall (1950), extended by Glenn (2004), Glenn (2011), and many others.
19 Glenn 2004. See also Bonilla-Silva and Mayorga (2011), Chavez (2020), De Genova (2002), and Ngai (2014).
20 Anyon 2014:172–73.
21 See also Michaels 2020.
22 Taft 2019.
23 Fine 1991; Lewis and Diamond 2015.
24 The 2012 teachers' strike in Chicago restarted the resurgence of mass education protests; 2014, 2015, and 2018 were also big years for massive strike waves. For examples, see Blanc 2019; Ewing 2018; Gordon 2009, 2021; Kwon 2013; and Rooks 2020. I also discuss this further in the book's conclusion.

CHAPTER 4. "BAD" KIDS
1 Carter 2005. See also Alonso et al. 2009; Harris 2006.
2 For examples, see Lewis and Diamond 2015; MacLeod 2009; and Valenzuela 1999.
3 See Tyson 2011.

4 See Gilens 1999:66; see also, Katz 1990.
5 My analysis shares similar threads with Oeur (2018). Both studies (Oeur's and mine) reveal how different kinds of neoliberal school reform imperatives motivated school practices that aimed to shape minoritized students into certain "regulated" selves, which in turn engendered higher intra-racial boundaries for students. In my case these were boundaries *within* the school for both Black and Latinx students. Oeur studied two neoliberalized schools that tried to improve Black male students' academic outcomes, largely through instituting a boys-only education. In that study, the boys learned that they were exceptional Black boys *because* they attended those schools, in contrast to other Black peers who did not attend their schools.
6 See Noguera and Syeed 2020.
7 See chapter 2.
8 See Golann 2021.
9 As described in chapter 2.
10 For example, see Oeur 2018.
11 See Ris 2015; see also Duckworth et al. 2007.
12 The "From Ghetto to Success" program and its title are likely inspired by a book of the same title published. This is a pseudonym but with the same spirit of the original. The book describes the ghetto as a "mentality." Therefore, one only needs change their mindset in order to achieve success.
13 See Cohen 2009.
14 See Oeur 2018.
15 See Golann 2021; see also Oeur 2018.
16 See Piven and Cloward 2012.
17 This finding also is like that of Valenzuela (1999), which showed that racialization in school undermined relationships between first- and second-generation Mexican immigrant youth. This was also partly the result of the "culture of poverty" narrative used to cast aside struggling students.
18 See Cairns 2013.
19 See Tyson and Lewis 2021.
20 See Giroux and McLaren 1989.

CHAPTER 5. ON (NOT) FIXING RACIALIZED POLICING THROUGH NEOLIBERAL ACCOUNTABILITY

1 Video accessed by the author from the school's website at the start of 2014. This video has since been removed from the school's website.
2 Sandview High's official record was that it suspended about *a quarter* of its students annually during my fieldwork. This number included the total number of students receiving at least one full day of out-of-school suspension. (In contrast, the neighboring high school to Sandview High with mostly White and affluent students suspended just roughly 5 percent of its students annually.) As well, about *20 percent* of Sandview High students received *formal* in-school suspensions

(ISS). I stress *formal* ISS because, as I discuss in this chapter, I also learned from students that *informal* suspensions were frequent. These did not count on their record but they were still suspended.
3   See Curran et al. (2019) for analysis of this pressure on schools generally.
4   See Fisher et al. (2022) and Higgins et al. (2022) for how school resource officers view students as populations that need to be controlled.
5   Recall that since the early 2000s, the US Department of Education has required that states identify and intervene in "low-performing" public schools in their state; this was (and still is) a central shift, with the reauthorization of 1965 Elementary and Secondary Education Act (currently under the Every Student Succeeds Act, ESSA), though the shift occurred under the former version, the No Child Left Behind Act (NCLB). Individual school districts with a "low-performing" status must participate in a state improvement plan. For Sandview High during my fieldwork, New York State selected a "District Comprehensive Improvement Plan" (DCIP), an approved federal program for "low-performing" schools. Sandview High's specific DCIP was called the "Turnaround Model," which was for schools in the lowest performance category. At the time, this category was called "Priority" Schools; in addition to participation in mandatory school restructuring led by the state, these schools also received funding from a three-year federal grant.
6   See Addington 2009; Kupchik 2010.
7   Kupchik et al. 2020:393.
8   See Brooks 2020:43.
9   See New York State Education Department (2013:8).
10 See chapters 1 and 2 for additional description of this law. "Low-performing" is the label currently used nationally to denote schools being sanctioned for their students having "too low" performance outcomes based on evolving state and federal metrics. For the first part of the NCLB era, the official general label for these schools was "failing," which was later re-named "struggling" during this study's data collection. Thus, when Sandview High was put into state receivership, it was because it was sanctioned as a "struggling" school for several years in a row. See New York State Senate (2015:5).
11 The behavior metric of "serious incidents" refers to violent incidents calculated from the state's student behavior indexing system. Violent incidents include events where no violence occurred but could have resulted from a student's action, such as throwing an object that could have seriously hurt someone but did not. In New York State this is called the "Violent and Disruptive Incidents Report" system (VADIR). It was enacted to comply with a new federal law to collect school-level data for the state, which is then used to calculate a "School Violence Index." See New York State Education Department (2018b).
12 New York State Education Department 2015c.
13 See Addington 2009.
14 Kupchik and Henry 2023.

15 See Annamma 2017; Kim and Venet 2023.
16 See chapter 2 for an introduction to school receivership programs specifically and neoliberal education reforms for school improvement broadly. Related, recall that the ESSA is the current version of the 1965 Elementary and Secondary Education Act (ESEA). Recall that under the ESSA and the state receivership programs, states still authorize the closure of schools as a final sanction for perceived "low-performance."
17 See Portz and Beauchamp (2022:721) for a discussion of the ESSA transition adding "non-test indicators" such as "school climate" and attendance measures. These were indicators on Sandview High's improvement plan before the ESSA, and they translated into measuring and evaluating based on suspension and "serious incident" metrics in terms of the school's evaluation on "non-test" indicators.
18 See Aldeman 2017:95; Jordan and Miller 2017; Welsh, Graham, and Williams 2019.
19 See Ravitch 2016.
20 See Jackson, Johnson, and Persico 2016.
21 See Dishon and Goodman 2017.
22 See Golann and Torres 2020.
23 See Brooks 2020; Marsh 2024; Sondel 2015; Sondel, Kretchmar, and Hadley Dunn 2022.
24 See Sondel 2015:301, 304.
25 For examples, see Ferguson 2020; Lopez 2003.
26 For examples, see Kupchik 2010; Morris 2016; Noguera 2003.
27 See Lerman and Weaver 2014.
28 Lerman and Weaver 2014:11.
29 See also Giroux (2003) for another analysis of how punitive school discipline undermines citizenship socialization goals of school. My analysis adds an empirical account of these policing mechanisms and examines intersectional aspects. I also differ by focusing on these harms related to informal punishment specifically, drawing attention to the seemingly "lesser" harms produced in a setting where formal exclusionary punishment is to be avoided.
30 See Shedd 2015 and Glenn 2004.
31 Shedd (2015) also analyzes students' perception of injustice in Chicago public schools, but with a focus on comparing their views by segregated/integrated schools and neighborhoods.
32 See Collins (2000) for more on intersectionality, the key analysis for identifying these layers of marginalization.
33 For examples, see Nolan 2011; Owens 2022; Rios 2011; Shedd 2015.
34 It is well established that punitive discipline policies disproportionately negatively impact Black and Latino *boys'* educational opportunities, however more recently it is being acknowledged that these policies also negatively impact Black and Latina girls (Crenshaw, Ocen, and Nanda 2015).
35 This was literally what the school's manual stated, and was also mentioned to anyone who complained, including parents. During the time of my

data collection, there was a webpage on the school website where parents routinely complained about the strictness and the overpolicing of the dress code for their daughters. In response, the school representatives reminded parents they were helping their children "dress for success" as aspiring professionals.

36 Collins 2000, 2004.
37 Edward Morris (2005) and Monique Morris (2016).
38 See also Rios (2017) for examples of added vulnerability for undocumented Latinx youth in school punishment systems.
39 Shedd 2015.
40 See Fong (2023) for an in-depth analysis of the trauma that the threat of a CPS investigation brings into many families' lives.
41 This is what I learned from both of the school professionals who spoke with me about this, including the person in the office in charge of making the calls.
42 I had a conversation with Eduardo when he returned to school. When I referenced the call home about CPS, he looked down at his shoes nervously, his head low into his shoulders. I then told him the school was not really going to send the government to his house.
43 See Jordan and Miller 2017; Mahowald et al. 2023.
44 See Jordan and Miller 2017.
45 See Mahowald et al. 2023.
46 See Lewis and Diamond 2015:57.
47 Servoss and Finn 2014; Welch and Payne 2010, 2018.
48 See Welch and Payne 2018.
49 See Ispa-Landa 2018.
50 Kupchik 2010.
51 See Welch and Payne 2010.
52 See White 2015.
53 See Lipman 2011.
54 Welsh 2019; Welsh and Williams 2018.
55 See Jordan and Miller 2017.
56 See Golann and Torres 2020.
57 See White 2015.
58 See Marsh 2024:340.
59 Lerman and Weaver 2014.

CHAPTER 6. GO GET THEM (AND NOT ME)

1 As Cairns (2013) demonstrated, school structure can focus on individual competition for resources in ways that are particularly motivating for students when it is combined with the neoliberal message that this competition is needed to be ready to participate in an increasingly risky society where individual economic instability is the norm. Cairns illustrates how this socialization can occur in school through the use of competitive games as an educational tool that also delivers the

message that the game is practice for their future adult roles, where they will have to compete against each other for scant resources.
2 Jones 2019.
3 Ochoa's (2013) analysis revealed how a California school overdisciplined the Latinx students compared to the Asian students, which, in turn, communicated to its students lessons about their racial and gendered selves that contributed to existing stereotypes of "model minority" Asians and "criminal" Latinx youth.
4 Valenzuela 1999.
5 The findings in this chapter are also an important addition to the existing literature demonstrating that racial antagonisms are fostered in school by the structure of academic tracking as well as discipline (Hardie and Tyson 2013; Ochoa 2013). Hardie and Tyson (2013) address the reproduction of White privilege, drawing on cases where the school's student population is mainly White and Black students. As stated earlier in this chapter, Ochoa's (2013) study examined a school with mostly Asian and Latinx students; there, the academic and discipline structure reproduced the stereotype that Asians are the "model" minorities and Latinxs are "criminals" and likewise undervalued. In that case, the school did tend to clearly police the Latinx students and let the Asian students go. Students then espoused racial stereotypes about their peers that mirrored these school experiences.
6 The "school violence index" (SVI) is the annual uniform violent incident reporting system "Violent and Disruptive Incident Reports" (VADIR) required by the State of New York. It represents different violent and disruptive incidents categorized and weighted to create a violence index for the school. It is part of the New York State SAVE Program (Safe Schools Against Violence) and used in part to determine "persistently dangerous schools" which require various interventions from the New York State Education Department. Sandview High is *not* a "persistently dangerous school."
7 As mentioned in note 11 of chapter 5, the "school violence index" is the standardized school level metric New York State requires schools to report on, using its student behavior indexing system. See New York State Education Department (2018b).

The records did indicate that for the 2013–14 school year there were several instances of "weapon possession" reported at the school, three of which were reported through screening. Yet, this weapon possession record for Sandview High was similar to that of the nearby White-majority high school, where an almost identical number of instances of "weapons" were reported at the school; yet there was no stated public concern over weapons and school safety for that school. Moreover, the nearby White-majority school did not perform weapon screening, meaning that Sandview High students were more likely to have a weapon confiscated and therefore show up in official records.
8 Author's review of the "juvenile arrests/ criminal activity" records for Sandview, New York State Division of Criminal Justice Services. Juvenile Arrests/Criminal Activity, 2010–2014.

9   According to author's analysis. (Data source: New York State Division of Criminal Justice Services "Crime, Arrest and Firearm Activity Report" for Sandview, issued March 6, 2015.)
10 Author's review of local news crime reports 2012–2015 as well as analysis of the New York State Division of Criminal Justice Services "Crime, Arrest and Firearm Activity Report" for Sandview (issued March 6, 2015.)
11 I learned from a school professional that the assembly was part of the new school administration's plans to demonstrate their new efforts to improve the school.
12 The special assembly was on a Friday afternoon, regular classes were cancelled for it but it was not mandatory for students to attend.
13 No official school data were available on the number and purpose of lockdowns. However, teachers shared that school lockdowns were not because of violence. As one teacher explained, "We have lockdown procedures for different things but nothing because of the kids." Teachers elaborated that the lockdowns happened typically because there was a building hazard. One teacher's example of a recent school lockdown was because a transformer broke, which left the school temporarily without power.
14 Data Source: Sandview High VADIR Incident Report Data. There were also *zero* incidents of serious injuries at Sandview High, as indicated by the category of "Assault with a Serious Physical Injury." For context, there were just over 70 "Minor Altercations" ("physical contact but no injury"), around a dozen incidents of "Assault with Physical Injury," and just under 10 incidents of "Bullying" during the 2013–14 academic year, which was average for the school.
15 As indicated in earlier chapters, Sandview High students described the two "races" at the school as Latinx or Black. And some Latinx students self-described their race as "Spanish" as well as Latinx, but it was still the same race to them. White students at Sandview High were so few (and isolated in the honors courses) that they were rarely referenced. Also, some students did not even believe that there were White students enrolled at Sandview High. As a student named Rocio put it, "I don't see no White students; I don't see them." I also hardly ever saw White students during my time at Sandview High.
16 See chapter 5.
17 Kupchik (2010:148) makes this theoretical argument that bullying among students is related to modeling the school's discipline structure; Kupchik and Farina (2016) test this empirically, finding that (nationally) schools with more authoritarian school discipline have higher rates of bullying. As they put it, "Harsh school punishment and invasive security practices may be providing students a model for bullying which they can imitate" (2016:4).
18 I learned from several different school professionals at Sandview High that some of the Black immigrant students also did not have their immigration papers. As one school professional at Sandview High put it, "There are so many Black students, Jamaican students, they are all undocumented." This individual also had

knowledge that they were undocumented because they came to her for letters of character support to help them in their immigration cases.
19 See Menjívar 2021.
20 See Chavez 2020.
21 See Gilens 1999.
22 Bashi Treitler 2013.
23 Specifically, Pyke and Dang (2003) found that second-generation Asian American youth called each other "FOBs" ("fresh-off-the-boat"). Ochoa (2013) found this applied to Latinx students too, where the FOB insult included them and was generally used to belittle immigrants (Latinx or Asian) who were more recently arrived and did not know English well. She also found the school bolstered this bullying, such as with "English Only" rules. I found "English Only" rules in practice at Sandview High too, which also likely fostered the reported bullying around immigrant students speaking heritage languages. Clearly this was awful, but in this chapter I highlight the most common insult for Latinxs and its meaning as a specific criminal frame, rather than an expression of bias on the basis of perceived foreignness related to race and immigration history.
24 See chapter 5.
25 See chapter 5 for a detailed analysis of why school dress code is a "100% girl issue" according to students.
26 Lewis and Diamond 2015.
27 Blumer 1958; Bobo and Hutchings 1996.
28 Bettie 2014.
29 Pascoe 2011.
30 See also Shedd (2015) on student perceptions. I engage directly with her work in chapter 5.
31 As stated earlier in this chapter, my work here should be considered in tandem with the broader empirical conversation documenting how authoritarian school regimes (e.g. Kupchik and Farina 2016) and neoliberal school programming (e.g. Cairns 2013) shape students' behavior toward each other and suggest concerning patterns in socialization related to school structure.

CONCLUSION

1 See Carver-Thomas and Darling-Hammond 2017. Furthermore, as previously noted, this is not about low-quality professionals; when teachers leave "bad" schools like Sandview High for "good" ones, those same teachers' performance based on their students' performance on state tests goes up (Shifrer 2022). In other words, teachers have "good" ratings when they don't work at "bad" schools. As a reminder, "bad" and "good" actually largely measure students' poverty levels (Berliner 2013; Reardon et al. 2019).
2 Simon and Johnson 2015.
3 Karp 2016; Meyers et al. 2023.

4 Kim and Venet 2023.
5 The 7mindsets program is a key example. According to their website, the 7mindsets program "has been implemented with more than 5 million students and educators across the country." See the website, https://7mindsets.com/.
6 Ravitch 2016:9.
7 Au 2016; Berliner 2005, 2013.
8 Fong 2023; Giroux 2018; Roberts 2011; Wacquant 2009.
9 Black and Rea 2021; Sunderman et al. 2017.
10 Close, Amrein-Beardsley, and Collins 2018.
11 Beckett 2018; Gottschalk 2016.
12 See Ewing and Green 2022; Lipman 2011.
13 See Tieken and Auldridge-Reveles 2019.
14 See Green et al. 2022.
15 See Pearman and Greene 2022.
16 See Candipan 2020; Pearman and Swain 2017. It is also important to note that when White gentrifiers do send their children to the local public schools, that scenario is not without its problems as well. In those cases, new White affluent parents also tend to produce new inequalities as they engage in resource hoarding when they enter predominately Black and Latinx working-class school communities (Posey-Maddox, Kimelberg, and Cucchiara 2014).
17 See Green et al. 2023; Pearman 2020.
18 See Weber, Farmer, and Donoghue 2020.
19 Deeb-Sossa and Manzo 2018; Deeb-Sossa and Moreno 2016; Syeed 2019; Tieken and Auldridge-Reveles 2019.
20 See Han et al. 2017; Tieken and Auldridge-Reveles 2019.
21 See Frankenberg and Siegel-Hawley 2024:51.
22 Frankenberg and Siegel-Hawley 2024:21.
23 Frankenberg and Siegel-Hawley 2024:7–8.
24 Ocejo 2024.
25 See Green et al. (2022) for an overview of the stages of gentrification as it relates to schools.
26 Goulas 2024:7.
27 Goulas 2024.
28 Averett 2021:91; Griffith and Burns 2024; Stewart 2023:31–33.
29 Tieken and Auldridge-Reveles 2019.
30 Tieken and Montgomery 2021.
31 See Daigon 2023.
32 Cowen 2023.
33 Daigon 2023.
34 Shaw 2024.
35 Cowen 2023.
36 See Rooks (2020) for a good recent summary of student activism across the United States related to K-12 education; see also Anyon 2014:158–61.

37 As Anyon (2014:172–73) reminds us, "feelings of efficacy" are critical for leading people into activism, and urging minoritized students to feel entitlement "would encourage them to hold the system accountable."
38 Lamont 2019.
39 Rooks 2020.
40 Darling-Hammond 2013; Ladson-Billings 2013; Tienken and Zhao 2013.
41 Carter and Welner 2013.
42 See chapter 1 for a detailed analysis.
43 For instance, in high-poverty regions of major cities like New York City, social justice organizations advocating for and organizing with under-served students in the Bronx can lobby the New York City counsel and mayor's office for funding (Su 2011).
44 Page and Gilens 2020.
45 Piven and Cloward 2012.
46 Prieto 2018.
47 Blanc 2019.
48 Thiel 2014.
49 Rooks 2020; Thiel 2014.
50 Anyon 2014.
51 Kwon 2013.
52 Gordon 2009.
53 Su 2011.

APPENDIX

1 See Goffman 1989.
2 Child assent forms are like informed consent forms but for minors.
3 This too was gendered, as it was more common for girls to talk about their aspiring adulthood and for boys to share traumatic stories. It is likely that sharing about trauma was more common among the boys because they tend to have fewer spaces to express vulnerability and hesitate to seek emotional support compared to girls. Regarding sharing about adult aspirations, this had to do largely with common elements of "girl culture" like femme tattoos, hair coloring and styles sported by celebrities, and boyfriends with professional jobs.
4 Bettie 2014.
5 See Mandell 1988.
6 See Bettie 2014:16–17.
7 See Thorne (1993) for details on trying to minimize being an authority figure when doing research with children.
8 See Downey, Dalidowicz, and Mason 2015.
9 As stated earlier, I examined administrators' public views from their writing in extensive public documents, local media interviews, and public videos of them that were posted to the school's website.

BIBLIOGRAPHY

7 mindsets, accessed March 8, 2024. https://7mindsets.com/.

Addington, Lynn A. 2009. "Cops and Cameras: Public School Security as a Policy Response to Columbine." *American Behavioral Scientist* 52(10):1426–46. https://doi.org/10.1177/0002764209332555.

Aggarwal, Ujju, Edwin Mayorga, and Donna Nevel. 2012. "Slow Violence and Neoliberal Education Reform: Reflections on a School Closure." *Peace and Conflict: Journal of Peace Psychology* 18(2):156–64. https://doi.org/10.1037/a0028099.

Aldeman, Chad. 2017. "The Case against ESSA: A Very Limited Law." Pp. 91–105 in *The Every Student Succeeds Act: What It Means for Schools, Systems, and States*, edited by Fredrick Hess and Max Eden. Harvard Education Press.

Allard, Scott W., and Elizabeth Pelletier. 2023. "Volatility and Change in Suburban Nonprofit Safety Nets." *RSF: The Russell Sage Foundation Journal of the Social Sciences* 9(2):134–160. https://doi.org/10.7758/RSF.2023.9.2.06.

Alonso, Gaston, Noel S. Anderson, Celina Su, and Jeanne Theoharis. 2009. *Our Schools Suck: Students Talk Back to a Segregated Nation on the Failures of Urban Education*. New York University Press.

Annamma, Subini Ancy. 2017. *The Pedagogy of Pathologization: Dis/Abled Girls of Color in the School-Prison Nexus*. Routledge.

Anyon, Jean. 1980. "Social Class and the Hidden Curriculum of Work." *Journal of Education* 162(1):67–92. https://doi.org/10.1177/002205748016200106.

Anyon, Jean. 2014. *Radical Possibilities: Public Policy, Urban Education, and a New Social Movement*. Routledge.

Apple, Michael W. 2007. "Ideological Success, Educational Failure? On the Politics of No Child Left Behind." *Journal of Teacher Education* 58(2):108–16. https://doi.org/10.1177/0022487106297844.

Apple, Michael W. 2013. *Educating the "Right" Way: Markets, Standards, God, and Inequality*. Routledge.

Au, Wayne. 2016. "Meritocracy 2.0: High-Stakes, Standardized Testing as a Racial Project of Neoliberal Multiculturalism." *Educational Policy* 30(1):39–62. https://doi.org/10.1177/0895904815614916.

Averett, Kate Henley. 2021. *The Homeschool Choice: Parents and the Privatization of Education*. New York University Press.

Ball, Stephen J. 2016. "Neoliberal Education? Confronting the Slouching Beast." *Policy Futures in Education* 14(8):1046–59. https://doi.org/10.1177/1478210316664259.

Beckett, Katherine. 2018. "The Politics, Promise, and Peril of Criminal Justice Reform in the Context of Mass Incarceration." *Annual Review of Criminology* 1:235–59. https://doi.org/10.1146/annurev-criminol-032317-092458.

Berliner, David C. 2005. "The Near Impossibility of Testing for Teacher Quality." *Journal of Teacher Education* 56(3):205–13. https://doi.org/10.1177/0022487105275904.

Berliner, David C. 2013. "Effects of Inequality and Poverty vs. Teachers and Schooling on America's Youth." *Teachers College Record* 115(12):1–26. https://doi.org/10.1177/016146811311501203.

Berry, Barnett. 2013. "Good Schools and Teachers for All Students: Dispelling Myths, Facing Evidence, and Pursuing the Right Strategies," Pp. 181–192 in *Closing the Opportunity Gap: What America Must Do to Give Every Child an Even Chance*, edited by Prudence L. Carter and Kevin G. Welner. Oxford University Press.

Bettie, Julie. 2014. *Women without Class: Girls, Race, and Identity*. University of California Press.

Black, William R., and Adam C. Rea. 2021. "Equity, Effectiveness and Control: The Every Student Succeeds Act and State Approaches to Defining School Turnaround," accessed July 22, 2022. *Policy Brief*, 7. https://scholarcommons.usf.edu.

Blanc, Eric. 2019. *Red State Revolt: The Teachers' Strike Wave and Working-Class Politics*. Verso Books.

Blumer, Herbert. 1958. "Race Prejudice as a Sense of Group Position." *Pacific Sociological Review* 1(1):3–7. https://doi.org/10.2307/1388607.

Bobo, Lawrence, and Vincent L. Hutchings. 1996. "Perceptions of Racial Group Competition: Extending Blumer's Theory of Group Position to a Multiracial Social Context." *American Sociological Review* 61(6):951–72. https://doi.org/10.2307/2096302.

Bonilla-Silva, Eduardo, and Sarah Mayorga. 2011. "On (Not) Belonging: Why Citizenship Does Not Remedy Racial Inequality." Pp. 77–90 in *State of White Supremacy: Racism, Governance, and the United States*, edited by Moon-Kie Jung, João Costa Vargas, and Eduardo Bonilla-Silva. Stanford University Press.

Bowles, Samuel, and Herbert Gintis. 2002. "Schooling in Capitalist America Revisited." *Sociology of Education* 75(1):1–18. https://doi.org/10.2307/3090251.

Brooks, Erinn. 2020. *Education Reform in the Twenty-First Century: The Marketization of Teaching and Learning at a No-Excuses Charter School*. Palgrave Macmillan.

Buras, Kristen L. 2014. *Charter Schools, Race, and Urban Space: Where the Market Meets Grassroots Resistance*. Routledge.

Cairns, Kate. 2013. "The Subject of Neoliberal Affects: Rural Youth Envision Their Futures." *The Canadian Geographer/Le Géographe Canadien* 57(3):337–44. https://doi.org/10.1111/cag.12012.

Calarco, Jessica McCrory. 2018. *Negotiating Opportunities: How the Middle Class Secures Advantages in School*. Oxford University Press.

Candipan, Jennifer. 2020. "Choosing Schools in Changing Places: Examining School Enrollment in Gentrifying Neighborhoods." *Sociology of Education* 93(3):215–37. https://doi.org/10.1177/0038040720910128.

Canizales, Stephanie L. 2024. *Sin Padres, Ni Papeles: Unaccompanied Migrant Youth Coming of Age in the United States*. University of California Press.

Carter, Prudence L. 2005. *Keepin' It Real: School Success beyond Black and White*. Oxford University Press.

Carter, Prudence L., and Kevin G. Welner. 2013. *Closing the Opportunity Gap: What America Must Do to Give Every Child an Even Chance*. Oxford University Press.

Carver-Thomas, Desiree, and Linda Darling-Hammond. 2017. "Teacher Turnover: Why It Matters and What We Can Do about It." *Learning Policy Institute*, August 16, 2017. https://learningpolicyinstitute.org.

Chavez, Leo. 2020. *The Latino Threat: Constructing Immigrants, Citizens, and the Nation*. Stanford University Press.

Close, Kevin, Audrey Amrein-Beardsley, and Clarin Collins. 2018. "State-Level Assessments and Teacher Evaluation Systems after the Passage of the Every Student Succeeds Act: Some Steps in the Right Direction." *National Education Policy Center*, June 5. http://Nepc.Colorado.Edu.

Cohen, Cathy J. 2009. *The Boundaries of Blackness: AIDS and the Breakdown of Black Politics*. University of Chicago Press.

Collins, Patricia Hill. 2000. *Black Feminist Thought: Knowledge, Consciousness, and the Politics of Empowerment*. Routledge.

Collins, Patricia Hill. 2004. *Black Sexual Politics: African Americans, Gender, and the New Racism*. Routledge.

Cowen, Joshua. 2023. "How School Voucher Programs Hurt Students." *Time Magazine*, April 19. https://time.com.

Crenshaw, Kimberle W., Priscilla Ocen, and Jyoti Nanda. 2015. *Black Girls Matter: Pushed Out, Overpoliced and Underprotected*, accessed September 25, 2024. https://scholarship.law.columbia.edu.

Curran, F. Chris, Benjamin W. Fisher, Samantha Viano, and Aaron Kupchik. 2019. "Why and When Do School Resource Officers Engage in School Discipline? The Role of Context in Shaping Disciplinary Involvement." *American Journal of Education* 126(1):33–63. https://doi.org/10.1086/705499.

Daigon, Glenn. 2023. "Why Red States Are Blocking New School Voucher Programs." *The Progressive Magazine*, July 3. https://progressive.org/.

Darling-Hammond, Linda. 2007. "Race, Inequality and Educational Accountability: The Irony of 'No Child Left Behind.'" *Race Ethnicity and Education* 10(3):245–60. https://doi.org/10.1080/13613320701503207.

Darling-Hammond, Linda. 2013. "Inequality and School Resources." Pp. 77–97 in *Closing the Opportunity Gap: What America Must Do to Give Every Child an Even Chance*, edited by Prudence L. Carter and Kevin G. Welner. Oxford University Press.

De Genova, Nicholas P. 2002. "Migrant 'Illegality' and Deportability in Everyday Life." *Annual Review of Anthropology* 31(1):419–47. https://doi.org/10.1146/annurev.anthro.31.040402.085432.

de Graauw, Els, Shannon Gleeson, and Irene Bloemraad. 2013. "Funding Immigrant Organizations: Suburban Free Riding and Local Civic Presence." *American Journal of Sociology* 119(1):75–130. https://doi.org/10.1086/671168.

Deeb-Sossa, Natalia, and Rosa Manzo. 2018. "Community-Driven Leadership: Mexican-Origin Farmworking Mothers Resisting Deficit Practices by a School Board in California." *Journal of Latinos and Education* 19(2): 199–215. https://doi.org/10.1080/15348431.2018.1499512.

Deeb-Sossa, Natalia, and Melissa Moreno. 2016. "¡No Cierren Nuestra Escuela! Farm Worker Mothers as Cultural Citizens in an Educational Community Mobilization Effort." *Journal of Latinos and Education* 15(1):39–57. https://doi.org/10.1080/15348431.2015.1045145.

Deeds, Vontrese, and Mary Pattillo. 2015. "Organizational 'Failure' and Institutional Pluralism: A Case Study of an Urban School Closure." *Urban Education* 50(4):474–504. https://doi.org/10.1177/0042085913519337.

Diamond, John B., Linn Posey-Maddox, and María D. Velázquez. 2021. "Reframing Suburbs: Race, Place, and Opportunity in Suburban Educational Spaces." *Educational Researcher* 50(4):249–55. https://doi.org/10.3102/0013189X20972676.

Dishon, Gideon, and Joan F. Goodman. 2017. "No-Excuses for Character: A Critique of Character Education in No-Excuses Charter Schools." *Theory and Research in Education* 15(2):182–201. https://doi.org/10.1177/1477878517720162.

Downey, Douglas B., Paul T. von Hippel, and Melanie Hughes. 2008. "Are 'Failing' Schools Really Failing? Using Seasonal Comparison to Evaluate School Effectiveness." *Sociology of Education* 81(3):242–70. https://doi.org/10.1177/003804070808100302.

Downey, Greg, Monica Dalidowicz, and Paul H. Mason. 2015. "Apprenticeship as Method: Embodied Learning in Ethnographic Practice." *Qualitative Research* 15(2):183–200. https://doi.org/10.1177/1468794114543400.

Duckworth, Angela L., Christopher Peterson, Michael D. Matthews, and Dennis R. Kelly. 2007. "Grit: Perseverance and Passion for Long-Term Goals." *Journal of Personality and Social Psychology* 92(6):1087–1101. https://doi.org/10.1037/0022-3514.92.6.1087.

Dumas, Michael J. 2014. "'Losing an Arm': Schooling as a Site of Black Suffering." *Race Ethnicity and Education* 17(1):1–29. https://doi.org/10.1080/13613324.2013.850412.

EdBuild. 2019. "23 Billion," accessed April 3, 2023. https://edbuild.org.

Ewing, Eve L. 2018. *Ghosts in the Schoolyard: Racism and School Closings on Chicago's South Side*. University of Chicago Press.

Ewing, Eve L., and Terrance L. Green. 2022. "Beyond the Headlines: Trends and Future Directions in the School Closure Literature." *Educational Researcher* 51(1):58–65. https://doi.org/10.3102/0013189X211050944.

Fabricant, Michael, and Michelle Fine. 2013. *Changing Politics of Education: Privatization and the Dispossessed Lives Left Behind*. Routledge.

Ferguson, Ann Arnett. 2020 [2000]. *Bad Boys: Public Schools in the Making of Black Masculinity*. University of Michigan Press.

Fernández, Jesica Siham. 2021. *Growing Up Latinx: Coming of Age in a Time of Contested Citizenship*. New York University Press.

Ferrara, Benjamin. 2004. "A Comprehensive State Response to School Violence: The New York Safe Schools against Violence Act." Pp. 57–80 in *School Violence: From Discipline to Due Process*, edited by James C. Hanks. American Bar Association.

Fine, Ben, and Alfredo Saad-Filho. 2017. "Thirteen Things You Need to Know about Neoliberalism." *Critical Sociology* 43(4–5):685–706. https://doi.org/10.1177/0896920516655387.

Fine, Michelle. 1991. *Framing Dropouts: Notes on the Politics of an Urban High School*. SUNY Press.

Fisher, Benjamin W., Ethan M. Higgins, Aaron Kupchik, Samantha Viano, F. Chris Curran, Suzanne Overstreet, Bryant Plumlee, and Brandon Coffey. 2022. "Protecting the Flock or Policing the Sheep? Differences in School Resource Officers' Perceptions of Threats by School Racial Composition." *Social Problems* 69(2):316–34. https://doi.org/10.1093/socpro/spaa062.

Flores-González, Nilda. 2017. *Citizens but Not Americans: Race and Belonging among Latino Millennials*. New York University Press.

Fong, Kelley. 2023. *Investigating Families: Motherhood in the Shadow of Child Protective Services*. Princeton University Press.

Foucault, Michel. 2012. *Discipline and Punish: The Birth of the Prison*. Vintage.

Frankenberg, Erica. 2009. "Splintering School Districts: Understanding the Link between Segregation and Fragmentation." *Law & Social Inquiry* 34(4):869–909. https://doi.org/10.1111/j.1747-4469.2009.01166.x.

Frankenberg, Erica, Jongyeon Ee, Jennifer B. Ayscue, and Gary Orfield. 2019. "Harming Our Common Future: America's Segregated Schools 65 Years after Brown." *Civil Rights Project UCLA*, May 10, 2019. https://escholarship.org.

Frankenberg, Erica, Christopher S. Fowler, Sarah Asson, and Ruth Krebs Buck. 2023. "Demographic Change and School Attendance Zone Boundary Changes: Montgomery County, Maryland, and Fairfax County, Virginia, Between 1990 and 2010." *RSF: The Russell Sage Foundation Journal of the Social Sciences* 9(2):75. doi: 10.7758/RSF.2023.9.2.04.

Frankenberg, Erica, and Gary Orfield. 2012. *The Resegregation of Suburban Schools: A Hidden Crisis in American Education*. Harvard Education Press.

Frankenberg, Erica, and Genevieve Siegel-Hawley. 2024. *Understanding Suburban School Segregation: Toward a Renewed Civil Rights Agenda*. Los Angeles: The Civil Rights Project/Proyecto Derechos Civiles, UCLA, February 22, 2024. https://escholarship.org.

Gilens, Martin. 1999. *Why Americans Hate Welfare: Race, Media, and the Politics of Antipoverty Policy*. University of Chicago Press.

Gilmore, Ruth Wilson. 2007. *Golden Gulag: Prisons, Surplus, Crisis, and Opposition in Globalizing California*. University of California Press.

Giroux, Henry. 2003. "Racial Injustice and Disposable Youth in the Age of Zero Tolerance." *International Journal of Qualitative Studies in Education* 16(4):553–65. https://doi.org/10.1080/0951839032000099543.

Giroux, Henry A. 2018. *The Terror of Neoliberalism: Authoritarianism and the Eclipse of Democracy*. Routledge.

Giroux, Henry A., and Peter L. McLaren. 1989. *Critical Pedagogy, the State, and Cultural Struggle*. SUNY Press.

Glenn, Evelyn Nakano. 2004. *Unequal Freedom: How Race and Gender Shaped American Citizenship and Labor*. Harvard University Press.

Glenn, Evelyn Nakano. 2011. "Constructing Citizenship: Exclusion, Subordination, and Resistance." *American Sociological Review* 76(1):1–24. https://doi.org/10.1177/0003122411398443.

Goffman, Erving. 1989. "On Fieldwork." *Journal of Contemporary Ethnography* 18(2):123–32. https://doi.org/10.1177/089124189018002001.

Golann, Joanne W. 2021. *Scripting the Moves: Culture and Control in a "No-Excuses" Charter School*. Princeton University Press.

Golann, Joanne W., and A. Chris Torres. 2020. "Do No-Excuses Disciplinary Practices Promote Success?" *Journal of Urban Affairs* 42(4):617–33. https://doi.org/10.1080/07352166.2018.1427506.

Gordon, Hava Rachel. 2009. *We Fight to Win: Inequality and the Politics of Youth Activism*. Rutgers University Press.

Gordon, Hava Rachel. 2021. *This Is Our School!: Race and Community Resistance to School Reform*. New York University Press.

Gottschalk, Marie. 2016. *Caught: The Prison State and the Lockdown of American Politics*. Princeton University Press.

Goulas, Sofoklis. 2024. "Breaking Down Enrollment Declines in Public Schools." *Brookings Institution*, March. www.brookings.edu.

Green, Terrance L., Andrene Castro, Emily Germain, Jeremy Horne, Chloe Sikes, and Joanna Sanchez. 2023. "'They Don't Feel Like This Is Their Place Anymore': School Leaders' Understanding of the Impacts of Gentrification on Schools." *American Educational Research Journal* 60(6):1059–94. https://doi.org/10.3102/00028312231191704.

Green, Terrance L., Emily Germain, Andrene J. Castro, Chloe Latham Sikes, Joanna Sanchez, and Jeremy Horne. 2022. "Gentrifying Neighborhoods, Gentrifying Schools? An Emerging Typology of School Changes in a Gentrifying Urban School District." *Urban Education* 57(1):3–31. https://doi.org/10.1177/0042085920974090.

Griffith, Michael, and Dion Burns. 2024. "Understanding the Cost of Universal School Vouchers: An Analysis of Arizona's Empowerment Scholarship Account Program." *Learning Policy Institute*. https://doi.org/10.54300/682.951.

Han, Chunping, Margaret E. Raymond, James L. Woodworth, Yohannes Negassi, W. Payton Richardson, and Will Snow. 2017. "Lights Off: Practice and Impact of Closing Low-Performing Schools, Volume I." *Stanford, CA: Center for Research on Education Outcomes (CREDO)*. https://credo.stanford.edu.

Hannah-Jones, Nikole. 2015. "The Problem We All Live With." *This American Life*. July 31. www.thisamericanlife.org/.

Hardie, Jessica Halliday, and Karolyn Tyson. 2013. "Other People's Racism: Race, Rednecks, and Riots in a Southern High School." *Sociology of Education* 86(1):83–102. https://doi.org/10.1177/0038040712456554.

Harris, Angel L. 2006. "I (Don't) Hate School: Revisiting Oppositional Culture Theory of Blacks' Resistance to Schooling." *Social Forces* 85(2):797–834. https://doi.org/10.1353/sof.2007.0006.

Harvey, David. 2007. *A Brief History of Neoliberalism*. Oxford University Press.

Harvey, David. 2012. *Rebel Cities: From the Right to the City to the Urban Revolution*. Verso Books.

Higgins, Ethan M., Brandon S. Coffey, Benjamin W. Fisher, Ivan Benitez, and Kristin Swartz. 2022. "School Safety or School Criminalization? The Typical Day of a School Resource Officer in the United States." *The British Journal of Criminology* 62(3):568–84. https://doi.org/10.1093/bjc/azab075.

Hursh, David. 2007. "Exacerbating Inequality: The Failed Promise of the No Child Left Behind Act." *Race Ethnicity and Education* 10(3):295–308. https://doi.org/10.1080/13613320701503264.

Hursh, David. 2020. "Editor's Introduction: The End of Neoliberalism." *Policy Futures in Education* 18(1):1–8. https://doi.org/10.1177/1478210319899776.

Ispa-Landa, Simone. 2018. "Persistently Harsh Punishments amid Efforts to Reform: Using Tools from Social Psychology to Counteract Racial Bias in School Disciplinary Decisions." *Educational Researcher* 47(6):384–90. https://doi.org/10.3102/0013189X18779578.

Jackson, C. Kirabo, Rucker C. Johnson, and Claudia Persico. 2016. "The Effects of School Spending on Educational and Economic Outcomes: Evidence from School Finance Reforms." *The Quarterly Journal of Economics* 131(1):157–218. https://doi.org/10.1093/qje/qjv036.

Jones, Jennifer A. 2019. *The Browning of the New South*. University of Chicago Press.

Jordan, Phyllis W., and Raegen Miller. 2017. "Who's In: Chronic Absenteeism under the Every Student Succeeds Act." *Washington, DC: FutureEd at Georgetown University*. September. www.future-ed.org.

Kandel, William A., Andorra Bruno, Peter J. Meyer, Clare Ribando Seelke, Maureen Taft-Morales, and Ruth Ellen Wasem. 2014. "Unaccompanied Alien Children: Potential Factors Contributing to Recent Immigration." *Congressional Research Service*, July 3. https://crsreports.congress.gov/.

Karp, Stan. 2016. "ESSA: NCLB Repackaged." *Rethinking Schools* 30(3):18–19. https://rethinkingschools.org.

Katz, Michael B. 1990. *The Undeserving Poor: From the War on Poverty to the War on Welfare*. Pantheon Books.

Kim, Rhiannon M., and Alex Shevrin Venet. 2023. "Unsnarling PBIS and Trauma-Informed Education." *Urban Education* 1–29. https://doi.org/10.1177/00420859231175670.

Klein, Alyson. 2018. "What's the Toughest Part of ESSA For District Leaders?" *Education Week*, August 12. www.edweek.org.

Kneebone, Elizabeth, and Alan Berube. 2013. *Confronting Suburban Poverty in America*. Brookings Institution Press.
Kozol, Jonathan. 2012. *Savage Inequalities: Children in America's Schools*. Crown.
Kupchik, Aaron. 2010. *Homeroom Security: School Discipline in an Age of Fear*. New York University Press.
Kupchik, Aaron, F. Chris Curran, Benjamin W. Fisher, and Samantha L. Viano. 2020. "Police Ambassadors: Student-police Interactions in School and Legal Socialization." *Law & Society Review* 54(2):391–422. doi:10.1111/lasr.12472.
Kupchik, Aaron, and Katie A. Farina. 2016. "Imitating Authority: Students' Perceptions of School Punishment and Security, and Bullying Victimization." *Youth Violence and Juvenile Justice* 14(2):147–63. https://doi.org/10.1177/1541204014557648.
Kupchik, Aaron, and Felicia A. Henry. 2023. "Generations of Criminalization: Resistance to Desegregation and School Punishment." *Journal of Research in Crime and Delinquency* 60(1):43–78. https://doi.org/10.1177/00224278221120675.
Kwon, Soo Ah. 2013. *Uncivil Youth: Race, Activism, and Affirmative Governmentality*. Duke University Press.
Ladson-Billings, Gloria. 2013. "Lack of Achievement or Loss of Opportunity." Pp. 11–22 in *Closing the Opportunity Gap: What America Must Do to Give Every Child an Even Chance*, edited by Prudence L. Carter and Kevin G. Welner. Oxford University Press.
Lamont, Michèle. 2019. "From 'Having' to 'Being': Self-worth and the Current Crisis of American Society." *The British Journal of Sociology* 70(3):660–707. https://doi.org/10.1111/1468-4446.12667.
Lerman, Amy E., and Vesla M. Weaver. 2014. *Arresting Citizenship: The Democratic Consequences of American Crime Control*. University of Chicago Press.
Lewis, Amanda E. 2003. *Race in the Schoolyard: Negotiating the Color Line in Classrooms and Communities*. Rutgers University Press.
Lewis, Amanda E., and John B. Diamond. 2015. *Despite the Best Intentions: How Racial Inequality Thrives in Good Schools*. Oxford University Press.
Lewis-McCoy, R. L'Heureux. 2014. *Inequality in the Promised Land: Race, Resources, and Suburban Schooling*. Stanford University Press.
Lewis-McCoy, R. L'Heureux, Natasha Warikoo, Stephen A. Matthews, and Nadirah Farah Foley. 2023. "Resisting Amnesia: Renewing and Expanding the Study of Suburban Inequality." *RSF: The Russell Sage Foundation Journal of the Social Sciences* 9(2):1–24. https://doi.org/10.7758/RSF.2023.9.1.01.
Lichter, Daniel T., Brian C. Thiede, and Matthew M. Brooks. 2023. "Racial Diversity and Segregation: Comparing Principal Cities, Inner-Ring Suburbs, Outlying Suburbs, and the Suburban Fringe." *RSF: The Russell Sage Foundation Journal of the Social Sciences* 9(1):26–51. https://doi.org/10.7758/RSF.2023.9.1.02.
Lipman, Pauline. 2011. *The New Political Economy of Urban Education: Neoliberalism, Race, and the Right to the City*. Routledge.
Lipman, Pauline. 2017. "The Landscape of Education 'Reform' in Chicago: Neoliberalism Meets a Grassroots Movement." *Education Policy Analysis Archives* 25:54–54. https://doi.org/10.14507/epaa.25.2660.

Lopez, Nancy. 2003. *Hopeful Girls, Troubled Boys: Race and Gender Disparity in Urban Education*. Routledge.
Love, Bettina L. 2023. *Punished for Dreaming: How School Reform Harms Black Children and How We Heal*. St. Martin's Press.
MacLeod, Jay. 2009. *Ain't No Makin' It: Aspirations and Attainment in a Low-Income Neighborhood*. Westview Press.
Mahowald, James Bear, Sarah Winchell Lenhoff, Erica B. Edwards, and Jeremy Singer. 2023. "Chronic Absenteeism in the School-Prison Nexus." *The High School Journal* 106(4):274–88. https://doi.org/10.1353/hsj.2023.a930440.
Mandell, Nancy. 1988. "The Least-Adult Role in Studying Children." *Journal of Contemporary Ethnography* 16(4):433–67. https://doi.org/10.1177/0891241688164002.
Marsh, L. Trenton S. 2024. "'We Aren't What We Say': Discontinuities of Teacher Beliefs and Instructional Practice at a 'No-Excuses' and High-Achieving Urban Charter School." *Whiteness and Education* 1–22. https://doi.org/10.1080/23793406.2024.2305475.
Marshall, Thomas H. 1950. *Citizenship and Social Class and Other Essays*. Cambridge University Press.
Martucci, Sara. 2024. *There Was Nothing There: Williamsburg, the Gentrification of a Brooklyn Neighborhood*. New York University Press.
Massey, Douglas S., and Nancy A. Denton. 1993. *American Apartheid: Segregation and the Making of the Underclass*. Harvard University Press.
McLaren, Peter. 2015. *Life in Schools: An Introduction to Critical Pedagogy in the Foundations of Education*. Routledge.
Menjívar, Cecilia. 2021. "The Racialization of 'Illegality.'" *Daedalus* 150(2):91–105. https://doi.org/10.1162/daed_a_01848.
Meyers, Coby V., W. Christopher Brandt, and Bryan A. VanGronigen. 2023. "State ESSA Plans and Comprehensive Support and Improvement (CSI) Status." *Educational Policy* 37(5):1277–1314. https://doi.org/10.1177/08959048221087209.
Michaels, Erin. 2020. "Beyond Academic Achievement Outcomes: The Impact of School on the Immigrant Political Incorporation of Undocumented Latinx Youth." *Youth & Society* 52(7):1285–1311. https://doi.org/10.1177/0044118X20913733.
Michaels, Erin. 2021. "The 'Structurally Adjusted' School: A Case from New York." *Critical Sociology* 47(7–8):1171–89. https://doi.org/10.1177/0896920521995535.
Monahan, Torin, and Rodolfo D. Torres, eds. 2009. *Schools under Surveillance: Cultures of Control in Public Education*. Rutgers University Press.
Morris, Edward W. 2005. "'Tuck in That Shirt!' Race, Class, Gender, and Discipline in an Urban School." *Sociological Perspectives* 48(1):25–48. https://doi.org/10.1525/sop.2005.48.1.25.
Morris, Monique. 2016. *Pushout: The Criminalization of Black Girls in Schools*. The New Press.
New York State Education Department. 2004. "Safe Schools Against Violence in Education Act, Report to the Governor and Legislature." December. www.p12.nysed.gov, accessed March 9, 2018.

New York State Education Department. 2012. "ESEA Flexibility Request." May 21. www.p12.nysed.gov, accessed March 7, 2018.

New York State Education Department. 2013. "Office of Accountability Memo. Progress of Priority Schools, Focus Districts and Focus Schools." June. http://p1232.nysed.gov, accessed October 30, 2017.

New York State Education Department. 2015a. "Commissioner Elia Identifies 144 Struggling and Persistently Struggling Schools to Begin Implementation of School Receivership in New York State." News Release. July 16. www.nysed.gov, accessed March 7, 2018.

New York State Education Department. 2015b. "Making Demonstrable Improvement: Request for Feedback. Presentation by Ira Schwartz, Assistant Commissioner of Accountability." July 31. www.p12.nysed.gov, accessed March 6, 2018.

New York State Education Department. 2015c. "School Receivership Demonstrable Improvement Indicators. Accountability office Webinar, Ira Schwartz." September 18. www.p12.nysed.gov, accessed December 1, 2017.

New York State Education Department. 2015d. "Student Assessments and Associated Growth Models for Teacher and Principal Evaluation, Form C. RFQ: Teacher and Principal Evaluation Service Provider—Assessments (App Period: 2015–16)." http://usny.nysed.gov, accessed March 9, 2018.

New York State Education Department. 2016. "2016–2017 State Aid Handbook." https://stateaid.nysed.gov, accessed March 7, 2018.

New York State Education Department. 2018a. "Race to the Top: Lists of Approved Student Assessments for Use by School Districts and BOCES in Teacher and Principal Evaluations under Education Law §3012-d." March 7. http://usny.nysed.gov, accessed March 8, 2018.

New York State Education Department. 2018b. "Violent and Disruptive Incident Reporting (VADIR), Using Data to Improve School Climate." February 28, 2018. www.p12.nysed.gov, accessed March 9, 2018.

New York State Education Department. 2023. "NY State Graduation Rate Data." https://data.nysed.gov, accessed June 27, 2024.

New York State Education Department. 2024a. "Accountability, Improvement Planning." www.nysed.gov, accessed June 27, 2024.

New York State Education Department. 2024b. "Diagnostic Tool for School and District Effectiveness (DTSDE) Resources." www.nysed.gov, accessed June 28, 2024.

New York State Education Department. 2024c. "Questions and Answers Relating to Evaluation Plans for the 24-25 School Year." www.nysed.gov, accessed October 14, 2024.

New York State Senate. 2015. "Amendment of Section 211-f of the education law, as added by section 1 2 of subpart H of part EE of chapter 56 of the laws of 2015. Takeover and restructuring [failing] OF STRUGGLING schools." April 17. http://legislation.nysenate.gov, accessed November 3, 2017.

New York State Teacher's Union. 2015. "Fact Sheet 15–14: School Receivership." July 8. www.nysut.org, accessed May 5, 2016.

New York State Teacher's Union. 2024. "Fact Sheet 24-7: Summary of Provisions of Chapter 143 of the Laws of 2024, Section 3012-e Relating to Teacher Annual Professional Performance Reviews (APPR)." August 8. www.nysut.org, accessed October 14, 2024.

Ngai, Mae M. 2014. *Impossible Subjects: Illegal Aliens and the Making of Modern America*. Princeton University Press.

Noguera, Pedro A. 2003. "Schools, Prisons, and Social Implications of Punishment: Rethinking Disciplinary Practices." *Theory Into Practice* 42(4):341–50. https://doi.org/10.1207/s15430421tip4204_12.

Noguera, Pedro A. 2016. "There's a Way to Help Inner-City Schools. Obama's New Education Law Isn't It. Kristina Rizga Interview with Pedro Noguera." *Mother Jones*, January 8. www.motherjones.com/.

Noguera, Pedro A., and Esa Syeed. 2020. *City Schools and the American Dream 2: The Enduring Promise of Public Education*. Multicultural Education.

Nolan, Kathleen. 2011. *Police in the Hallways: Discipline in an Urban High School*. University of Minnesota Press.

Oakes, Jeannie. 2005. *Keeping Track: How Schools Structure Inequality*. Yale University Press.

Ocejo, Richard E. 2024. *Sixty Miles Upriver: Gentrification and Race in a Small American City*. Princeton University Press.

Ochoa, Gilda L. 2013. *Academic Profiling: Latinos, Asian Americans, and the Achievement Gap*. University of Minnesota Press.

Oeur, Freeden Blume. 2018. *Black Boys Apart: Racial Uplift and Respectability in All-Male Public Schools*. University of Minnesota Press.

Owens, Ann, and Peter Rich. 2023. "Little Boxes All the Same? Racial-Ethnic Segregation and Educational Inequality Across the Urban-Suburban Divide." *RSF: The Russell Sage Foundation Journal of the Social Sciences* 9(2):26. https://doi.org/10.7758/RSF.2023.9.2.02.

Owens, Ann, and Gail L. Sunderman. 2006. *School Accountability under NCLB: Aid or Obstacle for Measuring Racial Equity?* Cambridge, MA: The Civil Rights Project at Harvard University.

Owens, Jayanti. 2022. "Double Jeopardy: Teacher Biases, Racialized Organizations, and the Production of Racial/Ethnic Disparities in School Discipline." *American Sociological Review* 87(6):1007–48. https://doi.org/10.1177/00031224221135810.

Page, Benjamin I., and Martin Gilens. 2020. *Democracy in America?: What Has Gone Wrong and What We Can Do about It*. University of Chicago Press.

Pascoe, C. J. 2011. *Dude, You're a Fag: Masculinity and Sexuality in High School*. University of California Press.

Pascoe, C. J. 2023. *Nice Is Not Enough: Inequality and the Limits of Kindness at American High*. University of California Press.

Pearman, Francis A. 2020. "Gentrification, Geography, and the Declining Enrollment of Neighborhood Schools." *Urban Education* 55(2):183–215. https://doi.org/10.1177/0042085919884342.

Pearman, Francis A., and Danielle Marie Greene. 2022. "School Closures and the Gentrification of the Black Metropolis." *Sociology of Education* 95(3):233–53. https://doi.org/10.1177/00380407221095205.

Pearman, Francis A., and Walker A. Swain. 2017. "School Choice, Gentrification, and the Variable Significance of Racial Stratification in Urban Neighborhoods." *Sociology of Education* 90(3):213–35. https://doi.org/10.1177/0038040717710494.

Piven, Frances Fox, and Richard Cloward. 2012. *Poor People's Movements: Why They Succeed, How They Fail*. Vintage.

Portz, John, and Nicholas Beauchamp. 2022. "Educational Accountability and State ESSA Plans." *Educational Policy* 36(3):717–47. https://doi.org/10.1177/0895904820917364.

Posey-Maddox, Linn, Shelley McDonough Kimelberg, and Maia Cucchiara. 2014. "Middle-class Parents and Urban Public Schools: Current Research and Future Directions." *Sociology Compass* 8(4):446–56. https://doi.org/10.1111/soc4.12148.

Prieto, Greg. 2018. *Immigrants Under Threat: Risk and Resistance in Deportation Nation*. New York University Press.

Pyke, Karen, and Tran Dang. 2003. "'FOB' and 'Whitewashed': Identity and Internalized Racism among Second Generation Asian Americans." *Qualitative Sociology* 26(2):147–72. https://doi.org/10.1023/A:1022957011866.

Ravitch, Diane. 2016. *The Death and Life of the Great American School System: How Testing and Choice Are Undermining Education*. Basic Books.

Reardon, Sean F., Demetra Kalogrides, and Kenneth Shores. 2019. "The Geography of Racial/Ethnic Test Score Gaps." *American Journal of Sociology* 124(4):1164–1221. https://doi.org/10.1086/700678.

Rios, Victor M. 2011. *Punished: Policing the Lives of Black and Latino Boys*. New York University Press.

Rios, Victor M. 2017. *Human Targets: Schools, Police, and the Criminalization of Latino Youth*. University of Chicago Press.

Ris, Ethan W. 2015. "Grit: A Short History of a Useful Concept." *Journal of Educational Controversy* 10(1):3. https://cedar.wwu.edu.

Roberts, Dorothy E. 2011. "Prison, Foster Care, and the Systemic Punishment of Black Mothers." *UCLA Law Review* 59:1474–500.

Rooks, Noliwe. 2020. *Cutting School: The Segrenomics of American Education*. The New Press.

Scott, Janelle T. 2011. "Market-Driven Education Reform and the Racial Politics of Advocacy." *Peabody Journal of Education* 86(5):580–99. https://doi.org/10.1080/0161956X.2011.616445.

Servoss, Timothy J., and Jeremy D. Finn. 2014. "School Security: For Whom and with What Results?" *Leadership and Policy in Schools* 13(1):61–92. https://doi.org/10.1080/15700763.2014.890734.

Shaw, Aly. 2024. "Billionaires Yass, DeVos Team Up to Dismantle Public Schools Across the US." *Network for Public Education*, April 30. https://networkforpubliceducation.org/.

Shaw, Linda. 2013. "Educators Debate Validity of MAP Testing." *Seattle Times*, March 2. www.seattletimes.com/.
Shedd, Carla. 2015. *Unequal City: Race, Schools, and Perceptions of Injustice.* Russell Sage Foundation.
Shifrer, Dara. 2022. "Contextualizing Educational Disparities and the Evaluation of Teacher Quality." *Social Problems* 69(2):841–86. https://doi.org/10.1093/socpro/spaa044.
Simon, Nicole, and Susan Moore Johnson. 2015. "Teacher Turnover in High-Poverty Schools: What We Know and Can Do." *Teachers College Record* 117(3):1–36. https://doi.org/10.1177/016146811511700305.
Smith, Neil. 2005. *The New Urban Frontier: Gentrification and the Revanchist City.* Routledge.
Sondel, Beth. 2015. "Raising Citizens or Raising Test Scores? Teach for America, 'No Excuses' Charters, and the Development of the Neoliberal Citizen." *Theory & Research in Social Education* 43(3):289–313. https://doi.org/10.1080/00933104.2015.1064505.
Sondel, Beth, Kerry Kretchmar, and Alyssa Hadley Dunn. 2022. "'Who Do These People Want Teaching Their Children?' White Saviorism, Colorblind Racism, and Anti-Blackness in 'No Excuses' Charter Schools." *Urban Education* 57(9):1621–50. https://doi.org/10.1177/0042085919842618.
Stewart, Mahala Dyer. 2023. *The Color of Homeschooling: How Inequality Shapes School Choice.* New York University Press.
Su, Celina. 2011. *Streetwise for Book Smarts: Grassroots Organizing and Education Reform in the Bronx.* Cornell University Press.
Sunderman, Gail L., Erin Coghlan, and Rick Mintrop. 2017. *School Closure as a Strategy to Remedy Low Performance.* Boulder, CO: National Education Policy Center. May. https://scholar.colorado.edu.
Syeed, Esa. 2019. "'It Just Doesn't Add Up': Disrupting Official Arguments for Urban School Closures with Counterframes." *Education Policy Analysis Archives* 27(110):n.p. https://doi.org/10.14507/epaa.27.4240.
Taft, Jessica K. 2019. *The Kids Are in Charge: Activism and Power in Peru's Movement of Working Children.* New York University Press.
Terriquez, Veronica. 2017. "Legal Status, Civic Organizations, and Political Participation among Latino Young Adults." *The Sociological Quarterly* 58(2):315–36. https://doi.org/10.1080/00380253.2017.1296756.
Terriquez, Veronica, and Hyeyoung Kwon. 2015. "Intergenerational Family Relations, Civic Organisations, and the Political Socialisation of Second-Generation Immigrant Youth." *Journal of Ethnic and Migration Studies* 41(3):425–47. https://doi.org/10.1080/1369183X.2014.921567.
Thiel, Elizabeth. 2014. "Victory for Portland Teachers." *Rethinking Schools* 28(3):10–11. https://rethinkingschools.org/.
Thorne, Barrie. 1993. *Gender Play: Girls and Boys in School.* Rutgers University Press.
Tieken, Mara Casey, and Trevor Ray Auldridge-Reveles. 2019. "Rethinking the School Closure Research: School Closure as Spatial Injustice." *Review of Educational Research* 89(6):917–53. https://doi.org/10.3102/0034654319877151.

Tieken, Mara Casey, and M. K. Montgomery. 2021. "Challenges Facing Schools in Rural America." *State Education Standard* 21(1):6–11.

Tienken, Christopher H., and Yong Zhao. 2013. "How Common Standards and Standardized Testing Widen the Opportunity Gap," Pp. 111–22 in *Closing the Opportunity Gap: What America Must Do to Give Every Child an Even Chance*, edited by Prudence L. Carter and Kevin G. Welner. Oxford University Press.

Treitler, Vilna Bashi. 2013. *The Ethnic Project: Transforming Racial Fiction into Ethnic Factions*. Stanford University Press.

Tyson, Karolyn. 2011. *Integration Interrupted: Tracking, Black Students, and Acting White after Brown*. Oxford University Press.

Tyson, Karolyn, and Amanda E. Lewis. 2021. "The 'Burden' of Oppositional Culture among Black Youth in America." *Annual Review of Sociology* 47:459–77. https://doi.org/10.1146/annurev-soc-090420-092123.

United States Department of Education. 2004. "No Child Left Behind, Unsafe School Choice Option." May. www2.ed.gov, accessed April 22, 2016.

United States Department of Education. 2017. "Every Student Succeeds Act Consolidated State Plan Frequently Asked Questions." June 16. www2.ed.gov, accessed August 16, 2020.

Valenzuela, Angela. 1999. *Subtractive Schooling: US-Mexican Youth and the Politics of Caring*. SUNY Press.

Wacquant, Loïc. 2009. *Punishing the Poor: The Neoliberal Government of Social Insecurity*. Duke University Press.

Weber, Rachel, Stephanie Farmer, and Mary Donoghue. 2020. "Predicting School Closures in an Era of Austerity: The Case of Chicago." *Urban Affairs Review* 56(2):415–50. https://doi.org/10.1177/1078087418802359.

Welch, Kelly, and Allison Ann Payne. 2010. "Racial Threat and Punitive School Discipline." *Social Problems* 57(1):25–48. https://doi.org/10.1525/sp.2010.57.1.25.

Welch, Kelly, and Allison Ann Payne. 2018. "Latino/a Student Threat and School Disciplinary Policies and Practices." *Sociology of Education* 91(2):91–110. https://doi.org/10.1177/0038040718757720.

Welsh, Richard, Jerome Graham, and Sheneka Williams. 2019. "Acing the Test: An Examination of Teachers' Perceptions of and Responses to the Threat of State Takeover." *Educational Assessment, Evaluation and Accountability* 31:315–47. https://doi.org/10.1007/s11092-019-09301-y.

Welsh, Richard O. 2019. "Recovery, Achievement, and Opportunity: A Comparative Analysis of State Takeover Districts in Louisiana, Tennessee, and Georgia." *Urban Education* 54(3):311–38. https://doi.org/10.1177/0042085918801884.

Welsh, Richard O., and Sheneka M. Williams. 2018. "Incentivizing Improvement or Imposition? An Examination of the Response to Gubernatorial School Takeover and Statewide Turnaround Districts." *Education Policy Analysis Archives* 26(124):n.p. http://dx.doi.org/10.14507/epaa.26.3679.

White, Terrenda. 2015. "Charter Schools: Demystifying Whiteness in a Market of 'No Excuses' Corporate-Styled Charter Schools." Pp. 121–145 in *What's Race Got to Do with It: How Current School Reform Policy Maintains Racial and Economic Inequality*, edited by Bree Picower and Edwin Mayorga. Peter Lang Publishing.

Willis, Paul E. 1981. *Learning to Labor: How Working Class Kids Get Working Class Jobs*. Columbia University Press.

Zimmerman, A. 2017. "'Despite Pushback, Education Panel Votes to Close Five Schools in de Blasio's Turnaround Program.'" *Chalkbeat*, March 23. www.chalkbeat.org/.

INDEX

academic achievement, 35, 37, 86; hyper-controlling behavior for, 78; K-12 schools and, 4, 81; segregation impacting, 23; standardized state-approved metrics for, 77

academic performance, 26, 51, 79, 148n14; neoliberalism and, 22, 81–84

accountability, viii, ix, 23, 101–3; neoliberal, 28–30, 79, 120, 122, 130, 145n7; neoliberal governance and, 128; social consequences and, 97–99

administration, school, 25, 31, 32, 140, 159n11; critique of state restructuring, 34; encouragement to drop out, 51, 53, 54–55; fear of Black youth, 95–97; hostility of, 96; teachers and, 119; turnover of, 32

affluent families, 15, 17, 20, 21, 124, 147n19

Annamma, Subini, 83

Anyon, Jean, 129, 162n37

Apple, Michael, 29

attendance, 78, 84, 120, 156n17; chronic absenteeism and, 94, 97; CPS (Child Protective Services) and, 93–95; state receivership enforcing, 82

authoritarian disciplinary practices, 29

authoritarian education, 63–65, 159n17, 160n31

auxiliary standardized tests, 37–39, 42, 48, 49–50

"bad" kids, 6, 59, 61, 63, 69–71, 72–73; myths of contamination and, 70, 75; stereotypes of, 62; students experience as, 100–101

"bad" schools, 5, 10–11, 23, 61, 160n1

Bashi, Vilna, 111

Beauchamp, Nicholas, 156n17

Bettie, Julie, 115, 139

Black students, 2, 3–4, 6, 10, 17, 19, 159n15; control of, 86; dress code and, 112–15; exclusion of, 55, 56; fear of, 95–97, 105, 107–9; identities of, 59–60; immigration history of, 53–54; policing of, 116–17; punishment of, 95–97; pushout of, 51–52; school security regime impacting, 105–7, 108–9; stereotypes, 91, 107–8, 117; stigmas of, 61–62

Bloemraad, Irene, 146n8

Brown v. Board of Education, 127

bullying, 159n17, 160n23

Cairns, Kate, 157n1, 160n31

Candipan, Jennifer, 161n16

"carceral continuum" (Shedd), 29, 93

carceral state, 2–3, 5, 28–30, 38, 68; K-12 schools and, 43, 119

Carter, Prudence, 59–60

Carver-Thomas, Desiree, 160n1

CBO. *See* community-based organization

"Challenges for youth in Sandview" (community forum), 13–14

character of students: children navigating racial stereotypes of, 75; school's focus on, 66–68; students' narratives about, 69, 70

Chicago schools, 148n35, 153n24, 156n31; education reform in, viii, 1, 21; neoliberalism in, 129, 145n1, 148n13

180 | INDEX

Child Protective Services (CPS), 93–95, 157n40, 157n42
chronic absenteeism, 94, 97
citizenship: socialization, 56, 99, 117, 156n29; students, 88–89, 91, 125–27; substantive, 56, 64, 76, 130
city council members, 14, 21
climate, school, 78, 80, 104, 141; ESSA and, 156n17; punitive, 87
community-based organization (CBO), 11, 12
competition for resources: pressure on marginalized youth populations and, 126, 127; role of school structure in, 114, 117, 157n1
conditionality, 43, 145n7; state standards and, 30–31
contamination myths, 70, 75
control of students: Black and Latinx, 86; dress code, 90; hyper-social, 88–89, 120, 125; in lunchroom, 85, 86; social, ix, 77–79, 80, 87, 101, 148n31
corporate malls, 12–13
CPS. *See* Child Protective Services
criminal frames of students, racialized, 7, 102, 112, 116, 117
criminalization, 104, 108, 121–22, 125, 158n3, 158n5; "illegal" immigrant frame and, 109–10, 111–12, 116, 117; punitive schooling and, 7, 88, 98, 101, 102, 103
criminal justice system, 28, 29, 121–22
critical education scholarship, 28, 29, 59
critical education theory, 76
"culture of high expectations," the school's techniques of and similarity to NECS, 84–86
culture of poverty: myth of and support for, 6; neoliberal ethos and, 97; schools' broad use of, 154n17; students' narratives about, 60, 70–71, 74
custodial citizenship, 88, 91

Dang, Tran, 112, 160n23
Darling-Hammond, Linda, 160n1

Data Wall in Sandview High School, 25–26, 61
DCIP. *See* District Comprehensive Improvement Plan
Department of Education, US, 30, 32, 147n8, 155n5
"Diagnostic Tool for School and District Effectiveness" (NYS), 36
Diamond, John, 113
disciplinary practices, 4, 7, 64, 110; authoritarian, 29; exclusionary, 83; "no excuses," 66, 67, 99; off-the-record, 89–91; punitive, 156n34; safety and, 80, 150n64; school security regime and, 116, 159n17; systems for, 100, 101; zero-tolerance, 107
disenfranchised populations: student, 21, 43, 64, 121; youth of, 8, 57–58
District Comprehensive Improvement Plan (DCIP), 35, 37, 38, 155n5
divestment, 11, 20–21, 24
"double free riding," 15–16, 128
dress code, 80, 89–91, 108, 112–16, 156n35
dropout. *See* pushout of students

educational outcomes, 128
educational systems, 4, 44, 125; authoritarian, 63–65, 159n17, 160n31; factors for positive outcomes in, 128
Education Department, NYS, 146n6, 146n7, 146n14, 149n50, 150n64; MAP testing and, 151n70, 151n71, 151n73, 152n9; SVI and, 158n7; VADIR and, 155n11, 158n6
education reform, 5, 35, 129, 154n5, 156n16; Chicago schools, viii, 1, 21; K-12 schools, viii, 4, 28; neoliberal, viii, x, 26–28, 30, 31, 124, 148n13; punishment and, 64; state-led, 1, 26
Elementary and Secondary Education Act (ESEA), 30–31, 32, 81, 98, 156n16; "New York Education Transformation Law"

and, 33, 82; "Unsafe School Choice Option" and, 35–36
ELL. *See* English Language Learners
English for Speakers of Other Languages (ESOL), 39, 52
English Language Learners (ELL), vii, 39–40, 52, 54
enrollment, school closures impacting, 122–23, 124
entitlement, 76, 88; student, 45, 50–51, 162n37; for youth, 57
ESEA. *See* Elementary and Secondary Education Act
ESOL. *See* English for Speakers of Other Languages
ESSA. *See* Every Student Succeeds Act
ethnographers, 139, 140
ethnography, 3, 4
ethno-racial group, 55, 72
evaluations, teacher, 38, 39, 48, 151n70, 152n9
Every Student Succeeds Act (ESSA), 27, 29, 30, 120, 147n8, 156n17; CPS and, 94–95; NCLB and, 81, 83–84, 127, 155n5; NECS and, 98, 99; threat of school closures and, 122
Ewing, Eve, viii, 147n2
exclusionary disciplinary practices, 83
exclusionary punishment, 36, 77, 81, 83, 90, 156n29
exclusion of students, 51; African American, 55, 56; Latinx, 55, 56
experiences of students, 4–5, 9, 40, 41–42, 44, 56–57; bad kids, 69–70, 71–73, 100–101; MAP exam and, 48–49; "School Isn't about Education Anymore," 45–47; Writing Project, 50

factory jobs, 12–13, 15
Farina, Katie A., 159n17, 160n31
fear: of Black youth, 95–97, 105, 107–9; of youth, 103, 104

federal government, viii, 27, 28, 42–43, 58; funding from, 3; state plans with, 30; threat of school closure and, 120, 121
Fine, Ben, 28
FOB. *See* "fresh off the boat" insult
Fong, Kelley, 157n40
Foucault, Michel, 29, 148n29
Frankenberg, Erica, 123, 147n24
"fresh off the boat" (FOB) insult, 160n23

gender, 88; in off-the-record discipline, 89, 91, 99, 113
gentrification, viii, 16, 18–19, 122, 123, 145n1; stages of, 161n25
Gilens, Martin, 128
Gilmore, Ruth Wilson, 29
girls of color, racialized policing of, 89–91
Giroux, Henry A., 156n29
Gleeson, Shannon, 146n8
Glenn, Evelyn Nakano, 88
Golann, Joanne, 150n65, 154n8
go-nowhere jobs, 13, 14–15
Gordon, Hava, 129
Graauw, Els de, 146n8
graduation rate, 34
Gramsci, Antonio, 76
grants, school: academic achievement and, 151n70; federal funding for, 35, 36, 80, 149n53, 155n5
Green, Terrance L., 147n2
grit narratives of students, 66–68, 74, 126, 127
gun violence, 103, 104, 105

Hardie, Jessica Halliday, 158n5
harmful socializing messages, 2, 5, 50–51, 54, 55, 75
Harvey, David, 28, 145n1
hegemony (Gramsci), 76
hidden curriculum, 6, 45, 51
high-stakes testing, 5, 62
homeschooling, 123–24
hostility of school administration, 96

hyper-social control of students, 88–89, 92, 120, 125

identities, Black and Latinx, 59–60, 75
"illegal talk," 110–11, 112
immigrants, student, vii, ix, 94, 154n17; Black, 53–54, 159n18; criminal frame threats, 109–10; gentrification and, 18–19; history of, 52, 160n23; "illegal," 111–12, 116, 117; Latinx, 52–53, 54–55, 92–93; punishments of, 91–93
immigration, 92; deportation threats, 94, 111–12; "fresh off the boat" insult, 160n23; unaccompanied minor and, 53; undocumented immigrant and, 9, 55, 94, 110, 111, 159n18
incentives, 28, 81; neoliberal school improvement orders and, 83; performance pressures and, 37, 55–56, 57; student pushout and, 51
informal suspensions, 80–81, 87, 154n2
inner-ring suburbs, 18–19, 122, 146n9
in-school suspension (ISS), 78–79, 81, 87, 89, 154n2
institutional racism, 4, 55
intersectionality, 7, 54, 89, 95, 99, 156n29
interventions, state, 4, 22–23, 27, 28, 127
interview subjects, 142, 142–44
ISS. *See* in-school suspension

jobs: factory, 12–13, 15; go-nowhere, 13, 14–15
Jones, Jennifer, 102

K-12 schools, ix, 5, 43; academic achievement and, 4, 81; carceral state and, 43, 119; education reform, viii, 4, 28
Kozol, Jonathan, 3, 16, 146n11
Kupchik, Aaron, F., 96, 159n17

Lamont, Michèle, 126
Latinx students, 7, 19, 123, 130, 146n1; control of, 86; dignity of, 74–75; dress code and, 112–15; exclusion of, 55, 56; identities, 59–60; illegal talk of, 110–11, 112; immigration history of, 52–53, 54–55, 92–93; policing of, 116–17; pushout of, 51–52; school security regime impacting, 105–7, 108–9; stereotypes, 91, 107–8, 117, 158n3; stigmas of, 61–62; students, ix, 2, 3–4, 6, 10, 17, 159n15
Lerman, Amy, 88, 99
Lewis, Amanda, 113
Lipman, Pauline, 145n1, 148n13
lockdowns, 105, 159n13
locked doors, during school hours, 79, 85, 91–92
low-income, 18, 128; Black and Latinx youth, 74; student population, 15, 17, 19, 43, 146n2, 146n12; suburbs, 15, 17, 21, 23, 146n1, 146n9, 147n24
low-performing schools, 5, 26, 28, 122–23, 156n16; conditionality and, 30; pressure in, 36–37
lunchroom, social control of students in, 85, 86

MAP. *See* Measure of Academic Progress
marginalization of youth, 57–58, 126
Measure of Academic Progress (MAP): teachers impacted by, 38–39, 48, 49, 50; testing for, 151n70, 151n71, 151n73, 152n9; Writing Project and, 47–49
meritocracy, ethos of, 6, 60, 73–74, 76
Milliken v. Bradley (1974), 17
"model minority" stereotype, 72, 158n3, 158n5
myths of contamination, 70, 75

NCLB. *See* No Child Left Behind Act
NECS. *See* No Excuses Charter Schools
neoliberal accountability, 28–30, 79, 120, 122, 130, 145n7
neoliberal governance, 27, 128, 145n7; punitive schooling and, 121; school

closures and, 119, 120; threat of school closures and, 42–43, 68, 120
neoliberalism, viii, ix, 97–99, 101–3, 154n5; academic performance and, 22, 81–84; accountability for, 28–30, 79, 120, 122, 130, 145n7; education reform and, viii, x, 26–28, 30, 31, 124, 148n13; experiments in, 123–24; NCLB and, 26, 27, 43; new immigrant destinations, ix; socialization and, 125–27
new immigrant destinations, ix
"New York Education Transformation Law" (2015), 33, 82. *See also* State Receivership Law 2015, NY
New York State (NYS), 22, 34, 149n42; "Diagnostic Tool for School and District Effectiveness," 36; Education Department, 146n6, 146n7, 146n14, 149n50, 150n64
No Child Left Behind Act (NCLB), viii, 3, 5, 11, 97, 127, 155n10; ESSA and, 81, 83–84, 127, 155n5; neoliberalism and, 26, 27, 43; state takeover and, 32–33
"no excuses," disciplinary practices, 66, 67, 99
No Excuses Charter Schools (NECS), 81, 85–86, 98–99, 120
Noguera, Pedro, 30–31
NYS. *See* New York State

Obama, Barack, 151n70
Ochoa, Gilda L., 103, 158n3, 158n5, 160n23
Oeur, Freeden Blume, 152n5, 154n5
off-the-record disciplinary practices, 89–91
opportunity gap, 23
opportunity hoarding, 5, 20; resource deprivation and, 23, 24
out-of-school suspensions, 77–78, 154n2

Page, Benjamin, 128
Pascoe, C. J., 115, 151n2

PBIS. *See* Positive Behavior Interventions and Supports
Pearman, Francis A., 161n16
performance: academic, 26, 51, 79, 148n14; low, x, 5, 26, 122, 123, 151n70, 155n10; punishments related to, viii, 18; student, 10, 18, 22, 37, 152n9
Philadelphia schools, viii, 21, 129, 148n35
police officers, 29, 79, 107
policing, school, 88, 100–101, 156n29; Black and Latinx youth, 116–17; dress code, 89–91, 108, 112–16, 156n35; racialized, 95, 102, 121
political membership, 6, 44, 45
Portz, John, 156n17
Positive Behavior Interventions and Supports (PBIS), 83, 120
poverty, 13, 14, 146n14
pressure: administrators impacted by, 119; in low-performing schools, 37–38; on school professionals, 67, 119, 121; on students, ix–x, 1, 65; on teachers, 25–26, 39–40, 42
punishment, 7, 80, 87, 95–97, 100–101; education reform and, 64; exclusionary, 36, 77, 81, 83, 90, 156n29; immigrant students and, 91–93; out-of-school suspensions as, 77–78, 154n2; performance related, viii, 18; state surveillance and, 25–26; system for, 89, 115, 157n38. *See also* suspensions
punitive schooling, x, 2, 3, 28–30; climate of, 87; criminalization of youth and, 7, 88, 98, 101, 102, 103; disciplinary practices and, 156n34; environment, 7, 35, 77, 78, 81, 98, 101; Giroux on, 156n29; MAP and, 38; neoliberal governance and, 121; regime of, 75
pushout of students, 51–53, 54–56, 153n14; CPS threat to, 93–94
Pyke, Karen, 112, 160n23

"Race to the Top" (Obama), 151n70
racial inequalities, 2, 3–4, 6–7, 10, 154n5; "savage inequalities" and, 16–17; segregation, 17, 123
racialization, 59, 75, 115, 116, 158n3
racialized policing, 95, 102, 121; population, 6, 72, 73; stereotypes, 60, 101, 105, 107, 108, 117, 158n5
receivership. *See* State Receivership Law 2015, NY
recruitment of students, 136–37
redistricting schools, 16, 20
Regents (state exam), 46, 47, 49, 152n6, 153n15, 153n17
regime, 40, 47, 51, 55–56, 65; punitive schooling, 75; school security, 7, 35–36, 98, 99, 105–7, 108–09; testing, ix, 6, 7, 35, 36–37
resource deprivation, 5, 11, 147n23, 161n16; competition and, 114, 117, 157n1; opportunity hoarding and, 23, 24
respect, students desiring, 7, 62, 63, 64–65
Rooks, Noliwe, 127, 161n36
rural communities, threats of school closure in, 123–24

Saad-Filho, Alfredo Saad, 28
safety and security, student, 35–36, 82, 105–6, 138, 158n7; disciplinary practices and, 80, 150n64
salvaging dignity, students, 59, 63, 74–75, 101, 107, 113, 125
Sandview, New York (pseudonym), ix, 3, 9, 15, 146n9, 147n19; city council members, 14, 21; community forum, 13–14; corporate malls in, 12–13; education reform in, viii; jobs in, 12–13, 14–15; redistricting schools in, 16, 20; school districts, 17, 19–20, 21, 147n23; tax base in, 12, 13, 14–15
Sandview High School (pseudonym). *See specific topics*
Sandview School District (SSD), 11, 22

"savage inequalities" (Kozol), 3, 16–17, 146n11
SAVE Act (Schools Against Violence in Education), 36, 150n62, 158n6
scholarship, 2, 4, 5, 44, 102; critical education, 28, 29, 59
school closures, viii, 1, 147n2; enrollment impacting, 122–23, 124; gentrification and, 122; neoliberalism and, 119, 120; performance impacting, 27–28. *See also* threat of school closures
school environment, 5, 148n35; punitive, 7, 35, 77, 78, 81, 98, 101; suburban, 3–4
"School Improvement Grant" (SIG), 151n70, 152n9
"School Isn't about Education Anymore," experiences of, 45–47
school professionals, 46, 54–55, 66, 109, 157n41, 159n18; experience with, 141–42; local, 58; pressure on, 67, 119, 121; students and, 2, 3, 35, 51, 63, 65, 129
Schools Against Violence in Education (SAVE) Act, 36, 150n62, 158n6
school security regime, 7, 35–36, 98, 99, 105–7, 108–09; disciplinary practices and, 116, 159n17
school violence index (SVI), 103, 150n58, 155n11, 158n6; Education Department and, 158n7
security personnel, 79–80, 84–85, 86–87, 91–92
segregation, 20, 127; academic achievement impacting, 23; racial inequalities and, 17, 123
self-presentation of students, 67–68
Shedd, Carla, 88, 156n31, 160n30; "carceral continuum," 29, 93
Shifrer, Dara, 39
Siegel-Hawley, Genevieve, 123
SIG. *See* School Improvement Grant
Smith, Neil, 145n1
social control of students, ix, 77–79, 80, 87, 101, 148n31; dress code, 80, 89–91,

108, 112–16, 156n35; hyper-social, 88–89, 92, 120, 125; overpunishment vulnerability in, 96; student efforts to normalize, 85, 86–87

socialization, 6; citizenship, 56, 99, 117, 156n29; neoliberalism and, 125–27; youth, 2, 88, 125, 130

social movements: role in challenging neoliberal governance, 128–29; youth participation in, 57

SSD. *See* Sandview School District

state: auditor observation, 46, 63, 97, 121; carceral, 2–3, 5, 28–30; interventions, 4, 22–23, 27, 28, 127; performance expectations of, 41, 77–78, 82, 101; takeover by, 26, 27, 32–35, 38, 119; testing, 25, 42, 51, 53, 61, 64, 65; test scores, x, 25, 45–47, 61–62

state exams, ix, 25, 31, 52; Regents (NY), 46, 47, 49, 152n6, 153n15, 153n17; student scores on, 44, 45–47, 48, 51, 57, 153n15

state improvement plan, x, 32, 33, 58, 77, 79–80, 97; DCIP, 35, 38; disciplinary incidents and, 81–84; ESEA, 82; MAP and, 38, 47; Sandview High Data Wall, 25; school security measures and, 35, 43, 78–80, 82, 98, 102; student attendance and, 81–84, 93–94, 98, 120; test scores and, 36; Writing Project as, 42

state-led education reform, 1, 26

state performance expectations, 41, 77–78, 82, 101

State Receivership Law 2015, NY, 30, 148n35; metrics, 83, 120; schools under, 33–34, 78, 82, 84; students impacted by, 34–35; threats of closure through, 97–98. *See also* "New York Education Transformation Law" (2015)

state standards, 11, 37; conditionality and, 30–31; improvement programs, 22–23

state surveillance, ix, 79–80, 83, 88, 99, 102; punishment and, 25–26

stereotypes, 61, 62, 71, 91, 101–2, 129; Black and Latinx, 91, 107–8, 117, 158n3; "model minority," 72, 158n3, 158n5; racialized, 60, 101, 105, 107, 108, 117, 158n5

stigma: of being "bad," 62–63; Black and Latinx youth and, 61–62; threat of school closures and, 59–60, 75–76

structural inequalities, 4, 34, 57, 67, 71, 126; racism and, 2, 72

student populations, 59; disenfranchised, 21, 43, 64, 121; low-income, 15, 17, 19, 43, 146n2, 146n12; racialized, 6, 72, 73

students, 7, 61–62, 69, 72, 90, 136–37; academic achievement, 101; affluent, 16, 154n2; bathrooms incidents with, x, 85–86, 91–92, 101; criminal frames of, 7, 102, 109, 112, 116, 117; disenfranchised populations, 21, 43, 64, 121; ELL, 39–40; entitlement for, 45, 50–51, 162n37; experience of, 4–5, 9, 40, 41–42, 44, 45–47, 56–57; grit of, 66–68, 74, 126, 127; harmful messages for, 2, 5, 50–51, 54, 55, 75; immigrant, vii, 18–19, 52–53, 54–55, 91–93, 94; performance, 10, 18, 22, 37, 152n9; phones, 40, 85, 87, 107–8, 136, 137; pressure on, ix–x, 1, 65; pushout of, 51–53, 54–56, 153n14; safety and security, 35–36, 82, 105–6, 138, 158n7; school professionals and, 2, 3, 35, 51, 63, 65, 129; self-presentation of, 67–68; social control of, ix, 77–79, 80, 87, 101, 148n31; state exams scores of, 44, 46, 48, 51, 57, 153n15; State Receivership Law impacting, 34–35; teachers relationships with, 63–64, 65–66, 100–101; test prep tools and, 47, 50; test scores, vii, x, 1, 71. *See also* Black students; Latinx students; White students; *specific topics*

Su, Celina, 129–30

substantive citizenship, 56, 64, 76, 130

suburban free riding, 15

suburban poverty, 5, 9–10, 11, 21–22

suburban schools, viii, ix, 128; poverty in, 5, 9–10, 11, 21–22; racial inequalities in, 3–4, 6–7, 10, 16–17; school closures at, 123
suburbs, 123, 128; inner-ring, 18–19, 122, 146n9; living in, 9; low-income, 15, 17, 21, 23, 146n1, 146n9, 147n24
"super minorities," 6, 72, 73
Supreme Court, US, 17
suspensions, 35, 36, 82, 86, 97; data for, 150n62, 154n1; informal, 80–81, 87, 154n2; ISS, 78–79, 81, 87, 89, 154n2; out-of-school, 77–78, 154n2
SVI. *See* school violence index
Swain, Walker A., 161n16
systems: criminal justice, 28, 29, 121–22; disciplinary, 100, 101; educational, 4, 44, 64, 125; punishment, 89, 115, 157n38

Taft, Jessica, 57
tax base, 12, 13, 14–15
teachers, ix–x, 16, 37, 40–41, 69–70, 150n62, 150n68; evaluations of, 38, 39, 48, 151n70, 152n9; "illegal talk" and, 110–11; interviews with, 141–42; MAP impacting, 38–39, 48, 49, 50; "no excuses" and, 66, 67; pressure on, 25–26, 39–40, 42; school administrators and, 119; students relationships with, 63–64, 65–66, 100–101; threat of school closures impacting, 64; turnover of, 119; union of, 21, 38, 129, 151n73, 152n9, 152n19; Writing Project and, 41–42
Terriquez, Veronica, 152n2
test-and-punish policies, 31–32
testing, 40, 47, 51, 65; auxiliary, 37–39, 42, 48, 49–50; high-stakes, 5, 62; MAP, 151n70, 151n71, 151n73, 152n9; regime, ix, 6, 7, 35, 36–37; standardized, 29, 64, 127; state, 25, 42, 51, 53, 61, 64, 65
test prep tools, 47–49, 50, 65–66
test scores, 32, 36, 72, 149n42; authoritarian education and, 63–65; MAP, 38, 39,

48; state, x, 25, 45–47, 61–62; students, vii, x, 1, 71
Thorne, Barrie, 162n7
threat of school closures, ix, 1, 10–11, 23, 28; ESSA and, 122; federal government and, 120, 121; low performance, x, 5, 26; neoliberal governance and, 42–43, 68, 120; state carcerality and, 2–3, 5; stigma of, 59–60, 75–76; teachers impacted by, 64; test and punish policies, 31–32, 44; trends, 122–25
Trails High School, 20, 147n19
"Turnaround Model," 36, 155n5
tutors, vii, 1, 135–36; after-school, 52, 53
Tyson, Karolyn, 158n5

unaccompanied minor, 53
undocumented immigrants, 9, 55, 94, 110, 111, 159n18
union, teacher's, 21, 38, 129, 151n73, 152n9, 152n19
United States (US): child labor in, 41; Department of Education, 30, 32, 147n8, 155n5
"Unsafe School Choice Option," in ESEA, 35–36
urban centers: school closures and, 122–23; school inequalities and, 16; strained public school and, 5, 10
US. *See* United States

VADIR. *See* Violent and Disruptive Incident Reports
Valenzuela, Angela, 103, 154n17
violence: gun, 103, 104, 105; SAVE Act, 36, 150n62, 158n6. *See also* school violence index
Violent and Disruptive Incident Reports (VADIR), 155n11, 158n6, 159n14
violent crime, 103–4, 150n58, 155n11

Weaver, Vesla, 88
White, Terrienda, 97

White flight, 16, 19–21
White students, 158n5, 161n16; academic achievement of, 23; school district funding for, 146n12; school district shifts of, 17, 147n19, 159n15; suspension rates of, 154n2; weapon possessions of, 158n7
Writing Project (standardized test), 41–42; experiences of students during, 50; MAP and, 47–49

youth, 3, 4, 6, 45, 142; "Challenges for youth in Sandview," 13–14; criminalization of, 104, 108, 121–22, 125, 158n3, 158n5; disenfranchised, 8, 57–58; entitlement for, 57; fear of, 103, 104; immigrant, ix, 53, 55, 154n17; involvement of, 129–30; marginalized, 57–58, 126; political development of, 57, 125, 152n2; political incorporation, 6, 44–45, 56–57; socialization, 2, 88, 125, 130. *See also* Black students; Latinx students

zero-tolerance, disciplinary practices, 107

ABOUT THE AUTHOR

ERIN MICHAELS is Associate Professor of Sociology at the University of North Carolina, Wilmington. She received her PhD in Sociology from the City University of New York (CUNY) Graduate Center. Dr. Michaels specializes in the sociology of youth, education, race and ethnicity, immigration, and political sociology. She has also published on these topics in *Youth & Society*, *Critical Sociology*, the *Journal of Contemporary Ethnography*, *Cornell University ILR Press*, and *Progressive Planning*.

www.ingramcontent.com/pod-product-compliance
Lightning Source LLC
Chambersburg PA
CBHW031151020426
42333CB00013B/612